WELCOME TO THE
OUTBACK

Sue Williams is the author of a number of bestselling books, including *Women of the Outback*, *Outback Spirit* and *Getting There – Journeys of an Accidental Adventurer*.

Her other books include *Peter Ryan: The Inside Story*; *Mean Streets, Kind Heart: The Father Chris Riley Story*; *No Time For Fear* – the story of shark attack survivor Paul de Gelder – as well as *And Then The Darkness*, about the disappearance of the British backpacker Peter Falconio, which was shortlisted for the prestigious Golden Dagger Award in the UK for the true crime book of the year, and the Ned Kelly Awards in Australia.

Also an award-winning journalist, Sue was born in England, and worked in print and television in the UK and New Zealand. She spent many years travelling around the world before falling in love with Australia in 1989. Since settling here, she has written for many of Australia's leading newspapers and magazines.

In stark contrast to the Outback, Sue's apartment is in the most densely populated part of Australia – Sydney's Kings Cross – where she lives with her partner, writer Jimmy Thomson.

For more information, please visit **suewilliams.com.au**

MICHAEL JOSEPH
an imprint of
PENGUIN BOOKS

MICHAEL JOSEPH

Published by the Penguin Group
Penguin Group (Australia)
250 Camberwell Road, Camberwell, Victoria 3124, Australia
(a division of Pearson Australia Group Pty Ltd)
Penguin Group (USA) Inc.
375 Hudson Street, New York, New York 10014, USA
Penguin Group (Canada)
90 Eglinton Avenue East, Suite 700, Toronto, Canada ON M4P 2Y3
(a division of Pearson Penguin Canada Inc.)
Penguin Books Ltd
80 Strand, London WC2R 0RL England
Penguin Ireland
25 St Stephen's Green, Dublin 2, Ireland
(a division of Penguin Books Ltd)
Penguin Books India Pvt Ltd
11 Community Centre, Panchsheel Park, New Delhi – 110 017, India
Penguin Group (NZ)
67 Apollo Drive, Rosedale, North Shore 0632, New Zealand
(a division of Pearson New Zealand Ltd)
Penguin Books (South Africa) (Pty) Ltd
24 Sturdee Avenue, Rosebank, Johannesburg 2196, South Africa

Penguin Books Ltd, Registered Offices: 80 Strand, London WC2R 0RL, England

First published by Penguin Group (Australia), 2012

1 3 5 7 9 10 8 6 4 2

Text copyright © Sue Williams 2012
Illustrations copyright © Sue Williams 2012 (unless stated otherwise)

The moral right of the author has been asserted

Design by Laura Thomas © Penguin Group (Australia)
Cover photograph by Peter Walton Photgraphy/Getty Images
Typeset in Fairfield by Post Pre-press Group, Brisbane, Queensland
Printed and bound in Australia by McPherson's Printing Group, Maryborough, Victoria

National Library of Australia
Cataloguing-in-Publication data:

Williams, Sue, 1959–
Welcome to the outback / Sue Williams.
9781921518638 (pbk.)
Country life – Australia.
Frontier and pioneer life – Australia.
Rural men – Australia – Biography.
Rural women – Australia – Biography.

994.0099

penguin.com.au

CONTENTS

AN OUTBACK ITINERARY:

Where I went looking for the heart of Australia

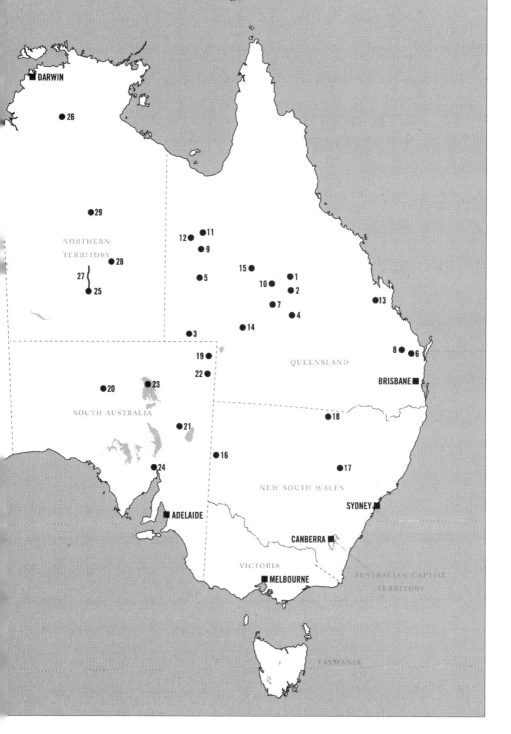

PROLOGUE

The woman looks at me and scowls. 'You're not from round here, are you?'

I shake my head in a way I hope will convey my sorrow that I'm not, in fact, from round here.

She says nothing, but looks me up and down, taking in the wash 'n' wear travel trousers that zip off neatly at the knee whenever the occasion warrants, the shiny new R. M. Williams boots, the fashionable BPA-free stainless-steel water bottle and the pristine white hat, which now seems to glow against the orange dust of our surrounds.

'No, I knew it,' she says finally, with a heavy sigh. 'Well, I suppose you'd better come in then.' She takes off, at what feels like quite unnecessary speed, down the dark corridor into her home.

I'd knocked on the nearest door to ask for help after an accident on the road just outside the ramshackle opal-mining town of South Australia's Coober Pedy.

This wasn't quite what I'd been expecting.

'It's very kind . . .' I start before realising she's already out of earshot, and scurry to make up ground.

'I'm in the middle of my dinner, but I've got some chops you can eat and some cold beer,' she throws over her shoulder as we come into the light. Is it my imagination or does her voice sound marginally less chilly? But, absorbing her words, my heart sinks back down again. We've only just managed to scramble over the first hurdle and now she's about to discover I'm a vegetarian. And, even worse, a vegetarian who doesn't drink. I sense this will end our blossoming friendship before it's even had the chance to bud.

'That sounds great,' I begin meekly. 'But I don't want to be any trouble. I'd just love a glass of water and . . . um . . . maybe a piece of fruit?'

'Fruit? Got peaches,' she grumbles. 'My last tin. Drink the juice cos the water tastes like shit. Welcome to the Outback.'

1

OLD DROVERS NEVER DIE;
THEY GO TO THE ETERNAL MUSTER

I can't breathe. I'm choking. The more I try to swallow, the more I can feel my throat close up. I gasp and try to gulp in air. But it doesn't work. I just cough and rasp for breath. I'm suffocating . . .

'Get some water!' I can hear someone shout at me. 'Over there! Over there! In the trough!' I spin around to see a trough full of muddy brown water. I dash over and greedily scoop up handfuls, slurping down the water as if my life depends on it. Because it well might. At last, I can breathe again, but I race back to the table, where another square of dry damper is waiting for me. I have to get that down to move onto the next challenge.

When I was first invited to take part in the 'Battle of the Greenhide' Drovers' Cook Ironwoman Competition, I wasn't sure what it would entail. 'But you should do it!' urged Sonya Cullen, events manager at Longreach's Australian Stockman's Hall of Fame. 'It's hard, but it'll be fun.' Fun? *This?* I've had more fun in a waxing salon.

We begin by lying in a swag, then, when the starting bell

sounds, scramble out, roll it up (and I'm surprised to discover how heavy and cumbersome it is) and run to the trough of dirty water. There, we splash the freezing water onto our faces, then race to the table of damper. Coughing and spluttering, we have to chew and swallow it – opening our mouths for the judges' inspection to make sure it has really gone down – before we can move onto the next stage. But it seems if you're prepared to risk your life by swallowing some of the filthy water just to get the damper down, then the rules are the least of your problems.

When finally I manage to swallow enough damper, I have to run off to pick up a hessian bag full of straw, which doubles as a sheep, sling it over my shoulder and then traverse a muddy dam to get it safely to the other side. I fall flat on my face in the mud almost as soon as I step into the dam. It's a struggle to get up again, with my wet 'sheep' now feeling more like it's stuffed with bricks. Then I go back to get another one . . .

But I try to smile as I flounder my way through the race. After all, this is nothing compared to the discomforts the real drovers used to face every day in the Outback. I know that now. I'm here at the 21st anniversary drovers' reunion weekend to learn all about droving from the men who did it over a lifetime, pushing stock throughout the country, swimming them across treacherous, crocodile-infested rivers, and over some of the most desolate land to help make the Outback, and Australia, what it is today.

While I've heard so much about the Outback, its luminous landscapes, the tough characters it breeds and the romance of its wide open spaces – so much a part of our national psyche – I've never really spent much time there. I've met some of its extraordinary people and written about how much they love living in some of the most remote areas of the country. I've been told firsthand how they'd often had to overcome enormous challenges to survive in such incredible isolation, but I could never quite work out what they liked about the Outback and why they stayed. I always wondered what stopped them from just upping sticks at the first sign of trouble and moving to the nearest city – where, let's be honest here, there were far easier jobs available, plenty of transport, good roads, neighbours next door rather than a three-hour drive away, neat quarter-acre blocks (or even pleasant apartment buildings), the choice of thousands of people to socialise with, fresh food, 24-hour medical centres, nice cafés, hairdressers you didn't have to book weeks in advance for a quick trim, cinemas, ice-cream . . . Yet few ever did; they'd shudder at the very thought. Instead, they invariably chose to stay in the Outback, which always looked to me to have pretty much nothing there but dust and dirt and sand and flies and unbearable heat and hardship.

But after having heard from so many people how wondrous the land out back is, I felt it was finally time to see for myself. I had a few months spare from pressing work deadlines so why not spend that time scouring the Outback, battling the elements in search of the real heart of Australia? What is the Outback? Where is it? Is it really worth preserving? And am I really up to the challenge of finding out?

That, perhaps, was my greatest worry. After all, English-born, I've spent my whole life in cities. Even as an enthusiastic new Australian who's been here for over 20 years, I still rarely roam beyond cities' outer suburbs. The ridicule I faced a couple of years ago out in the bush after I excitedly called a newborn lamb a 'sheepling' still burns. So even now as a cityslicker living in a high-rise apartment in Sydney's Kings Cross – the most densely populated area of the country's biggest city – I know

I am perhaps not the ideal person to solve the mystery of the Outback's appeal. Wide open spaces scare me. Far horizons just don't look right without skyscrapers. I thrive on noise, crowds, traffic, stress, 24-hour cafés and a supermarket three minutes away that stays open till midnight.

What's more, I'm a vegetarian teetotaller with a slight gluten intolerance and an over-sensitivity to caffeine. I know it's tough getting by in places where the traditional diet is often steak, damper, billy tea and oceans of beer. Turning up at cattle stations and asking for cheese in lieu of meat isn't the best way to guarantee a warm welcome, surprisingly. Refusing alcohol is perhaps even worse. And I'll never forget when I first turned down an offer of tea and produced my own herbal teabag instead. 'What?' the elderly lady barked at me. 'Our tea not good enough for you?'

Then there was the time I tried to drive down the Gibb River Road through the Kimberley. The heavy rain of the approaching wet season had turned the track into a swamp and all I could do was sit on the ground and watch the thunderstorms light up the sky for hundreds of kilometres around – and wonder how on earth I'd get out again. Or the pitch-black night I went for a stroll in the desert near South Australia's Oodnadatta, and couldn't find my way back again. Or that afternoon I went out with an elderly Aboriginal tracker to search for bush food and watched him nimbly leap over a chasm, and felt too embarrassed to tell him that there was no way I could do the same. Sadly, I was right. Although my guide tried gamely to catch me, he couldn't, and my dislocated shoulder took six months of physio to heal. After each trip to the Outback, I'd returned to the city with a huge sigh of relief.

Even so, this trip, I vowed, would be different. I'd work

hard to find the true heart of Outback Australia, in all its glory, desolation, laughter, lunacy, romance, passion and spirit of adventure.

So I pulled out the maps and started researching interesting Outback-y things to do and good people to see. One of the first things that jumped out at me was a cattle drive in Aramac, in Outback Queensland. And the second was this drovers' reunion in Longreach, where old-timers would gather and share their stories of life in the saddle. I thought the coincidence was an excellent omen for the start of my Outback travels. The drovers would doubtless be able to offer a wealth of great tips for surviving the cattle drive and I'd be a superb listener – as only a person who can't ride and, to be honest, is just a teensy bit scared of cows, could hope to be.

Jack 'Goldie' Goldsmith is one of the first to offer me a few pointers. He not only drove cattle for years, he also spent a fair bit of time stealing other people's. But back in those days, even cattleduffers and poddy-dodgers – those who stole unbranded calves – had their own code of conduct.

'You'd never take them off anyone who had less than you,' he says, with pride. 'You never took off a little fella, either. That wasn't done at all. We all lived by that code.'

Goldie, today 77, and only a touch less hardy than he used to be, lived as colourful and as dangerous a life as any Outback drover. Leaving home in the Blue Mountains of NSW at 16 to escape an abusive stepmother, he dreamt only of working with cattle on a huge Outback station. It took him a while to get there. He spent a few years sleeping rough and picking up odd jobs along the way, trapping rabbits, picking potatoes and tobacco, building fences, being a tent boxer, a shearer, a ringer – someone who works with cattle or sheep, I'm helpfully informed when my blank look is noticed – a horse-breaker and working for the railroad.

Finally, he got his big break in Mungallala, between Charleville and Roma, where he was hired to be a drover, taking a mob of 4500 sheep to Muckadilla, 85 kilometres away, accompanied by just the boss drover, a cook, horses and ten dogs. He found he loved the life, and did everything he could to become a drover.

'I loved the freedom of it,' he says, that spark still in his pale-blue watery eyes. 'Just loved it. The vast empty spaces, the sound of the horse bells at night, the murmur of the cattle. They'd get used to you over time, and be almost tame. You're moving them and see them start to swing out and you just ride up and call out, "Move over, boys", and they will. And if you need to, you crack a whip and they'll all move.'

How about when there's a stampede? Goldie fixes me with a stern look, and adjusts his battered old hat. 'We don't use that word here,' he admonishes. 'That's American. We call it a "rush". That's why you always sleep by the fire near a tree. If you hear the mob coming, you'll have time to get out of your swag and hide behind the tree and the fire will divide them.' I swallow, and take careful note of his advice. I had no idea a cattle drive could be so dangerous. It did look terribly dramatic in the movie *Australia*, of course, when even Hugh Jackman was forced to put his shirt back on over his rippling abs to save the day, but that was just a movie . . .

Goldie, however, hasn't noticed my worried look. 'I've always been lucky,' he continues. 'One time I was drafting horses and one of them rushed the rail and I got knocked down. Twenty horses followed him. I was lying on the ground half-unconscious but not one hoof touched me. Not one. One of the blokes there said they thought I'd be a crushed and mangled wreck.' This time, we swallow in unison.

Happily, that luck stayed on his side throughout his life, more or less, right up to his last big droving run ten years ago, moving 1100 bullocks from Tambo to Roma. Before that, he survived a shoot-out at Normanton in the Gulf Country in 1956, when an Aboriginal stockman risked his life to save him. Goldie reckons he's the first white man since the First Fleet landed to name his sons after the tribal names of an Indigenous person. Then there was that time he swam across the Norman River, home to the largest saltwater crocodile ever shot, at 8.64 metres long. He was one of only three men to have successfully swum over, one of the others being the famed cattleduffer Harry Redford, after whom the cattle drive I've signed up for is named. Three days later, a drover swimming his mob across had a beast taken by another massive croc. Goldie was also lucky to get away with a lot of his cattleduffing. These days he's pretty ashamed of it, even though he proved incredibly entrepreneurial. Sometimes, he and his mates – 'I got mixed up with the wrong crowd,' he claims – would duff cattle, walk them hundreds of kilometres away, put their own brand on them, and sell them back to their original owner.

One of the people he'd regularly come up against as a result was Gordon Storer, a police officer with the stock squad, who worked 'however many hours we could stay awake' to catch Goldie and his ilk for the station owners who 'expected us to know every inch and block of land in 349 000 square miles'. Back then, they were enemies. Today they're friends.

'Stealing was a crime and it was my job to catch him,' says Gordon, now 70. 'I was earning a living with the stock squad and it was a way of keeping my family fed and a roof over our heads. Jack was on the other side of the fence. But then if he hadn't been doing what he was doing, along with the others, I wouldn't have had a job. So it was him who kept me working.'

The pair now meets up every year at the drovers' reunion to swap stories about those days in the saddle, one determined to hunt the other down, the other equally determined to get away. But both agree on one thing: it's a joy to live and work in the Outback.

'Bush people are God's own,' says Gordon, a much bigger, bluffer bloke than Goldie, and probably much more than a match for his old foe. 'Even today, you can pick who's from the bush and who's from the city. The young people from the bush are more adult somehow, more mature and have a different outlook on life. They're more sensitive to other people's feelings. It's easy to tell with the older people too. Older people from the bush look at you when they're talking to you; they look you right in the eye, not like city people.'

Goldie, who's released a CD of his harmonica music and has even had a song written about him by country singer Graham Rodger, agrees that people in the Outback are just different.

'The Outback has changed, with all the bitumen roads and road trains and technology and electric light,' he says. 'It's more comfortable living now. But there's still that element of comradeship there. If anybody's down and out, people will pull him in, give him a feed and help him get back on his feet. That spirit is still alive.'

It's the thought of that spirit that's now driving me on through this drovers' ironwoman contest. With my 'sheep' both safely dumped on the other side of the bog, I'm given a star picket, which I assume is a kind of fence post, and a thing that looks like a section of steel pipe, closed at one end, as a makeshift hammer. I just copy my competitors, banging the picket into the hard ground with all my might. I'm puffing and panting, but I draw heart from the groans of the woman next to me as we all run to the next stage, for a hay bale to carry around the course.

People certainly had to be fit to be drovers, but they started young. Georgie Booth, for instance, who worked as a drover up in the Gulf Country, was only 16 when he was given his first mob of nearly 1300 bullocks to muster between Richmond and Hughenden.

'The only time I saw a road was when I crossed one,' he says, now a tough old man of 81, smartly dressed in immaculately ironed blue denim, with a neat white moustache and a wooden cane. 'With droving, there were good times and bad. Sometimes you'd be walking in drought, other times in floods. In 1950, it rained every day and every night but you'd still do the eight miles a day you were contracted for. You'd be paid two and six per head per 100 miles.'

There was also the hazard of snow for Victorian high-country drovers like Noel Elliott, 69, for whom getting trapped in a snowfall or drift was a constant threat.

'You'd try to get in for the three to four months when the snow had melted,' he says. 'You never saw many people up there. You'd only see them later in the pub, where Outback hospitality was always good.'

Some of these blokes may look frail today, but they were as tough as nails back then, and sometimes still can be when the occasion warrants. These annual reunions started back in 1990 and while many of the faces in the first photo taken of Australia's droving past are no longer with us – gone to the eternal muster, as they say – there's just as much fire in the bellies of those who remain. In 1993, former drover Hank Cosgrove and his ex-nurse wife, Berry, set out a program of activities for the reunions, with traditional Outback games, which have been held ever since. The tug o' war, however, was banned after the enmity between the two sides grew too ferocious. Another year, there was a fight over the billy-boiling competition.

This morning, as the men each lit a fire and fanned the flames in the quest to make their billy boil first, happily all has been peaceful. The mood isn't quite so mellow for the damper competition, however. When Berry says, 'Go!', we pack around the table laden with bowls, flour, baking powder, salt, milk and oil to see who can make the most delicious damper, cooking it carefully over hot coals. As an ex-Brit, I'd only tasted my first damper earlier that day – a piece of Berry's that she'd got up at 5 a.m. to make, which had come smothered in butter and Golden Syrup, and was absolutely delicious – but I felt sure it'd be simple.

After a great deal of mixing and kneading, a little fighting over the salt, and having someone else help me put my mixture in a camp oven over coals, I fondly imagined replicating Berry's handsome, crusty, golden-brown concoction. But my damper, sadly, is pale and pasty and decidedly soggy around the edges. And those aren't its worst faults. Berry picks it up during the judging, looks at it critically, turns it over and taps it. 'No drum,' she snaps. 'Listen to that. Hear anything?' I hear not a thing. Who'd have known I'd need to have it double as percussion?

Yet my damper still doesn't come last. Just number 14 out of a field of 18. Loyally, I even have a taste of it later to check how wrong the judges might have been. It's disgustingly underdone. 'Oh, it's not so bad,' Berry says consolingly. 'One year, I put them all in the bin. They looked like doggy doo-doos. They were all burnt. We judge damper on the look of them, the drum, the consistency and the taste.' Hank kindly points out how hard it is to judge the heat of the fire, made up from gidgee wood, which creates a charcoal that burns very, very hot.

'You really have to take your time with it,' he advises. 'Every year, Goldie comes in and goes, *bang, bang, bang* and his damper ends up looking like something a donkey's dropped.'

Luckily, none of these blokes had me as their cook on a cattle drive, which, in the lean drought-hit years, could often see them away from home for up to nine months at a time, ensuring cattle could get fed on the long paddock. For the drovers themselves, it was a diet mostly of damper, corned beef, mutton and billy tea.

One of former drover Azzie Fazulla's favourite memories centres on food. A man from Broken Hill who started out droving in 1939 at the age of 13 with a mob of 5000 sheep, he'd spent weeks out in the middle of nowhere not seeing another person. But then, just near the NSW–South Australian border, a station owner's wife approached, carrying a big tray of roast meat and vegetables, and a bottle of beer. 'I could see her from five miles away,' he says, grinning. 'I thought Christmas had come.'

Azzie, now 85, but a sprightly, trim man full of energy, is today Australia's oldest living male descendant of the original Afghans. His grandfather came from the Punjab, and his father opened up the land with camels, carting sleepers for the railway lines. Azzie then helped to open up the land through droving, and is sad that now road trains have mostly taken over.

'You look at a mob of cattle now and think you'd like to go with them,' he says. 'You wouldn't want to put them in a truck. Droving is a much more humane way of getting them around.'

I hadn't expected the old drovers to have been so concerned

11

about their cattle, assuming they'd regard them merely as their meal tickets. But again and again, they talk of how the welfare of the livestock was their top priority. If the stock were in poor condition, the drovers would often insist on taking it slower to give them more time to feed along the way, often in direct contravention of owners' orders.

'If the cattle were having a hard time, you'd feel it and know it,' says Jim Kennedy, 80. 'But it was your job to look after them. You'd sing to them at night to settle them. If they could hear you singing, they'd usually be OK. Most of it was off-key and you'd go through all the corny songs you knew, but they didn't seem to mind. And to see big mobs moving off in the morning, at daybreak, and to be close to your horse, that was the real romance of the life. You loved being with the animals. When you delivered the cattle, by God, you'd miss them. Then you'd be told there was another mob going in another couple of weeks . . .'

Ken 'Stumpy' Hartland feels much the same. Often, while droving, you'd have no one to talk to, so you'd speak to the cattle or horses. 'You'd go to camp and hop off the horse and light a fire,' says Stumpy, 72, who started droving, like Azzie, at 13. 'Then you might go to the toilet. There wasn't any toilet paper, and they say never pick up a straight stick in the Outback to stir your tea with – someone might have used it to wipe their bum. But the horse would then come and bump your shoulder to tell you to unpack them. When you're out in the country, your animals, the dust and the breeze look after you.'

With the hay bales successfully dumped, it's time to climb astride one of the sawhorses on which horse saddles have been placed, and make a stockwhip crack. By this stage, I'm coming second in the race, but I know this is where it all might come crumbling down. And I'm right. I thrash and I thrash and, despite having had a lesson or two earlier in the day from old drover Bill Ward, who'd earlier won a separate whip-cracking contest, it resolutely fails to do as I command. The only sounds are a dead thud when the whip hits the ground, and a scream from me when I inadvertently catch the side of my face with the lash.

This must all be hard to watch for a bloke like Lindsay Black, one of Australia's champions at pretty much all things Outback, including roping bullock, bronco and bareback-bronco riding, steer wrestling and every kind of rodeo event. Starting out droving at the age of 12 with his dad, who he describes as part-Aboriginal, he went on as a young man to travel the entire country between 1949 and 1965, performing and competing as one of its most famous rough riders.

'In the US, we're called cowboys, but here we're rough riders,' Lindsay, now a thickset man of 81 and wearing a tall black hat, tells me. 'You'd be born on a horse back in those days. But it was a dangerous sport. I saw three fellas get killed and a lot of blokes break limbs. I got horned in this arm by a steer. Its horn came out the other side. But rodeos have changed a lot these days; they're not so dangerous now.'

He does fear for the future of the Outback, however. 'Scrub-pulling with no plan has buggered up a lot of the country, and the mines are doing a lot of damage now,' says Lindsay. 'They're taking up so much land, there's going to be no room left for growing food, and being a food bowl. We're being sold out. One day it'll all be gone. There'll be nothing left.'

Whatever happens, at least these reunions will ensure that some of the proud history of Outback droving will continue to be celebrated, both by those who lived it, and blow-ins like me.

'The stories and memories mean a lot to us all,' Ben Maguire, CEO of the Australian Stockman's Hall of Fame, said the previous day at the start of the special weekend. 'We always look forward to keeping these alive.' Hank, now 79, who began droving at the age of eight, and Berry, 74, will be there every year too, keeping the Outback games going, and making sure the traditions continue for as long as they've got something to do with it.

That's despite those who seem equally determined to trash them, of course. I look as though I'm doing my best to ruin the proud tradition of whip-cracking, and I know how disappointed my mentor, Bill, must be. Mind you, he was doing this kind of stuff from the age of 14 when he went off to work in a big property in the Outback.

'At 6 a.m., I was a 14-year-old boy,' Bill, 68, tells me. 'By dinnertime, I was a man.' The Outback was his home and his life for so many years, and he loved it. 'You could camp wherever you wanted to and no one would bother you,' he says. 'When you worked, you worked as a team with other people. You had the peace and quiet so you could hear yourself think. And you had that precious thing, one word: freedom. That's what the Outback is all about.'

I'm doing so badly with this whip, with no hope of being able to make it crack within the next 50 years, one of the judges comes over and kindly allows me to move onto the next challenge. This is the final one, and the one I've been looking forward to the least: drinking a glass of warm beer as quickly as possible. I asked beforehand if I could drink something other than beer, and they'd been happy to oblige. Only trouble is, they've given me a can of ginger beer that is just about the fizziest thing I've ever tasted, let alone tried to skol.

After every fast slug, I dry retch. I can see a few of the spectators turn away from the sight. Drinking, and the ability to drink fast, is a bit of an Outback necessity, especially when you've a herd of bullocks to look after, and a horse to jump back onto at a moment's notice.

Two competitors have finished and have put their glasses on their heads to signal they're empty before I drain the last of my ginger beer. Third. I guess that's not too bad. But is it good enough to ever make me a drover?

I guess I'm going to find out in just a few days, when I go on a cattle drive for real.

2

GET OFF! GET OFF THE HORSE! CATTLE DROVING FOR THE FIRST-TIME RIDER

The tall woman in jeans, chequered shirt and a huge cowboy hat looks me up and down.

'Hmmm,' she says finally, putting her hands on her hips and pursing her lips. 'You haven't ridden a horse before? Righto.'

I wonder what's going through her mind. The same thing, probably, as is going through mine. *You've signed up to go on a cattle drive and yet you can't ride? What the bloody hell were you thinking?!* But her face doesn't give anything away. 'Yes,' she says. 'I think we'll give you Starlight to ride.'

This is the moment I've been dreading. Weeks ago I'd booked a place on the tenth annual Harry Redford cattle drive, billed as one of the great authentic experiences of Outback Australia, and my mouth had dried up every time I thought about climbing onto a horse or getting up close and personal with cows. It's not that I don't like horses, or cows for that matter. They both look lovely from a distance. But that's precisely where I've always liked to keep them.

16

Out here, about 70 kilometres north-east of the small settlement of Aramac in central-west Queensland, having no experience of livestock is about as oddball a notion as living happily in an apartment block, nestled among two dozen others, in one of Australia's busiest suburbs. Whenever I mention where I live to any of these people, they look at me with such deep sympathy, such incredible pity. Personally, I felt I was doing quite well – a snazzily minimalist apartment in a fashionable building – but to these folk, I was a terribly sad ne'er do well, someone who couldn't even afford a block of dirt in a tiny sneeze of a place like Aramac. To make matters worse, my childhood was obviously deprived too. Growing up, the only place I'd ever seen horses was on TV, and cows were the creatures on the pages of a picture book about Old MacDonald and his farm.

I hadn't come to Aramac completely unprepared, however. In the week before leaving Sydney, a friend – incredulous that I'd signed up for such a thing – bought me a birthday present of an hour's riding lesson at a stables in the eastern suburbs. I knew I'd need all the help I could get. As a kid, pretty much the first time I got on a bike I fell off and broke my arm. As an adult, I fell off a moped and broke my wrist. Horses could prove to be even more problematic. Another friend, this one a keen rider herself, and markedly less supportive, tried to talk me out of the whole thing.

'You know, even I wouldn't do a cattle drive without weeks of preparation first,' she said. 'And I've been riding for years. You'll be galloping after strays, racing up and down banks, jumping over ditches . . .' Each time she started this way, I tried to change the subject. Even if any of that were true, I'd rather not think about it. But sometimes she just wouldn't take the hint. 'Even the most experienced riders have accidents,' she told me another time.

'Think of Christopher Reeves. Horses are very unpredictable animals. They work with two notions: survival and procreation. Fear of predators has never been bred out of them so you must always remain alert and engaged. I was once thrown by a silly Arab mare who was spooked by a leaf on the track.' A leaf? Won't the Outback be full of leaves?

On the plus side, though, my friend did offer to lend me her riding helmet, boots and shirt. The day she dropped them over in a big plastic bag I felt my spirits sink, just a little. This crazy idea was too quickly firming up as reality. I took the boots out and tried them on. Too small. I took the shirt out. Too white. I could imagine what that'd look like after the first five minutes in the red dust of the Outback. I then pulled out the helmet and put it on my head to see how it would feel. Itchy and uncomfortable. I took it off and a shower of dried mud fell down around my shoulders. I touched my hair and it was caked in mud too. I phoned my friend to ask why the helmet was so dirty.

'Oh, sorry about that,' she said. 'I haven't used it since the accident.' *The Accident?* It turned out the last time she rode, she was cantering back from a jumping lesson when she lost her balance and went under her horse, which came down hard on her right foot. She was taken to hospital by ambulance to have a plate and five screws inserted. 'Thanks, but the hat's a bit big,' I said. There was no way I wanted to start my riding career with an unlucky helmet on my head.

The day of the riding lesson came around very quickly. A girl who looked no older than 12 selected boots and a hat for me from a pile, and then held the horse for me to climb onto. I asked if there was a stepladder. She sighed and coaxed the horse to a block that she told me to stand on. It was a hell of a struggle but, eventually, with a helpful shove, I managed to get on the thing's back, and sat nervously looking out over its head, and feeling unstable as the trainer coaxed us into a ring covered in sawdust and dirt.

The girl led me around and then finally ordered me to ride the horse without her at the other end of the rope. I had to try to persuade it to go, stop and turn left and right. I couldn't really refuse. The only other students in the ring were five- and six-year-old girls who trotted and cantered and performed somersaults on their horses, while all the time regarding me with undisguised contempt and sighing theatrically when I cut in front of them, apologising for not being able to steer properly. It was one of the longest hours of my life. By the time my young instructor had helped me yank my leg over to prepare to dismount, and then watched me crumple to the ground as my legs failed to hold my weight, I felt thoroughly disheartened.

That evening, I started watching TV to take my mind off the whole thing. The ABC's 7.30 program began, and presenter Leigh Sales looked solemn. 'If I asked you which animal kills the most Australians each year, what would you say?' she asked us viewers. 'Maybe snakes, crocodiles, sharks? The answer's actually horses. Tonight we bring you the story of one young woman killed two years ago after she came out of the saddle during a TAFE riding course. The horse industry's unregulated, except for racing . . .' I switched it off.

I tried not to think about the drive much after that until it was almost upon me and I had no choice. With a few days to spare around Longreach before heading off to Aramac, 1200 kilometres west of Brisbane and 66 kilometres north of Barcaldine, I was passing through a tiny settlement, and stopped at a café. I started talking to a knot of people sitting at the tables out the front. They asked me where I was on my way to, and why.

I told them about the cattle drive and asked, 'Is there anywhere around here to buy a helmet and boots?'

The daughter of the café owner said she knew just the place and jumped into her car and drove off. A few minutes later, she returned with what looked like a brand-new pair of boots in a box. 'Try these on,' she said. 'I've only worn them once and now I'm selling them.'

'But they look so nice,' I said. 'Why don't you want them?'

She sighed. 'I'm never going to ride again. Not since my accident.' She indicated her left arm, which I now noticed was encased in plaster. 'I broke it in two places,' she explained. 'And it's not healed right, so now they're going to have to break it again and reset it.'

I looked at the boots, and they looked at me. First an unlucky hat, now unlucky boots. I tried them on. They were a touch too big. Relieved, I apologised. I would've loved to have bought them if they fitted, I lied.

In Longreach, I bought a new pair of boots and a helmet for my riding debut. At least I'd be creating my own luck.

But now, the time has finally arrived and it's far too late for second thoughts. I am standing at the first gathering point of the cattle drive, being told that Starlight is my mount. Starlight. That sounds like the name of a fast horse. I'd been hoping for a Dobbin or a Tiny or a Plodder. In truth, I wouldn't even have minded a smallish donkey or a Shetland pony or something slow and low enough for me to keep both feet on the ground. But I smile and nod, as if Starlight is the horse of my dreams.

The woman in charge seems, however, to be having something of a change of heart. As she and her fellow workers lead the horses through, allocating them to the various riders, she brings Starlight along and suddenly calls someone else's name.

I feel a little aggrieved. I'd been getting used to the idea of riding Starlight, which after all was part of the nickname of the infamous cattle rustler Harry Redford, or Captain Starlight.

He was an excellent horseman whose career highlight came in 1870 when he stole, with three others, around 1000 head of cattle and a white bull from various big properties. In three months he drove them 800 miles down Cooper Creek through country that had defeated Burke and Wills just ten years before. The route he pioneered became known as the Strzelecki Track. When he was finally caught, he was put on trial at Roma, with the white bull the prize exhibit. Against all expectations, an admiring jury found him not guilty. Despite being a cattle thief, these days he's considered something of an underdog hero – in the Ned Kelly vein – who succeeded in traversing some of the toughest country in Australia and showed what could be done with big mobs of cattle, a few people, and a huge amount of determination.

But now Starlight has been stolen away, and a different horse is being selected.

'Here we go,' says the cowgirl Chrissie Nott, leading out a huge black horse named Stutter. She brings the horse right up to me and tells me to hold its lead. It's *massive*. 'About 16 hands,' someone tells me later. In non-horse-speak, that's about five metres tall.

'Is this the biggest horse you've got?' I ask, astonished. 'Couldn't I have a little one?'

A voice comes from somewhere behind me. 'It's much better to have a taller horse,' it says. 'With a small horse you can get hurt bad. You fall off and don't have time to protect yourself before you hit the ground. A bigger horse is better. If you fall, you're less likely to get seriously injured.'

That sounds neither convincing nor reassuring and, given the choice, I'd much rather have less far to fall. I look at Stutter and gingerly put a hand up in the vague direction of his head. He snorts and I leap back and everyone around us laughs. Hell, what's so funny?

'All these horses have won cups before,' Chrissie is saying. 'But just don't ask if it's for racing or bucking . . .' Hilarious. She turns to me. 'We're not riding till tomorrow but if you like, you can hop up on him now and get used to him.'

I force a smile. 'Thanks,' I say, 'but I'll wait till tomorrow. No sense in rushing a relationship.'

As I walk away, full of trepidation for what tomorrow will bring, Bob Marshall canters up on his horse, a good-looking golden-brown one with a white mane. A Palomino, I learn later. The horse, that is. As for Bob, he's the ex-Aramac mayor who was one of the founders of this drive, and for the first years acted as boss drover. Recently, he's suffered a few health setbacks and so relinquished that role but he still works on the drive as a drover, looking after both cattle and tourists – he won't be drawn on which are the most troublesome. Sitting up on his horse, with the reins casually draped over one hand, he looks happy, relaxed and comfortable. I envy him.

He must be reading my mind. 'I've got a great tip for you,' he tells me. I pull my notepad out of my bag. He's been riding horses all his life. This could be gold. 'First and foremost . . .' he says before pausing. I lean forward encouragingly. His voice drops to a conspiratorial whisper . . . 'Take notice of what they tell you.' My pen halts midsentence. He grins and trots off. Caught out already. Thanks, Bob.

Chrissie overhears and chuckles. 'You'll be fine,' she says. 'We're yet to lose a tourist.' It sounds ominously like a challenge.

22

'You know, we even had a man come along once who'd had two hip replacements,' she continues. 'He had trouble getting on and off, so he had a polypipe to pee into.' I wonder how that might work out for a woman. It could be a great help for a novice rider like me, anxious about drinking anything for fear of having to clamber off and back on the horse whenever the need struck. Chrissie looks aghast at the very suggestion.

These days, the new boss drover is local grazier David 'Chook' Hay. The son of a drover who often used to join his dad, he volunteered when Bob had to take time out. Now he also supplies most of the cattle and over half of the horses, since he loves introducing people to the bush-droving life. The modern generation has lost its link to the Outback, he believes. The cattle drive is the perfect way to reacquaint the two, and show people what life was like for the pioneers who opened up Australia. Some are quicker to learn than others.

'I like introducing people to the peace and quiet,' says Chook, 52. 'There's no mobile phone coverage, and you ride all day and just hear a beast bellow and a horse whinny. We had a bloke come with us once who loved it. When I asked him why he liked it so much, he said he loved the sounds. I said, "I can't hear anything!" He said that's what he liked about it. He'd been living with artificial sounds all his life.'

The sun is fast fading into the dusty scrub, so I heave a swag from the back of one of the cars and lug it out into the bush. My new friend Jan D'Auria, whom I'd met the day before when we both stayed at the same motel in Longreach, comes with me, and we spread our swags out close by each other. I feel relieved. I wasn't sure about swag etiquette and was dreading having to set up home a kilometre away from everyone. Instead, we giggle as we try to work out how to unroll them – at least the ironwoman challenge had taught me something – and then zip them up to avoid insects and snakes slipping inside before we get in them at night.

It sounds as if we'll be out of them before the insects have a chance to wake up in the morning, anyhow. Breakfast, we're told, is at 5.40 a.m., so we'll probably be up by 5 a.m. I ask one of the drovers what time the sun rises. 'Not by then,' is the gruff answer.

Once our beds are made, we take a stroll around, admiring others' set-ups. One guy is obviously an old hand at this – he has a very elaborate swag-tent contraption with a roof, mosquito net, pegs and guy ropes. 'All you need,' I joke, 'is a chandelier.' He points smugly to a light he's clipped to the inside. Close enough.

An hour later, we all assemble back on the dirt near the horses and get into a minibus. We drive to a concrete stage next to a tennis court by Lake Dunn, where local kids have been participating in 'bush Olympics' all afternoon, with kayak races, gumboot throwing, a sack race, a '$20 between the knees' race, a spitting competition and a 'get dressed quickly' race. The hit of the program proves to be the 'find a Kool Mint in a bowl of flour' event, where children go down on their knees, find the mint and pick it up in their mouths. While the small kids emerge white-faced, the older ones simply blow the flour away, then take hold of the mint. No flies on these bush kids!

Afterwards, the local people cook us a meal, and everyone tucks into steak and snags and chicken and mince and vegies. I tuck into the vegies.

As the sun sets, sending up a brilliant purple hue around the horizon, the lake glitters in the moonlight. It's a stunning sight. The coolibah trees drip into the water, and I wander away from the party to look up at the sky. I've never seen so many stars in my life. It's a clear night, warm and balmy, and there's only the sound of a breeze ruffling the leaves, the cry of a lonely bird, and the creak of frogs. I sigh. This could be perfect . . . without the riding. I shake my head as if to banish the thought and wander back to the crowd.

We mix and mingle, talking to each other and to locals. My fellow tourists, or 'guest drovers' as we're known, are from all over Australia, as well as one tiny young woman from Hong Kong who's always wanted to take part in something like this. She is, of course, an accomplished rider. Most of the others are too. A couple have a grandfather or a father who once worked as a drover, and want to see what life had been like for them. A few had worked on cattle stations and want the chance to relive their youth. There's a girl who's doing the drive for her Duke of Edinburgh Award, and her mum has come along for the ride, as it were.

My friend Jan, from the Sunshine Coast, has always dreamt of going on a cattle drive and this is a birthday present to herself. Recently, she discovered that her great-grandfather Patrick Darcy had actually been a drover and now she wonders if it's been in her blood all along.

'I wanted to take time out and smell the eucalypts,' she says. 'The pioneering spirit of England and Europe has long faded away, but it's still living here. It's our heritage and it's so raw and it's from not that long ago. Now I have this amazing feeling of coming home.'

Another woman, Di, has her own cattle station but loves droving, and wants the chance to ride among cattle without taking responsibility for them, or for cooking her own meals. There's also a little group of people in the area taking part in an arts workshop, staying in cottages nearby.

'How long have you been riding?' one asks.

'I start tomorrow,' I reply. She looks surprised.

'Is that wise?'

'I'm not sure,' I answer. 'I think I'm about to find out.'

The next morning I wake up tired and full of dread. I'd slept in the clothes I'd been wearing – it had been too dark and too difficult to even think of getting changed – and I'd hardly slept for worrying about the drive. The swag did prove surprisingly cosy, though, and it was hard to leave it in the night to wander into the bush to pee. I walked a long way from our swags but then found myself near others' and so had to walk further still. Then I stumbled around in the darkness, trying to find my way back again. The next night, I'll check out everyone's sleeping location first, I vowed.

In my dreams, Stutter had bolted, bucked, thrown me to the ground and stomped on me. I woke with a start just as everyone was gathering around me, saying what a shame there were neither ambulances nor hospitals out here. I told myself to stop being such a baby before going back to sleep.

Yet I'm evidently not the only one who'd been unable to sleep, or feeling anxious. While most of us left the party around 10 p.m., a second group stayed on. When they came back to the camp, blundering around, making noise and shining torches, Jan sat bolt upright and started scrabbling for her shoes. 'Wake up!' she called to me. 'It must be time to get up!' Heart pounding, I grabbed for my clothes and fumbled for my torch. When I eventually found it, down the bottom of my swag, I shone it on my watch. It was 12.15 a.m. It took me a good hour to calm down and fall back to sleep.

Jan and I still get up way too early, however. We rise about 4 a.m., in the darkness, with the fire the only distant glow. It seems the workers in the camp are feeding the flames and getting their cooking implements ready. We roll up our swags, repack our bags and dump them in a horse box set up to carry everything to the next evening's campsite.

There are big cast-iron grilles over the fire, sizzling with steaks, sausages, chops, bacon and fried eggs. A big pot of porridge is also bubbling away, another of homemade spaghetti is cooking and there's hot water and a billy full of tea being swung around in the traditional way by one of the cooks. It's to force the tealeaves to the bottom, he says. I'm full of admiration. Obviously, tea bags would be cheating.

I put my own peppermint tea bag in a cup and ask one of the cooks, with the nickname 'Mad Dog', for some hot water. He looks at me curiously but says nothing as he pours it in. I then help myself to a bowlful of porridge and slap some honey on it. It's the best porridge I think I've ever tasted.

Chook then shouts that it's time to go to the horses. The horse tailers – the two workers looking after the horses, one of whom is Chook's daughter Alison – bring them out of their enclosure one by one. Stutter looks like he had a good night, judging by how alarmingly fresh and full of energy he is. He stands looking at me with what I swear is a smile. I go over and gingerly stroke his face. 'Good boy,' I whisper. 'Please be a good boy today.'

Riders can put on their own saddles or wait for help. 'But if you don't do it yourself, we will call you "Princess" for the rest of the trip,' warns one of the workers. That seems a small price to pay, and I stand with Stutter, having a quiet horse-whispery word with him, while Chook's wife, Anne, fetches a blanket and then the saddle and bridle and sets him up. I start planning ahead.

'What time's smoko?' I ask her. 'What time will we be getting off the horses for our first break?'

She frowns. 'We won't be getting off the horses till lunchtime,' she says. 'We're handing out snacks now, so you'll just have something to eat and drink as you go.'

'But we've been told to be careful if we take off our jackets as it might startle the horses. Won't eating on its back startle it?'

She looks amused. 'Not if you're careful,' she replies.

A milk crate is floating around and eventually that comes my way too. 'OK, then,' says Chrissie, who's materialised next to me. 'Up you get.' I take a deep breath and wave my foot half-heartedly towards a stirrup. It's so high, I miss completely. I can see her trying to suppress a smile. I try again, a bit harder this time. I miss, but I think I'm getting the hang of it. Third time lucky. I lift my leg towards the stirrup, look up and notice something's missing – the horse. Stutter, evidently bored, has wandered off, leaving me standing on the milk crate by myself. There's laughter all around. There's nothing to do but join in, hoping like hell no one caught the moment for *Australia's Funniest Home Videos*.

Chrissie leads Stutter back, catches my foot and physically pushes it into the stirrup. This time, there really is no escape.

'Just hold the saddle here, and heave yourself up,' she instructs. 'One . . . two . . . three . . .' I grit my teeth and lunge for the horse's back and, to my surprise, suddenly find myself, with the help of a push, on Stutter's back. And facing the right way too. Not bad at all. Chrissie shows me how to hold the reins and then suddenly I'm on my own in charge of a bloody great big horse. Stutter senses my indecision and starts walking towards the rest of the group. I'm glad one of us has taken control.

It's now about 7 a.m. and the cattle have been set free. They thunder off into the distance. A few heartier souls kick their horses and go galloping out towards the front, where the boss drover is directing the whole operation. Stutter and I plod along at the back. This suits us both. Most people overtake us, but neither of us minds. Every so often, when I can summon the courage, I lean forward and give Stutter an encouraging pat. Otherwise, I hang on grimly to the reins, squeezing my legs around Stutter's girth, keeping my heels down, just as I've been told, trying to ignore the numbness that's gradually seeping into the entire lower half of my body.

I'm incredibly thirsty but having a drink would entail taking at least one hand off the reins to reach for the water bottle slung on a cord across my body, so that's out of the question. I've been given a muesli bar and a mandarin for my morning tea but there's no way I'm eating, either. The crackly muesli wrapper could easily scare Stutter and as for trying to peel the mandarin – forget it. I'm not willing to do anything that might jeopardise my tenuous position on his back.

It's pretty bare landscape around here, orange dirt, green spinifex and rocky soil, dotted by black gidgee trees. As the sun climbs higher in the sky, it's getting gradually warmer too. I wonder if it'll soon be time for lunch, time to get off the horses. It feels like we've been going for hours. I sneak a quick look at my watch. It's just 7.30 a.m.

More and more thickets of gidgee trees gradually appear, and Stutter keeps heading for them. He often walks so close that I have to duck under the spreading branches. Other times, he goes straight through the centre, leaving me lying forward on his neck, trying to avoid the worst of their spiny arms. I'm getting constantly whacked and scratched, and I suspect Stutter is doing it on purpose, to see how quickly he can get me off his back. I catch sight of a huge golden orb spider with yellow-banded legs sitting hunched inside his silvery wheel-shaped web between two of the branches, and wonder how many more there might be, waiting for the chance to scuttle down a passing rider's shirt.

'Hey, Sue! How are you going?' I look to my side and see Jan has hung back to check I'm OK. She looks deliriously happy.

'You're doing great,' she says, obviously trying to be encouraging. 'Isn't this fantastic?' I look at her shining face surveying everything before us: the red and black landscape, the dots of brown ahead, which I assume must be the cattle, and the brilliant blue sky.

'Yes,' I answer. 'Fantastic.' I almost mean it.

By about 10 a.m., I'm beginning to feel a little more confident. The trees have thinned out here, and Stutter seems to have resigned himself to having me on board, and to walking steadily at the back of the drive. I congratulate myself; this can only get better.

A group of the others ahead has paused and we slowly catch up to them. There's sandy ground in front of us now, on what was obviously once a river bed. Our horses step down towards the bank to walk along its base. Stutter, however, seems to have other ideas. He suddenly halts and goes down on both his front legs and is kneeling in the sand. I'm intrigued. This is interesting; I didn't know horses did this. It's a bit like camels getting down to allow you on or off their backs. If only I'd known Stutter could do this, I'd ask him to do it every time I had to mount or dismount.

But then a voice breaks through my reverie. I can hear someone shouting.

'Sue! SUE!' 'Get off! GET OFF THE HORSE!' I wonder

why the sudden urgency, but there's something in the voice that makes me take heed.

'Get your feet out of the stirrups! Get off the horse and get away from him!'

I do as I'm told, pulling my feet free and then crawling on my hands and knees off the horse and away up the river bank. I have no idea what's going on. When the shouting stops, I turn around to see Stutter happily rolling around in the sand.

I still have no idea what the problem is, but Chrissie has jumped down from her horse and grabbed me. 'Are you OK?' she's asking. 'Are you all right?' I tell her I am. But she looks shaken. It turns out that a rolling horse can be quite dangerous as it can easily roll onto its rider – something else I've now learnt. By now, a few people have gathered around me to also check I'm OK. I assure them that, really, I'm perfectly fine. If I was going to fall off, it seems to me that actually scrambling off on soft sand was probably the best possible outcome.

But Chrissie has gone over to Stutter, seized his bridle, pulled him to his feet and led him back up the river bank to beside me. Now I have the struggle of getting back on with no milk crate this time to assist. Chrissie's thought of that, however, and leads us both to a fallen tree, telling me to stand on the trunk. She then helps to hoist me onto Stutter's back once more, and get both feet into the stirrups. We set off again.

A few minutes later two of the other riders pull up close. 'Are you all right?' they ask. 'But good on you for getting back on! That's great you did that!'

I realise too late that maybe I'd actually had a choice.

3

AN EXTRA IN A COWBOY MOVIE

That evening, around the flickering flames of a roaring camp fire, I discover I'm not the disgrace I imagined I'd be in claiming the title of first person off their horse in this year's Harry Redford cattle drive. I felt sure I'd be the butt of all the jokes, and have to wear a fair amount of disdain for not even being able to ride a horse across a bit of sand successfully. But, no, it turns out I'm a bit of a hero. Not only did I come off and not hurt myself, I didn't complain and I got straight back on.

My friend Jan is also enjoying something like champion status. An hour on from the sand, we reached a waterhole, and were told to be careful as we approached it to allow the horses to drink, as it may well have been boggy and muddy. The horses might have got their front legs stuck and then reared up in an effort to extract them. Chrissie was riding close by me, and I asked her if Stutter really needed a drink. Perhaps he wasn't thirsty, and we could both hang back to stay clear of danger. She wouldn't have a bar of it, even when I said I'd be more than happy to give him a drink from my own water bottle. I'm sure she thought I was joking.

But as Jan approached, her horse, Sneezer, waded across the muddy bank and straight into the water, right up to its thighs. At that point, it went down on its back legs, as if ready to swim. Jan, completely composed, merely pulled at the reins, slapped him on the flanks, shouted at him to get back up, and kicked him lightly with her feet. He immediately rose back out of the water, and Jan was congratulated on her riding skills. After watching her, Stutter and I stealthily inched our way to the water's edge, each waiting for just one false move from the other. Thankfully, neither of us put a foot, or hoof, wrong.

Lunch came as a blessedly welcome break, with the chance to climb down from our mounts and stretch our legs. I hadn't been able to feel mine for about two hours, and my legs bowed as I touched the ground. For the next hour, I felt as if my legs were barely there, and I limped around, trying to get some blood back in them. I was ravenously hungry and thirsty, and the food looked wonderful, but I was too afraid to eat or drink much in case I needed to go to the toilet later and had to get down off the horse again.

Sitting near the camp fire, Chrissie says it'll get easier with time. I tell her I don't believe her. It seems as if she'd been born in a saddle and, in her jeans and cowboy hat, she looks impossibly cool and comfortable in these surrounds. What would she know about being scared of horses? But it hasn't always been like this, she protests. Her first time Outback had been the inaugural Harry Redford cattle drive in the Year of the Outback, in 2002, and she'd come along from the Gold Coast as a tourist, just like us, as a first-time rider.

That first night, she'd cried herself to sleep. 'I hurt so much all over,' Chrissie said. 'Even my eyelashes hurt. I just wanted to go home. But then your body gets used to it, and you fall in love with it.' She's been coming ever since – apart from the one year, in 2003, when the drought was at its worst. That year's drive had to be cancelled: there wasn't a blade of grass in sight, and every property had been de-stocked of cattle. Now she's a regular volunteer, integral to the drive's success. 'So you never know,' she says. 'It could happen to you too.' Yeah, sure.

But it is that evening I start to understand the lure of a cattle drive. The cattle have been rounded up into a makeshift yard, ringed with electric fence wire, the horses have been hobbled, the dogs have been fed and tied up, our swags have all been spread out and a big crowd of us are sitting around the fire, either with cups of tea or the first beer of the day, talking about how it all went. Many of my fellow guest drovers say how wonderful it is, riding a horse and seeing all the cattle in front of them, but I can't join in. I'd barely caught a glimpse of the cattle from my position at the back of the pack; this is definitely something I should remedy tomorrow.

Behind us, dinner is being cooked in camp ovens on another fire, and a battery of different smells is wafting across to us. As we eat and the sun slips down, above us a million stars suddenly appear alongside a silvery sliver of moon. 'I bet the evenings aren't like this in the city,' Bob says, sitting down beside me. 'You just can't beat nights out here.' I have to agree.

When we've all finished eating, a few of the guys start yarning around the fire. They talk of the old days of droving – something I now feel very familiar with – and the first ever Harry Redford event, started as a way to give Australians, as well as overseas tourists, a taste of what it would be like to be on a real cattle drive. For that, they went out and begged, borrowed and stole horses, saddles, hobbles and bridles, and won support from the local Aramac Shire Council, the Queensland government and some corporate sponsors. Local stations all along the 600-kilometre route donated cattle to be auctioned in Roma at the end of the three-month ride, with the proceeds going to charity. It proved such a massive success, it's been held every year since, bar 2003, with the shortened 200-kilometre drive lasting a total of three weeks.

Guest drovers take part in it for anything from three days to the whole three weeks, and now come from all over Australia and the world. This year, there are 24 guest drovers on my section of the drive, and by its end a total of 62 will have taken part. Meanwhile, all the workers who stage the drive do so purely as volunteers in their free time.

'Everyone takes a holiday from their job or pays other people to look after their stations or businesses,' says Bob, aged 70. 'We've all got the passion for it, and here in the Outback, we're community minded and community spirited. It's nothing short of bloody incredible.'

Naturally, there have been hiccups along the way. In past drives, people have fallen off horses and, occasionally, have been bucked off. There are stories about the different personalities of the horses, many of whom really are ex-racehorses; Stutter, apparently, included. And there was that one year when the electric fence hadn't been turned on and there was a midnight rush – thanks to the old drovers, I now knew that meant a stampede – of all the cattle. It'd been impossible to find them at night, so they'd had to wait till light the next morning to round them back up. But it's amazing how things seem to work themselves out. One year, Bob lost his socks on the cattle drive. He found them just where he'd left them, four years later.

That night Jan and I gaze up at the stars from our swags and remark on how stunningly beautiful is it out here.

'It was a great night!' I say to her. 'What fabulous people, and interesting stories . . . Jan? Jan?'

She's already asleep, and within minutes I am too.

The next day proves much easier. I've started to relax and I'm even – kind of – enjoying myself. I ride closer to the front now and can see the cattle rumbling along in front and beside us. It is indeed a spectacular sight to climb over a ridge and watch them spread out on the glorious red and green Mitchell grass plains. It has an almost magical, timeless quality about it, with just the cries of the drovers to keep the cattle in check, along with the shouts to the dogs, the whistles, the occasional crack of a whip, and the thunder of hooves. I feel like an extra in a cowboy movie, with the sun on my face and the wind behind my back, following our leader, Chook, the boss drover. He looks all tough and manly with a hobble casually slung over his shoulder. Back in the city, that could be the perfect fashion accessory.

At other times, though, I still feel the agonising cramping of my legs, knees and thighs, and the terror of Stutter misbehaving and dumping me. I'm getting braver about leaning forward, patting his neck and whispering sweet nothings in his ear, as if that's going to help.

But naturally I've still got a long, long way to go to make a passable guest drover.

One minute, Jan and I are keeping watch over a couple of cattle stragglers and the next, they've completely vanished. We just took our eye off them for a couple of seconds and they were gone. While we can't stop laughing at our incompetence, it makes you realise what a tough job droving really is. It's an art. I'm constantly surprised by how timid the cattle are, and I realise how different they are to dairy cows. It takes just one wrong step too close to them to have them shrink away in fear, or try to make a run for it. I'm anxious now about causing a stampede – whoops, no, a rush.

As well, I still struggle to get on and off the horse. The only art I've perfected is that of riding up to one of the helpers and asking them to give me a hand dismounting, which usually means they have to actually lift me off. I have little pride when it comes to horses, I've discovered. The first time Chrissie suggests I hobble Stutter myself, I look at her aghast. 'What, get down there?' I ask. She nods, as if it's the most natural thing in the world to crawl under a horse, close to its heavy, trampling hooves and try to tie its front legs together with a bit of leather and chain. Stutter had probably been waiting all day for just that moment.

'I'm sorry,' I say eventually. 'I don't think I can . . .'

That afternoon there's a real bonus, though: camping close to a dam. As soon as our horses are hobbled, Jan and I race up there, strip off and wade in through the slimy reeds, feeling the mud underfoot and ducking under the water to rinse all the dust off. It feels wonderful – our first wash since we've been on the drive.

We feel almost like real drovers, who used to bathe in dams or in troughs anywhere they could. 'And it didn't really matter if there wasn't any water for weeks,' one of the old drovers had told me at the reunion. 'You all smelled the same.' But now smelling sweetly, Jan and I stop and look all around us. The horses are grazing contentedly on the grass by the water. Butterflies are fluttering around the banks. Birds are twittering around the branches of trees. Even Stutter looks at peace.

The evenings around the camp fire are still my favourite time, however. The food is pretty fabulous – I can't believe how those roasts, stews, vegetable bakes, Golden Syrup dumplings and apple crumbles are all cooked over a simple fire – and the chefs are even preparing me special vegetarian dishes a lot of the time. I'm effusive in my praise. As a non-cook myself, I'm always extremely grateful to anyone who prepares food for me, especially if they make a special effort to exclude meat.

Everyone's now a lot more relaxed, and we're getting to know each other. There are some surprises too. Robbie, one of the cooks, turns out to be another of Chook's kids, and he's brought his own child along, four-month-old baby Cooper, together with his wife, Emma, so there are actually three generations of the one family on this drive.

The woman from Hong Kong, Chance Xie, 27, sells hedge funds for a bank but is loving being part of such an incredibly different world to her own. 'I can't believe I am sleeping under the stars and they are all so bright,' she says. 'You don't see the stars in Hong Kong. And all the Australians have been so kind to me in the Outback. It has been wonderful.'

Meanwhile, the accomplished horsewoman and grazier Di turns out to be none other than Di Zischke, otherwise known as 'the Camel Lady'. She ran camel safaris for 25 years around the desert regions of the country and has travelled more than 37 000 kilometres on camel back during her career. Now 68, she still breaks in and sells camels, and teaches people how to handle them. 'But I've always wanted to do this cattle drive,' she says. 'I've loved cattle since I was a little girl, and I'm so enjoying this.'

Everyone's taking turns to tell jokes around the camp fire and some even recite bush poetry. There's plenty of yarning too, where someone tells a story that you become utterly convinced is true . . . before they get to the punch line and you realise you've been totally sucked in. I love it, and even have a go at telling one of my own. The rest of the time, I sit back and listen to the others, gazing at the stars above and chewing at a twig – until, with a start, I remember old drover Stumpy's words about where it might once have been, and spit it out and scrub my mouth out with toothpaste.

We're all now falling into a rhythm on the cattle drive. I'm growing to like being in the Outback, and I'm loving the romance of the vast open plains, the waterholes, the rivers, and being among the horses and cattle.

I know a couple of my fellow drovers are hoping each day that some beast will make a break for it and they can go after it for the thrill of the chase, but I'm quite content to hope none of them do. I'm also enjoying the people, the lack of stress, the simplicity of setting out at daybreak each day and sitting around a fire as the sun goes down.

The weather, so far, has been on our side, with the evenings quite warm and clear, and the mornings crisp. On our third night, it rains a little, but as I snuggle under the lid of my swag, it still feels pretty cosy. By now, however, we're into what the drovers are calling 'devil devil country', with the grass full of prickly burrs. The dogs whine when these get into their paws, and the rest of us have them everywhere in our clothes. Every time I turn over in my swag, I feel another cut into me somewhere on my body. It seems impossible to avoid them.

The next morning, however, is very cold and frosty. It's hard to prise ourselves out of the swags into the pre-dawn blackness. As we eat breakfast, the tailers bring in the horses. They're all whinnying and looking restless, as if they're spooked by the changing weather. Chook brings out his horse, which suddenly rears up and lashes out with his front hooves. Chook struggles to hold him. The horse is thrashing around and then catches his legs in the reins and falls over, crashing into the ground with a sickening thud. Then, just as suddenly, the horse becomes perfectly still. Watching, we all gasp.

Chook kneels beside his head, talking softly to him. Someone asks if he's dead. A few minutes pass, then the horse shakes his head and tries to stand. He'd simply knocked himself out with the force of his head hitting the ground. Chook walks him back to the water. He'll ride a different horse today.

Every day, two more volunteers – another Aramac ex-mayor, Gary Peoples, the chairman of this drive, and his mate Roger Warren – hitch up a beautiful big Clydesdale called Chester to an old-fashioned wagon, and trundle along the road, parallel with the route the cattle drive takes. They're there to provide back-up for the riders in case anything goes wrong, and to coordinate all of the services.

I ask them if I could maybe ride with them that day, in their wagon, just for a change. They seem surprised, but are more than happy for me to come along for the ride. When I tell Chrissie, she asks me if I'm sure.

'It might be nice to give Stutter a rest today.' She raises an eyebrow. 'Well, OK.' I have to admit to her that it's actually much more about taking a break myself.

I then spend a very happy day in the wagon, taking turns to hold Chester's reins, chatting to Gary and Roger, and admiring the sight of the horses and cattle from the comfort of four wheels. I feel cowardly, but surely riding a wagon is just as valid an Outback experience as being on the back of a horse? I don't quite manage to convince myself but, hell, I'm now having a lovely, relaxing time. This is the best. 'That over there is cattle class,' Gary smiles. 'This is business class.'

These days, a lot of the guest drovers are repeat visitors; they come along and enjoy it so much, they come back again and again. 'A lot of our custom is via word of mouth,' says Gary, who used to go droving as a kid with his father. 'People say they love the quietness of it; you're just riding along with the animals. It's been so successful, and it's really put Aramac on the map.' In 2011, the Harry Redford drive was even voted in the top 25 of the '100 Things to Do Before You Die' by readers of the country's highest-selling domestic travel magazine, *Australian Traveller*.

Indeed, while there are a couple of other cattle drives held around Australia that allow visitors to join in, the Harry Redford drive is widely considered to be the most authentic. After all, we're actually droving cattle from one place to another, from Lake Dunn to Bowen Downs and Muttaburra, and not simply around a permanent camp, with proper tents and showers. We're living pretty much exactly how the original drovers did – sleeping in swags, bathing in waterholes and on the move every day – albeit with much better food, lots of support, none of the responsibility and for a much shorter time. I'd learnt that much from those dear old drovers back in Longreach.

The next morning is my last of this cattle drive. It has been an amazing experience and, the previous evening, the real drovers had given a little speech at the camp fire about me and the other two guest drovers who'll be heading off at the same time. Their words are both generous and gracious. No one mentions how odd it is for a vegetarian to be taking part in a cattle drive, which is, after all, about taking meat to market, and everyone is very kind about my horse skills – or lack thereof. I feel touched and, I have to admit, privileged to have been a part of it.

But I also feel more than a tad relieved not to have to face another day on a horse. My two colleagues, however, don't feel quite the same about letting the drive continue without them. Chance is sobbing as if her heart will break, and the other person is quiet and subdued. I hug Chance and try to console her. She can always come back another year, I tell her. And she'll have her memories.

'But I just wish I could stay for the next two weeks,' she says, gulping for air.

I smile kindly but, on the inside, I know that I could easily burst into tears too – if they told me I had to stay.

4

GREY NOMADS AND DINOSAURS

We Australians are wonderful travellers – everywhere but in our own backyards. When we're young, we go off to Europe, to Asia and to Latin America to see the sights and it's usually not until much later in life that we even think to explore our Outback.

So I'm fast finding that almost everywhere I go I'm surrounded by grey nomads. But bloody good on 'em. They're the ones who seem to be playing a blinder at propping up the Outback tourism industry and, by God, they're working hard at it. There's now *The Grey Nomad's Guidebook*, grey nomad bumper stickers, grey nomad seminars, workshops and websites galore, and I'm rapidly learning that there's nowhere you can go in the Outback today without seeing a little caravan on tow, a motorhome, a campervan or a 4WD packed to the gills with bedding, saucepans and toilet rolls, being driven by someone in search of a new lease on life after they've retired from the old one.

Ironically, however, the timing of those Outback jaunts mean many things are no longer available to these travellers.

Clambering to the top of Kakadu's Ubirr rock to enjoy the panoramic views of floodplains and escarpments, riding a camel across the glorious red sand of the Simpson desert, striding over the picturesque Larapinta Trek of Central Australia or going scuba diving off some of the most isolated beaches in the world in Western Australia are more than likely to all be out of the question. Instead, they're happier to settle for a gentle stroll and a nice cup of tea almost anywhere else. But at least they're having a good time.

Back in Longreach after the cattle drive, I find I'm surrounded by grey nomads. They're everywhere: blocking up roads after jack-knifing while trying to reverse cars with caravans attached; buying the little supermarket out of groceries; dripping melted ice-creams on the floor of the Australian Stockman's Hall of Fame; and setting up home at the massive Discovery Holiday Park, a sprawling makeshift mega-city of caravans, cabins and tents. But I shouldn't be surprised. This part of Queensland isn't so much a golden circle for grey nomads as a kite-shaped golden pond, with Winton at the end of the tail, Longreach at the base of the mainframe and the towns of Isisford, Blackall and Barcaldine each making up a point of the triangle on the top. Of the 400 000 tourists visiting this part of Outback Queensland annually, 70 per cent are now grey nomads, many of whom stay two or three months around the region.

And it's little wonder, really. While there's a huge amount of rivalry between each of these towns over which is the friendliest (Winton claims that title), which is the tidiest, which was the first to strike artesian water (Barcaldine) or drill it (Blackall), and which has the best facilities for visitors, all have a surprisingly rich array of things to see and do, and they each cultivate a strong sense of history. The locals can be pretty welcoming as well.

'We *love* the grey nomads,' says the woman behind the counter at a chemist store in Longreach. 'If it wasn't for them coming out here and then popping in all the time with their prescriptions, we'd be having trouble making ends meet. A lot of the places round here would die without them. We've got a lot to be grateful to them for.'

Along with hordes of grey nomads, I spend a day checking out the Australian Stockman's Hall of Fame with its rich history of explorers, convicts and settlers, all pioneers in their own ways who battled the tyranny of distance, the harshness of the land and plagues of everything from dingos to mice. Life in the Outback could be so hard for so many, you wonder why more didn't turn around and flee back to the coast. But if any did, there's no section at the museum for them. Instead, there's the saying writ large, 'Once you swim the Barcoo River, you'll always come back to the Outback'. It's an echo of a maxim I've heard so many times before, but with marginally different geography – you'll always come back if you cross the Thomson River, the Parachilna, the Simpson Desert . . .

'Oh, they're all true, more or less,' says Eric, 73, a touring grey nomad I strike up a conversation with while shuddering over a little film showing thousands of mice hiding in a bale of straw, and hearing about how, during plagues, mice have been known to eat whole boats and nibble sleeping farmers. 'Once you discover what it's really like out here – mice plagues excepted – you get to love the places. It's so different from our lives in the cities.'

Another day I head off to the Qantas Founders Museum, which commemorates the founding of the airline and its impact on the Outback. I ask directions and get strange looks. I realise later why: it's the only building with a massive great jumbo jet parked out front, alongside an old Boeing 707, Australia's first international jetliner. While the grey nomads surge like their own mini-plague into the museum, I climb up onto the plane, sit at the controls in the cockpit, and even, with a safety harness attached, go for a walk out on one wing.

That afternoon, I drop into the Kinnon & Co. Station Store in the main street, which belongs to a particularly enterprising family who seem to have most of the tourist attractions of the area sewn up. Richard and Marisse Kinnon turned to tourism when it looked as though they'd lose their cattle property to years of drought. Now, with the help of their three children Abigail, 18, Jeremy, 15, and Lane, 14, the family run the store and café, and offer a number of tours and events, usually centring on history, for which they dress as early settlers. It contributes to a whole-some other-era worldliness about them; they're nothing like any family I've ever met. The children were all homeschooled, and they look, and sound, like an early episode of the TV soap *The Waltons*, yet don't even have a TV! But they do seem perfectly happy, living and working all together.

In the 21st century, how can this be? 'I don't know,' says Marisse, but she still sounds as if it's the most natural thing in the world. 'They're free to pursue other opportunities if they want to, but they all seem to just like being here. We get on fine.'

I go on one of their tours, a replica Cobb & Co. stagecoach 'gallop thru the scrub'. For half of the ride, I sit inside the carriage and for the second half, up the front next to Richard, holding the reins of the four horses. Clouds of dust rise up to blanket us, and we're thrown around with surprising violence because of the uneven ground, the carriage springs and the galloping of the horses – but it's exhilarating. It's also atmospheric, with the horses' hooves thundering across a landscape that hasn't changed much in the past 100 years.

Later, I take a riverboat cruise, and have dinner on the Thomson River as the whistling kites perch on the coolibah trees that fringe the river. Eventually the kites take off, gliding slowly above our heads, and the tiny heads of turtles pop out of the water all around us. When the red of the sunset fades to gold and then goes to black, the boat flicks its lights onto the riverbank to show us what's stirring in the ghostly haze, and then turns them off again for some star-gazing as the white moon shimmers above. In my hardy explorer's shirt and cargo travelling pants, I freeze. The grey nomads come up trumps. They're all dressed sensibly in cardies and jackets.

The next evening, my last in Longreach, I go over to the holiday park to check out how the other half is living. Very well, it seems. In the great hangar of the Woolshed Restaurant on the site, there are dozens of grey nomads tucking into steak and chips, fish and chips and oversized bowls of pasta and salad, while a country singer croons in the corner. Maureen and Michael from Bendigo are at the next table and, seeing me dining solo, invite me to join them. They've been in town for three weeks and are preparing to move on the next day. They've spent two months in this part of Outback Queensland and are loving every day. They have plans to travel for a full year, they say.

'We had no idea it would be this nice, and there'd be so much to do here, eh?' says Michael. 'We wanted to get away somewhere warmer for the winter, and save on the electricity bills, but we're honestly shocked by how good it's been.' So they're not missing home at all? 'I am,' Maureen says pointedly. 'I wanted to just be away for three months but . . .' she tails off as their meal arrives. One meal, curiously, between two.

Maureen carefully carves up the steak and they take turns with the fork. Michael murmurs his assent through his chews.

'Bloody great people,' he says when he's finished. 'Not like they are in our part of the world, eh? Here, they're always ready to have a chat with you, they're so welcoming and they can't do enough for you.' I have to agree with him here. 'Bloody great, they are, eh?' he repeats.

And what's more, the locals' largesse seems to be infectious. The couple offer me a lift to Winton, where I'm going next. I accept happily. The car I've been travelling in isn't available for the next few days, so I was planning to catch the bus. This sounds much easier and, what's more, it'll give me a chance to study the grey nomad species up close.

The next morning, Michael and Maureen pick me up at 6.30 a.m., which feels pointlessly early, but I'm hardly in a position to complain. Michael insists I sit up front with him, while Maureen is banished behind to a sideways seat in the living room of their cosy Toyota Hilux Nica motorhome. I soon appreciate, however, why she looks perfectly content to sit and knit by herself. She's obviously fuming about the thought of being on the road for a year. *'For a year!'* she mutters a couple of times, as if she can hardly believe it herself, and appreciates having an audience.

After a while, I can't believe that this couple will even make it through to the end of the day together, let alone a year. I've found travelling can be tough for any couple, even, sometimes, for a weekend away. So two people spending a year wedged tightly in a confined space could turn out to be the stuff of nightmares.

Michael seems to be completely oblivious to Maureen's mood. He's a man who hates a chat, as they say around here; in fact, he just doesn't shut up. By the time we've reached Darr, 20 kilometres away, and still haven't yet hit fourth gear, I feel I know pretty much everything there is to know about him: his boyhood, his school years, how he was robbed of a promising footy career by a knee injury, the evening classes and his first job in a bank – which turns out also to have been his last.

'Was there for 50 years,' he says proudly. 'Still sitting at the same desk where I started, eh! Not many people today could say that, could they? Kids now could never hold down a job that long.' Or want to, I almost say. I just smile and smile until my face aches. He's a nice man, but I can see why the prospect of a year on the road with him isn't exactly filling his wife with joy.

At Morella, just another 35 kilometres further, it's time to take a break. I wonder if there's a nice café in town but we drive straight through and out the other side, then bump up onto the grass verge. Maureen takes that as her cue to bang the cupboards around and get the kettle out, and Michael as his to show me the minute workings of their motorhome: where they sleep, where they eat, where they cook, where they do crosswords, where they like to have their cups of tea, where one of them might be murdered by the other . . . It takes 45 minutes, which is an extraordinary feat for such a small space. The tea takes another 20. I guess at their time of life – Michael is 75 and Maureen 71 – there's no need to rush, but I see my life flitting past in slow motion, as well as a bus out of the corner of my eye. But Michael's only just warming up.

For their year away, he says, they plan to do many things: go to Birdsville to watch the races; stay underground at the opal-mining town of Coober Pedy; and check out the Mt Isa rodeo. They'd seen a documentary just before they left home about the world's last outback boxing tent, where a professional boxing troupe takes on all-comers, at Mt Isa, and Michael particularly wants to see that. Run by fourth-generation showman Fred

Brophy, the fighting was bloody and brutal but, he says, it looks like good fun to be there. As part of the audience in the tent that is, Michael adds quickly, definitely not fighting on the mat. 'A taste of the *real* old Outback, eh, darl?' he says, turning to Maureen. She grimaces. 'I don't know if I'd be game to go in,' she replies. 'It was very violent. People seemed to get hurt.'

It does sound interesting, though, and I imagine Fred Brophy would be a fascinating bloke to talk to, especially if he's been doing it for years, and his boxing tent would be a sight worth seeing. I'm not sure, however, how I'd go watching a boxing match. I've never liked boxing, I'm with Maureen on that. Why would people ever get involved in such a violent pastime – I don't even like to call it 'sport' – and what drives people to watch? But I make a note of Fred's name, and store it away for another time.

Michael and Maureen are now talking over their itinerary for the next few months; Michael eagerly, and Maureen not so much. But it seems they've rented out their home to provide them with their spending money for this trip. This was evidently his idea, and Maureen shoots him a dark look . . . obviously that's why she can't cut their travels short. Mind you, he continues, they hadn't realised how expensive it can be, what with fuel prices, the higher prices of fresh food in the Outback, repairs when things go wrong with the van, fees for powered sites in holiday parks, entry to attractions and the occasional meal out. That's something that had never really occurred to me before, either. 'We're self-funded retirees,' says Michael. 'We can't afford all that, especially with the sharemarket like it is. We've seen our savings go down all the time since the GFC, eh? So now we're on much more of a budget.'

This tallies closely with what I've heard about grey nomads on the road. While everyone in the Outback is immensely grateful for their adventurous spirit, they just wish they'd spend more money along the way. But some of them simply don't have much cash to spare. For a few, this drives them to desperate measures. 'I think they have a competition for who can nick the most toilet paper from public toilets,' one tourist operator says snidely. And someone in Longreach had reported that whenever grey nomads go into local stores, the assistants often keep a keen eye on them. 'Lollies, chocolate, anything, disappears,' she laughs. 'A few of them are so hard up, they really shouldn't be travelling at all.'

Occasionally, they can come unstuck too. Saving money on food means some eat poorly – bread bought weeks before in the last big town they visited served with plastic cheese slices for lunch, and tiny portions of whatever cheap cut of meat they can afford for dinner. Sometimes this can lead to illness, which can be exacerbated by many nights spent on the roadside, without water to wash in or electricity to stay powered up, so that drivers can avoid park fees. A police officer I spoke to one night mentioned that grey nomads are increasingly taking up beds in local hospitals because of bad health. Sometimes too, they don't pay enough attention on the roads, since they're often not used to driving such large vehicles.

Obviously, Michael and Maureen aren't doing it too hard. Yet. Being careful with their money at the moment means making their own tea rather than having it in cafés, and occasionally sharing meals. But if times get any tougher, they might be forced to pull their belts much tighter. 'We always know, if worse comes to worst, we can always sell our house and head off into the Outback indefinitely,' says Michael. 'The Outback's great for that. We'd camp for a month at a time in one place, so we're not using fuel, and the locals are always so hospitable here. They'll buy you a drink any time. Maybe invite you back for a meal from time to time too. That'd be all right, darl, eh?' He looks at Maureen. She's looking stonily out of the window. 'Let's hope it won't come to that,' she says.

It takes nearly all day to get to Winton, a mere 180 kilometres away. By the time we arrive, I'm exhausted. 'Can I give you something for petrol?' It's the least I can do, I say. Michael gladly takes up my offer.

I explore Winton over the next few days, and fall in love with the place. It's a neat little town, with lovely old buildings down the wide main road, residents constantly watering their bougainvillea, decaf coffee in not one but two cafés, and everyone so polite and smiley. It becomes pretty much my favourite Outback town.

I adore the Waltzing Matilda centre, a living love letter to the old swagmen of the Outback who drifted around, picking up shearing work and carrying all their belongings in their swags. With a sound and light show, recorded voices of swaggies telling their stories, a tiny hologram display and the story of Red Jack – a woman who dressed as a man and travelled Queensland for nearly 20 years – I spend the best part of a day there. I love the idea of working hard then playing hard, spending all those wages on beer, and then having to pick up work again. The romance and hardship of it all I find equally entrancing, and that longing for the freedom of the road . . . Would it be too much of a stretch to suggest some of the grey nomads are a kind of heroic nouveaux swaggies?

That night, I have dinner at the Tatts, the gorgeous old 19th century pub on the corner, with a wide verandah filled with tables, and watch the sun go down at the end of the road. Publican Paul Nielsen, dressed in his trademark shorts and zipping around everywhere chatting to customers – tells me how the town attracts so many. 'The secret is you make everyone feel welcome,' he says. He is trying to set up a Friends of Winton in Sydney. With his levels of energy, he might very well succeed.

The next morning I take a tour of the massive sheep and cattle property Carisbrooke Station with owner Charlie Phillott. I've been told he's a great guy and a marvellous guide, but to just keep off the subject of religion. I'm happy to do so; like with politics, talking about it can only ever lead to trouble. Charlie turns out to be an elderly pastoralist, with an almost military bearing, who knows this land like the back of his hand and loves it fiercely. And for good reason. It's some of the most spectacular landscape in Australia, with long low claypan country and open grasslands, watched over by towering red craggy cliffs. There's even a glowing sandstone mesa Three Sisters formation, far more awe-inspiring than the much better-known Three Sisters of NSW's Blue Mountains.

Charlie points out wedge-tailed eagles swooping down, and talks of the artesian bores that service the western half of Queensland and the curse of the rapidly multiplying gidgee trees, where once there were just bare plains dotted with spinifex.

'Fifty years ago, this used to be endless plains,' he says, shielding his eyes against the sun so he can see the distant horizon. 'But now the landscape's changing. My dad told me that his father told him he would catch his horse and ride 800 miles to inspect properties in the course of his daily work.'

The only other person on this tour is another grey nomad, Eileen, who's taking three months away from Brisbane to travel around and rediscover her love of the Outback. As Charlie stops and makes us billy tea on a fire, Eileen says how she once lived on a property but, when her marriage broke up, she returned to the city. She's regretted it every day since, she says.

Eileen seems so forlorn, I ask her why she doesn't just find a little house in a nice town like Winton and move there. She'd be able to sell her house in Brisbane for so much more than she'd pay for one here.

'I couldn't do that!' she says. 'Not on my own!'

'But why not?' I persist.

'I couldn't live here, a woman on my own, could I, Charlie?' she asks our host.

It's Charlie's turn to look baffled. 'Why not?' he asks.

Her face is getting redder. 'Well, I'd need a husband to come out here with.' She winks at Charlie. He looks embarrassed.

I don't give in. Eileen's probably only about 65, looks fit and active, and obviously has plenty of get-up-and-go to travel around on her own in the first place. 'But everyone's always saying there are a lot more single men in the Outback than in the cities,' I offer. 'Surely, moving out here would be the perfect way to find one?'

'Oh, no, I couldn't,' she says, looking coy. 'That just isn't done. I'll probably live the rest of my days in the city, looking out of my window on to other people's gardens and hearing the noise of traffic . . . I expect I'll die there too. And I'll only be found when the neighbours smell me.'

Charlie's looking positively alarmed by now. Eileen looks deathly serious. 'Oh, come on!' I laugh, trying to make light of it. 'She'd be all right out here, wouldn't she, Charlie?'

He looks uncertain.

After the tea, Charlie drops us off at Lark Quarry, an elegant hangar of glass and tin seemingly in the middle of nowhere. But, surprisingly, it's actually one of the most important paleontological sites in the world. Here, 95 million years ago, a bunch of small dinosaur-like coelurosaurus were peacefully grazing when a giant meat-eating theropod came upon them. The resulting stampede – or should that be 'rush'? – was captured for the rest of time in over 3000 fossilised footprints on the silt floor. It's the world's only recorded evidence of a dinosaur stampede and was used as the inspiration for the stampede scene in the movie *Jurassic Park*. Gazing at those footprints now, and realising how long they've been moulded into the earth, is a truly humbling experience.

'It's the largest collection of dinosaur tracks in the world,' says our guide Ian Pascoe. Eileen smiles fetchingly at him.

The next day, my interest piqued, I make my way to the Australian Age of Dinosaurs centre, just outside Winton. Built on top of a stark red jump-up, or mesa – a stand-alone flat-topped hill that remains when the surrounding land is worn away by erosion – this is home to the world's largest collection of dinosaur fossils, and the biggest fossil-preparation lab in the southern hemisphere. It was begun by sheep graziers David and Judy Elliott after they discovered a dinosaur bone on their property, from what turned out to be the largest dinosaur ever to be found in Australia.

The first formal dig started in 2006 and by 2009 it was officially announced that three new species of Australian dinosaur had been found: a carnivorous theropod nicknamed Banjo; and two kinds of giant plant-eating sauropods, dubbed Matilda and Clancy. After a number of digs, the material now in storage at the centre represents 25–35 more years of fossil-preparation work. 'You have the fossils but they're like a massive jigsaw puzzle to be put together, without a picture on the box,' says guide Freddy Hill. 'One way to tell if a bone is from a dinosaur is by licking it.

If your tongue sticks to it, it means the bone has dried out and it could be a dinosaur. But be careful before you lick; it could also be a cow pat.'

Volunteers come to help on the digs and also pay for the privilege of helping in the lab to prepare the fossils, drilling them with tiny dentists' drills to free them from their 100-million-year-old rock tombs. Watching the volunteers bent over lumps of rock, peering at them through a huge magnifying glass and patiently drilling infinitesimal quantities of dust off them, makes me feel so happy I'm not doing it. Or, even more, paying to do it. Patience was never my strong suit. Time may not have been able to destroy the evidence of these dinosaurs roaming the earth, but an accidental whack from me might do the job.

Work's still being done on the centre and, by 2015, it's likely to be a world-best natural history museum displaying our prehistoric past. 'This will be the dinosaur capital of Australia,' says chief of operations Dr Brant Bassam. 'It'll be for anyone interested in our ancient history. It'll have sculptures of dinosaurs, 3D film shows and virtual effects to bring them back to life. It's going to be amazing.'

I wonder if Eileen's coming over to see it. Just as grey nomads are reinventing themselves around Australia, by either neces-sity or choice, so the local dinosaurs will now hopefully have a second coming. But as well as the spectacle, Eileen might particularly enjoy the company of one of the technicians and guides, 'Gorgeous' George. A very nerdy, but immensely like-able, dinosaur-obsessed fossil cleaner and tour guide, he recently appeared on the reality TV show *Beauty and the Geek*. He was voted off before he could find a partner but is still looking . . .

The next day, I reluctantly leave Winton to head back to Longreach. This time, on the Greyhound bus, it takes only two hours. It's cheap, it's comfortable, you're sitting up high enough to see all the scenery and you can choose who you talk to. I sit next to a man called Gordon who's living the grey nomad nightmare. He lost all his money through a bad investment in an apartment block on the Gold Coast and so came, with his wife, to live in the Outback. He's now got a job as a driver and his company allows him to park his caravan on a patch of waste ground out the back of the office, rent-free. Apart from the money they spend on food, the couple are saving every cent of Gordon's wages to enable them to pay back their creditors.

'The Outback's giving me a chance to get my life back together,' he says. 'I could never survive like this in a city. Sure, it's hard. We used to live in a lovely house overlooking the water, and it's lonely, especially for my wife. But the Outback's a very forgiving place. There's no social ladder out here. People accept you for what you are, and are willing to give you a chance, no matter what your age.'

Back in Longreach, I pick up the car again and join the procession of neat campervans, solar-powered off-road caravans and converted vans and coaches, all bristling with names like Cruise 'n' Snooze, Advencha B4 Dementia, Anzac Gypsy and Neva Inn, to drive to the picturesque little town of Barcaldine, 100 kilometres to the east. Once there, I check into a motel and go for a walk to find a café. In the window of one are two women who look very much alike, apart from their different coloured T-shirts, and both are lathering scones with jam and cream. I immediately want what they're having and go inside to sit down. When I order, they smile over at me.

'It's hard to resist, isn't it?' says the one in black. They turn out – surprise, surprise – to be sisters.

Denise, a retired teacher from Brisbane, and widowed Ann from Bribie Island, have long dreamt of travelling around Australia for a year. They're in just their first month and, apart from the mice plague they discovered when the pillows on their campervan beds became covered in black dots, they're having a fabulous time. 'It was a kind of yearning to get away for a while,' says Denise, 67. 'You want the kind of freedom you can only get in the Outback. These kinds of places get under your skin; there are great people living here.'

Before they left, they learnt simple mechanics, like how to change a tyre, through the Campervan & Motorhome Club of Australia but, at the end of the year, both are adamant they'll return to their urban lives.

'We won't become highway wanderers,' says 72-year-old Ann firmly. I ask what she means and it turns out there are a number of well-defined classes of grey nomads. The sisters say they fall into the 'once in a lifetime' group, those who just take time out of their regular lives to travel for three months to a year. 'Highway wanderers' are the grey nomads who sell their homes and spend the rest of their lives on the road, often only moving on after they've collected their pensions each fortnight.

'I am enjoying it, but I'm not *that* adventurous,' says Ann. I wonder if, one day, I'll ever be doing the same – or maybe I already am, simply in another guise?

Scones finished, we say our goodbyes, and I go in search of Doug Stewart. He's the man running Barcaldine Council's grey nomad volunteers program, an incredibly innovative project encouraging retirees to stop by during their stay and share their skills with the local community. While the town benefits from their voluntary work, they get to meet locals, make enduring friendships, receive vouchers to use in local stores and have the chance to give back to the Outback.

It's a scheme that's been going since 2008 and has proved immensely successful with both locals and visitors alike. In addition, it's attracted the interest of more than 30 other towns around Australia which say they'd like to introduce it into their communities too. Yet despite starting with Queensland government backing, and having been praised by a high-powered independent academic study, it's now in real danger of falling over for lack of funds to support it.

'Grey nomads often spend about three months here and have the kind of skills that many of us in the Outback could really use,' says Doug. 'It can be hard to get tradespeople to come to places so far out, but the grey nomads, although retired, have really valuable skills, talents and knowledge that are wonderful for us to tap into. We've found they get as much out of it too. It's a chance for them to really engage with the local community and get a lot of satisfaction out of helping, and it's a great way of bridging the gaps between the bush and the cities.'

The idea is a wonderful one, and the results seem to speak for themselves. The kind of tasks that have been undertaken are enormously varied, from a former CSIRO scientist giving a talk to local schoolkids, to retired chippies and builders helping fix up some of the buildings around town, from a restoration program at a local church to painting an aged-care building, from helping build a raised garden for wheelchair patients to enjoy at the hospital to teaching a belly-dancing class for the elderly.

The program's oldest volunteer, an 80-year-old, arrives every year to swing a hammer with the vigour of a man half his age. A visiting musician came one time to play the flute to a woman lying in a coma in hospital who nurses feared was brain dead.

As the haunting music filled her hospital room, a tear slid down her cheek. 'It was beautiful!' says Doug, shaking his head. 'No one could communicate with her, and she couldn't communicate with us, but the music had shown us she was still there . . .'

We drive out to the Lloyd Jones Weir, an area 14 kilometres out of town, where many of the grey nomads park their vehicles among the gum trees that line the Alice River. It's a nice spot. The river is apparently teeming with yellow belly perch and redclaw crayfish, there are wood-fired barbecues close to a bench and tables in the middle of the grounds, and the council maintains a public toilet and shower block, with campers contributing to the cost of toilet paper (or perhaps donating from their own supplies!) Some wag has even erected a tombstone over a mock grave, inscribed with the words: 'Here lies the last person caught stealing toilet paper', and there's a 'thong tree' nearby, a tree with dozens of thongs hanging on pieces of wire down from its branches.

This has been Max and Mary Guthrie's home for the past two months. Two of Doug's regular volunteers, these grandparents park their caravan with its sunshade extension, solar shower and gas-bottle heater here on what a sign declares to be 'Geriatric Drive' for three months every year and are happy to muck in with pretty much anything that needs attention.

'I've been painting tables and helping with the church and the theatre and painting the rails at the pony club,' says Max, 75. 'I also did an audit with the Harry Redford cattle drive. We like to lend a hand with anything, really. We enjoy it. It's nice to meet people and you have fun working; there's a real camaraderie about it. It's nice to be able to give back. And besides, I don't like to sit around too much doing nothing. It's a fantastic scheme.'

Mary, 72, agrees. 'It keeps us out of mischief,' she says,

laughing. 'And it's always a great atmosphere wherever you go. It's very friendly.'

Otherwise, the couple spend their days reading, knitting and chatting with their friends who park nearby every year, or with the newcomers they're quick to introduce themselves to. There's also fishing, walks and the town to drive into, and they'll hear from their kids who phone on Skype through their laptop or text them every other day. Sometimes, they'll just go and do some shopping at Mitre 11. Mitre 11? They laugh. 'That's what we call the tip,' explains Mary. 'You get little bits and pieces from there, and sometimes just wood for the fire. You get into trouble if you're caught nicking off with stuff, but who's going to catch us?'

The couple seem extraordinarily content, not only with their chosen grey nomad lifestyle, but also having been given the opportunity to help others on a casual, part-time basis. I ask them if they think they're living the best of all worlds, and they don't hesitate to reply.

'We're just loving being grey nomads,' says Max. 'We love travelling. You just can't do this sort of thing when you're young and you've got a young family to support and a job to go to. But now, with our children settled, it's great to be able to live like this. You go to different places and learn so much from people you meet. I'm only sorry we didn't do this in our 50s, when we could still have done so much more. And to be able to help others as you go . . . well, it doesn't get better than this.'

5

EVEN THE CROWS FLY BACKWARDS

Their hooves thunder down the track as their riders hunch low. The crowd's roar builds to a frenzy. 'Come on, Toe Cutter!' someone yells. 'Dirty Harry!' another cries. The shouts become louder, more guttural and intense.

Suddenly, one animal veers towards the rails and, for a moment, it looks like he might hit the metal and it will be all over. But his jockey heaves at the reins and yanks him back onto the straight and narrow just in time. Another twists and his jockey tumbles off. The crowd gasps, helpers rush to check he's not injured, and then lift him up to get back in the race.

'This is a great day,' says John de Groot happily, as the winner finally streams past the post and then keeps on running and running and running . . . until he nearly knocks the gate down at the end of the track. 'I've always seen goat racing as the poor man's horserace. It's *very* exciting.'

I've never really given much thought to goats before but it seems I really should have. Goats helped settle the Outback,

John de Goat, sorry, *de Groot*, tells me. They were harnessed into teams to pull wagons, carting wood and manure, they were astonishingly low-maintenance, eating anything and everything, and they provided milk and, at the end of the day – well, the end of *their* day – meat. They have also always been great sport.

When John, now a very proper Brisbane lawyer, was growing up in Barcaldine, he became a champion bareback goat rider on his favourite mount, Thunder. His winning tactic? To make sure the race was always in the direction of his house, so the goat would think he was running for home. Today, John helps keep the proud tradition of goat racing alive by sponsoring races every year and putting up prizes for the children who win, travelling in the specially designed racing carts the goats pull.

What's more, he's even written a book, *Memoirs of a Goat Racer*, and is well advanced in his plans to set up the world's first goat-racing hall of fame and museum in Barcaldine's Australian Workers Heritage Centre. 'They're such an important part of our history,' says John, whose eccentric passion for goats sits oddly with his lawyerly bearing. 'They were part of working men's survival. Without goats, the west would never have been settled.'

This all feels slightly surreal, but everyone involved in the sport is deadly serious. Goats need to be handled sensitively, apparently. They're smart and can sometimes prove obstinate. They can refuse to start, deliberately face the wrong way, drift to the left or right or even flick the cart to get rid of their jockey. They're a cross between a horse and a dog, with the haughtiness of a cat thrown in.

Another expert on all this is Tom Lockie, dubbed the Bart Cummings of goat racing, who has one of the biggest goat-racing stables in Australia. A short, squat man with a big voice and an enormous laugh, who also runs Artesian Country Tours, he began by catching feral goats, breaking them in and training them. In the early days, he could sell them for $2.80 each; last year a good racer fetched $680.

'Most goats enjoy racing,' he says. 'They understand what it's all about. And we're now using them to teach kids about animal husbandry, through handling and breaking in goats as part of the Year 11 and 12's education at school. But I've had good goats and bad. I've got one at the moment who's a mad bastard. I've been feeding him and looking after him and keeping him on a chain for months now, but I still can't tame him. I've called him Tyson. Someone said I should just eat him, but I don't think I could. The bastard would still be galloping around the camp oven . . .'

I ask if I can have a ride in a goat cart and resist the advice that, to make it go faster, I have to lean forward and twist my goat's tail. Sitting in the little cart, my feet dangling close to the floor, I decide I far prefer this to riding horses. It all feels safer and more comfortable, and the goat seems so much friendlier than my cattle-drive horse Stutter ever was.

This is the aspect of the Outback I'm warming to: this quirky kind of make-your-own-fun side. Of course, there are more serious and worthy attractions in a place like Barcaldine, but it's this knockabout aspect I'm getting to appreciate. People don't seem to take themselves too seriously, and no one ever seems afraid of wearing their heart on their sleeve.

You'd have little trouble guessing, for instance, where the Globe Hotel publican Pat Ogden's allegiances lie. Massive posters of past and present Labor Queensland premiers – Anna Bligh, Peter Beattie and Wayne Goss – hang outside the pub he's run for the last 47 years. One of the six hotels on the short main street, it's decorated with all sorts of federal and state election posters for the party. 'I'm a life member of the Labor Party and this is a Labor pub,' he says, grinning. 'I was born in Barcaldine nearly 83 years ago, brought up here and have never been outside Queensland. I don't need to. Everything anyone's ever needed is in this town.'

Pat isn't alone in his fervour. Since today's May Day (Labor Day in Queensland) there's a steady crowd pouring into the Australian Workers Heritage Centre, the nation's only commemoration of the history of the working man and woman. The most important part is its special exhibition about the Great Shearer's Strike of 1891 in Barcaldine, which proved to be a watershed moment in the fight to better the nation's working conditions. Many of the strikers' meetings were held around a large ghost gum by the town's railway station, where the unionists tried to stop strike-breakers getting off the train. As a result, it was dubbed 'the tree of knowledge', and it's popularly believed that the Labor Party was founded beneath its branches.

By 1899, the state had the world's first Labor government but, sadly, the tree didn't fare so well. When I rent a bicycle one day for a gold coin donation to tour the town, I can't seem to find it. The reason? It isn't there any more. In 2006, the 200-year-old tree was poisoned; it's a mystery that endures to this day. Some blame an over-enthusiastic railway worker spraying weedkiller around the tracks, others say it was a local with a grudge.

Happily, some cuttings were able to be taken from the tree, however, and these are being propagated as clones. A massive $5 million timber sculpture now hangs over the site in homage, dominating the streetscape. Admirers call it 'Barcy's box'; detractors have nicknamed it 'box costalot' and 'the gallows'.

*

There's a fair bit going for the Outback, but there are aspects of it I still loathe. Every morning at every single motel I stay in, I'm woken before the crack of dawn by the Outback alarm call. The sweet sound of birdcall? The chirping of frogs? The lowing of cattle? No, the roar to life and then steady throbbing of a diesel engine. That mightn't be so bad if you've slept well, but regularly sleep is broken by the thunder of cattle trucks driving past during the night – as the non-meat-eater, I always imagine the cattle inside are crying, 'Help! Help!' – and then there's the drone of mosquitoes in the room.

'Make sure you turn on the air conditioning before you go to sleep,' one helpful motel owner tells me.

'But it's so noisy,' I protest. 'It sounds like a factory in my room with it on.'

'That's what I mean,' she says triumphantly. 'It means you don't hear anything else.'

There's also the issue of Outback food. Some of it is good, some of it is very good, and some of it is absolutely dire. If you're a fan of fried food, fried battered food and even food that's fried, battered and then fried again, you'd be in your element. In nearly every roadhouse, there's all kinds of meat on offer, clad in batter and deep fried to death, hot chips and more hot chips, rissoles, sausages and, in one place, memorably, even fried eggs in batter.

In most high streets, the bakery claims pride of place, many stacked with white bread, with not a grain in sight to interrupt the slices, cakes and pies. Then, of course, there's all that beer and soft fizzy drinks to wash it all down.

Locals regularly complain about the quality of some of the vegetables and fruit their stores are sent. People in Barcaldine still talk about the time the store sold square oranges. *Square* oranges! Is it any wonder that Australia is now among the world's fattest countries?

But then again, I'm finding plenty that's good about the Outback. Every time I pull over on a road to take a photo, someone stops to ask me if I'm in trouble or need a hand. I'm always being offered lifts – even if I'm only going 200 metres – as many Outback people don't seem to like to walk anywhere that they could drive instead. Everywhere I go, people don't hesitate to say hello and have a chat. As well, that community spirit I hear about all the time is endearing to a city-dweller. It might well take 20 years before you're no longer considered a blow-in in some of these places, but you'll always be treated with friendly civility.

'The Outback has to be community spirited to survive,' the grey nomad guy Doug Stewart had told me. 'If we weren't community minded, we'd perish. You can't sit around and wait for people to help; that might never happen. You have to get up and get involved yourself.'

Another local says she loves how tolerant the Outback community can be. While there will always be a few rednecks in every place, there are often fewer in the Outback because so many have had the experience of living and working with outsiders – Afghans, Chinese, Italians, Greeks – from the early days. 'It's a simpler, gentler life,' another local goat enthusiast tells me. 'You can live cheaply in the Outback and you can live well. The quality of your life can be better.'

Although to make the most of all that, you have to learn to relax, advises Doug. 'If something doesn't happen today, it might happen tomorrow. It can be frustrating, but you can't let it get to you, otherwise you'd go crazy.'

I've never been a patient person, so I tell myself that I'm going to take Doug's advice to heart, and try to be more laidback. For the first ten minutes, it goes well. I'm driving out of Barcaldine south towards Blackall when I close in on a giant road train, full of cattle. It's heavily laden and travelling pretty slowly, so I take a deep breath and dawdle along behind it. We continue grinding along at about the pace of a snail with a heart condition until I realise that most of my day might well be spent travelling the next 100 kilometres.

I've always been nervous about overtaking road trains. It's hard to see from behind how long they are, and sometimes they can swing across the road and the wind they generate can push you off-course too. And on a narrow two-lane road, there's always the danger of something suddenly appearing travelling the other way ready to collide head-on. Patience, I tell myself, between gritted teeth, is a virtue.

After about 20 minutes of this, there's an end in sight. The road train is signalling right. I sit back. Patience has triumphed. He's going to turn off any second and leave a clearway ahead. But he doesn't. Five minutes later, he signals again. He obviously misjudged his turning. But again, he doesn't turn. I wonder what the hell he's playing at.

Then I hear a thundering in my ears and notice another massive road train overtaking both me, and him. Then another. Then another. This strikes me as ridiculous. If they can overtake, why can't I? It suddenly occurs to me why he was signalling – to tell me to overtake as the road's clear ahead. I await my moment, but he's evidently decided that, since I ignored all previous signals, any more efforts would be wasted on such a moron. I move to the right to look as far ahead as I'm able, take a deep breath and go. I glance over as I pass his cab. He's shaking his head.

*

My next stop, Blackall, is known historically as a centre for sheep and, since my cattle-droving days have taught me all I need to know about cattle, and goat racing about goats, I feel obliged to level the score. The town's major claim to fame is its wool scour, a steam-driven wool-washing plant to remove dirt, dead skin, sweat residue, pesticides, grass and anything else that's become tangled in the wool before it parted company with the sheep. It started up in 1908, using 200 000 gallons a day of the hot water that bubbled up from an artesian bore nearby, and continued in operation until 1978.

It was the only wool scour in the world with shearing sheds attached, so drovers could bring their sheep directly there and shear them on site with steam-operated shears. The wool would be washed in tanks with ash and soap made from mutton fat and caustic soda, dried and pressed into bales, weighing 40 per cent less than before it was cleaned. The scour worked throughout Australia's so-called golden age of wool, a time when our sheep numbers hit a record 180 million, wool dominated our exports, sheep-breeder John Macarthur was put on the $2 note and the entire country was happy to ride on a sheep's back.

Ten years after the plant's closure, however, a group of locals got together and came up with a plan for its restoration, forming a delegation to travel to Canberra to ask the then Prime Minister Bob Hawke for a grant to help them. He agreed and the result is now the lovingly restored wood and tin building, together with its fully functioning steam engine driving the mass of belts and pistons and whatever else. It's kept in full working order by dedicated volunteers, who also run regular tours. Last year alone, they had over 11 000 visitors.

Bob Harvey is one of those five-day-a-week volunteers, a man who did a bit of selling fruit at the age of 13 when he left school, as well as driving, serving in a shop, cattle work, dozer driving, coal mining, working on the roads for the council, digging graves. He's already dug his own, and built a coffin for when he'll need it, even lying in it to check it for size. 'I couldn't decide whether to buy an expensive coffin or not, so decided to make it instead,' he says. As you do.

The Outback in those days was, despite that, a livelier place, Bob believes. 'You couldn't afford drink, there weren't drugs and you played games in the claypan and went to dances,' he says. 'We entertained ourselves. We used old condensed milk-tins as horses and bones as the cattle we were droving. You could pick the wool off dead sheep and always find a way to make a quid. Now life is a lot more complicated. I can't believe the thousands of toys my grandchildren have. To even shoot a roo you need a gun licence, two tags and a permit from national parks. Back then, your parents taught you gun safety from the age of eight.'

Yet he'd still live nowhere else but the Outback. Even Blackall is too busy for him; he lives 3 kilometres out and drives to the scour, where he works the steam engine. 'I could never live in the city,' says the 71-year-old. 'There's all that hustle and bustle. Then there's all that traffic and people driving like maniacs. You've got to think for them and work out what the silly buggers are going to do. There's none of that stress in a place like this. It's that stress that kills you. Out here, even the crows fly backwards to keep the dust out of their eyes.'

He's aided and abetted by good mate Bob 'Wilo' Wilson, a retired wool presser. As such, he's something of a rarity. They say a morning of wool pressing is like playing football for eight hours straight, and many died young of heart strain. His love of the wool industry is equalled, however, by his passion for art. He paints, he makes leatherware, like whips and saddles, and he does copperwork. He also cooks, and makes bush dinners once a month at the scour during the tourist season. 'It's a great life here,' he says. 'The Outback's so laidback, you don't have too much to worry about. The sheep are gone now, so life's a bit tougher, but it's a pretty strong little town, and life is good here.'

I take my cue from these old guys and try to be as laidback as them. I choose a local motel for its boast of having several amenities, and try not to get annoyed when it actually has none. The internet is down for the whole time I'm there, its café on the premises is closed for renovation – and has been for some time apparently – and the phone in the room has such crackly line it's worse than useless. The owner's pet poodle also keeps leaving dismembered dolls outside my front door. But today, not even the stink of sulphur from the tap water can douse my spirits. Instead, I let the water run for a few minutes until the smell goes and then make myself a nice cup of peppermint tea. Afterwards I walk to the hot artesian spa at the aquatic centre, have a soak for the grand sum of $3 and sleep better than I have for weeks. I wonder if I'll be able to maintain this sangfroid back in the city.

The next morning I visit a cattle saleyard, just to see what it's like. I've never been to one before but it takes me a while to work out what's happening. Wandering between the steel yards, I keep having to flatten myself against fences as cow hands (should I call them that?) push along groups of animals, ushering them into their pens. Walking down another muddy corridor, I'm startled when a man walking towards me suddenly stops, unzips his trousers and pees into another pen. 'There are public toilets over the other side,' I want to say to this man, 'don't be so bloody lazy.' But then this is his world, not mine, and I don't have a clue about the rules.

Instead, I stop dead in my tracks, turn around and walk back the way I've come. It doesn't do me any good. As I pass another of the pens, a cow pees in a long arched projectile that hits me at knee-level and drips down onto my shoes.

I wonder if the higher route is the safer way to go, and climb up the steep ramp to reach the narrow walkways over the pens. But here feels just as precarious. At the cry of 'Sale-O! Sale-O! Sale-O!' crowds of men race along the platforms, stopping above each one of the enclosures just long enough to shout an incomprehensible stream of auction-sales babble, declare that a lot is sold, tick forms and rush onto the next sale. I'm always a little way behind, and keep bumping into a man sloshing around a pot of pink paint with which he daubs the animals that have either been sold, or not sold, I have no idea.

After 20 minutes of this, I'm exhausted from running and trying to get out of the way, and my right trouser leg is drying as stiff as a board. I take my leave and head back to the motel where, happily, at least the shower is working and there's a coin-slot washing machine in the laundry.

After Blackall, I drive west to Isisford, where I stop at a café on the main road. It appears the kind of dreamy small town where nothing ever happens but, like many places in the Outback, looks can be deceiving. One of the coffee drinkers is Dutchman Hans Budding, who, while at home in Holland, spotted the local hotel opposite, Clancy's Overflow Hotel, for sale on the internet. He came, he saw, he fell in love; he bought it for $400000. Now he's restoring it into a classic Outback pub.

'I know this is in the middle of nowhere, but it feels to me like a little paradise,' he says. 'I have a cottage out the back so I walk to work, the locals are nice and I've tripled the revenue.' The only downside seems to be that his wife didn't feel the same way.

After a short stay, she returned to the Netherlands – a country that could fit 220 times into Australia yet has roughly the same number of people – and she won't, by all accounts, be coming back. 'But I love it here,' Hans says. 'And I'm too busy now to search for love.'

And the surprises just keep on coming. Upstairs from the café is an old picture theatre converted into a fabulous museum devoted to Isisfordia, the oldest crocodile ever discovered and, at 95 to 98 million years old, the granddaddy of all crocodiles that ever followed.

Arriving back in Longreach, where I'm going to catch the train back to Brisbane, I realise I have a problem with the car. It's suddenly developed a terrible smell. At first, I wonder if it's my imagination but it grows steadily worse. I hope it might go away of its own accord but it doesn't, and I know there's no way I can give it back with such a stink. At the motel in Longreach I stay in, I can't even bring myself to park it outside my front door, leaving it around the corner out on the road instead.

'You know there's plenty of room to park your car here,' the motel owner tells me. 'You don't have to park it so far away!' I say that I'm happy parking it where I have. When he says the same the next day, I finally tell him about the smell.

'Did you hit a roo somewhere?' he asks. I shake my head. I've made it a policy not to drive at dusk or dawn to avoid roo rush hour. 'Well, did you run over an old dead one then?' I suppose I might have done. 'I'll come and have a look at it for you,' he says. I could kiss him.

He walks over to the car and screws up his nose. 'I see what you mean,' he says with a grin. 'It's foul! You've probably run over a dead one and part of it is stuck. Their stink gets worse because they start to cook onto the underside of the car. We call it the roo's revenge. There's nothing for it but to get under and scrape it all off.' I look at him in horror. I don't think I can do that. What if there's a bit of the head or an eye? It's the stuff of nightmares. He sees the look on my face. 'Don't worry,' he says. 'I'll do it for you.'

'You can't possibly . . .' I start, hoping to hell that I don't sound convincing. 'You can't do that for me.'

Thankfully, he shrugs. 'Why not? We always try to help our guests out.'

Later that day, with the car newly scraped and deodorised, I'm so deeply, profoundly grateful, I buy a slab of beer and deliver it to the front desk. He's genuinely embarrassed. 'It's part of the service,' he protests. 'You didn't have to do that.'

'Oh, yes, I did,' I reply.

The Spirit of the Outback leaves Longreach on Mondays and Thursdays, departing at 7.15 a.m. and arrives in Brisbane early the next morning.

I've always loved trains, being able to relax and watch the scenery out the window, and chat to other people on the trip. I have a twin sleeper to myself and I spend the first 15 minutes happily pottering around the cabin, working out what's what: discovering one of the bank of cupboards opposite the seats is a fold-down sink, another has a mirror and power point so I can use my computer and recharge my phone, and another is where you can hang your clothes – if you have any worth hanging, of course. There's even a little table that slides out from under the seat. I wind up the blinds at the windows, and those at the windows in the corridor, so I have a view both sides, and settle down contentedly to enjoy the ride from the Outback to the city.

It's a gloriously sunny day, and outside the red earth glows beneath the pale-green scrub, dotted with acacias, wattle, gidgee trees, gums and my new favourite, discovered in Barcaldine, grevillea glauca, whose hard wooden fruit when split in the middle can be used as clothes pegs. There are old fences and front gates of properties with battered metal letterboxes and dirt tracks leading off for kilometres into the bush. On the other side, we pass regularly close to the main road, with the occasional road train being tailed by a hesitant grey nomad – or a dumb city person like me. *This*, I think, *is the way to go.*

A couple of hours in I wander down the train's corridors to the Captain Starlight Club Car – I just can't get away from Harry Redford – for some tea and a chat with the staff. The train's three-quarters full, mostly with city folk coming back from their trips to the Outback, but they're all ensconced in their cabins, presumably enjoying the view.

I go back to watch the desert uplands slowly give way to thickly wooded hills, get out for a quick look at the small settlement of Alpha where we stop for a few minutes, and gaze at some of the steep rock ravines with their emerald glades before the beautifully named Bogantungan, wondering how on earth they managed to build the line there.

Gradually, the landscape changes. The towns grow bigger and neater and look wealthier, and the red earth turns dusty pink and then to brown. There are still windmills, but there are lakes and ducks and fisherman in boats, new houses, proper shops, regular cars and storage warehouses. In Emerald, there's a 24-hour gym, a business centre, fast-food restaurants and big family stores. This, I remember, is where a woman from Barcaldine told me she has to come to buy extra-large knickers. All those bakery delicacies have their price.

As the afternoon wears on, I go back to the club car. Already I can tell these are city people; I smile and say hello, and they look surprised – *Do we know you?* But I start up a conversation with a couple, Bruce and Margie. They've been part of a tour around many of the same places I've been, and they've loved it. 'But we saw so much more than you, being on a tour,' Bruce insists. 'You should have done that. It would have been much better.'

I say I had a good time, and met lots of interesting people anyway. 'But not as good as we had,' he persists. 'You wouldn't have believed the people we met.' My new sangfroid is in danger of evaporating already, and I itch to tell him he has no idea of the things I've done and people I've seen, like the wool scourers, the cattle drovers and the goat racers. But instead, I merely nod, smile, make my excuses and move off. I think being in the Outback where people are pretty generous with their conversation, I'm just not used to such competitive exchanges.

As the evening arrives, I have a drink at the train's onboard Stockman's Bar. 'Hello!' I say to another couple. 'How are you?'

They nod tightly. 'Fine, thanks,' they reply, and look the other way. The only friendly person seems to be an Aboriginal woman who's sitting on her own. She pushes conversation until people have to respond. I admire that; it's obviously what it takes. Eventually, someone asks her what she does. 'Me?' she laughs. 'What do I do? I drink.' There's an audible gasp around the bar. She grins. 'I'm just joking!'

At dinner, I sit with a man and his son and we chat happily over the entire meal. He talks about all the great places he's been to in the Outback, and says I've got to make it to Birdsville. 'And if you get there for the races, make sure you go to Fred Brophy's boxing tent,' he tells me. 'Watching his boxers wipe the floor with their challengers is an experience and a half!'

My ears prick up at the mention of Fred's name again. He seems to be a pretty popular bloke. I'll make sure to phone him when I'm back in Sydney and go to see him. Meanwhile, the man opposite carries on talking, asking me where I've been and what I thought of it. We finish the meal and shake hands warmly before going off to our cabins. 'Where are you from?' I ask him as he leaves. 'Barcy,' he says.

When I return to my cabin, the seat's already folded down into a bed, and I sit and watch the darkness passing by. Soon I'll be back in the city but, somehow, I'm just not as excited by the prospect as I usually am.

6

WATER, WATER EVERYWHERE

Soaring at 4000 feet over the great deserts of central Australia in a tiny four-seater plane, I have a sudden creeping sensation that something is wrong, terribly wrong.

It's not the stomach-churning lumps and bumps of the occasional thermals, nor the realisation that there's nothing – and no one – to be seen in any direction on the vast plains below. It's simply the fact that the earth here is not its usual raw, sun-burnt red. Instead, it's a brilliant green.

What's more, in place of the dry, desolate wilderness encrusted with the sand and salt of popular Outback fable, there's a land that's covered with water, water everywhere. Lakes that haven't seen rain in almost forever are full to their brims, and knotted veins of milky rivers and creeks criss-cross the earth like lines on Aboriginal paintings.

The pilot turns on one wing and we drop a couple of thousand feet, drawn to a flash of searing blue, and what looks from this distance to be a crystalline eruption on the South Australian landscape. As we draw nearer, I realise it's a gigantic cluster of waterfowl; the birds somehow knew there was going to be more water to be found around here than there has been for decades, perhaps centuries. They started arriving the year before, the pilot says. That's when the locals began to suspect something astonishing was about to happen in the mysterious, empty heart of Australia.

This is the first time I've ever seen anything like this – and, I know, it'll probably be the last too. One of the wettest summers since records began, and possibly since the climate around the massive Lake Eyre basin changed from wet to arid, has turned the normally parched deserts into living, breathing wonderlands of water, birdlife, animals and wild greenery.

And now this miraculous once-in-many-generations transformation is laid out like some giant tapestry before us. The pilot swoops down to take a closer look at a huddle of pelicans on a tiny sand island in a sheath of water stretching past the horizon, only to be distracted by a flock of wild ducks and cormorants.

This is a glorious way to see the Outback and all the better, somehow, for being so unexpected. I hadn't intended this to happen. I'd always imagined driving two of the most famous routes of Outback Australia: the Strzelecki and Birdsville tracks, and so I'd been busily trying to hire a 4WD, find a co-driver and organise maps, food and a satellite phone.

But I was also following the weather reports with increasing worry. Rain had begun falling in places that hadn't seen it for years, and great swathes of the historic stockroutes through the north of South Australia were completely cut off by flooding.

The road reports made for discouraging reading. Rain damage to road. Road travel not recommended. Warning: soft conditions. Caution at creek crossings and floodways. Caution: washouts and detours. Road closed, road closed, road closed.

As the rain continued and there were forecasts of even more wet weather from the coast on its way, I was forced to revise my plans. This was the Outback after all; the place where the most unpredictable things happen. One day, you've got a magnificent sheep property and Australia's riding on your woolly back, the next the market has collapsed and you're staring ruin in the face. One moment, you're swimming in a gorgeous little waterhole in the Northern Territory, the next you're between a crocodile's jaws. You can be driving through one of the most stunning deserts in the world, and the next minute you're totally lost among the sand dunes and out of diesel, wondering whether to stay in your car or go walking to look for help. (Answer: *Stay in the car!*)

When disaster strikes in the Outback, it's often of biblical proportions. There's drought and fire, and then there's flood. There's famine, then plenty, then there's famine again. Pestilence, plagues of locusts and mice as well as horse flu and the Hendra virus . . . The only thing missing is war, yet there've been plenty of skirmishes over issues like water allocations, the live-export trade, land being bought up by mining companies, fracking and nuclear-waste dumping. Yes, the only thing you can ever expect in the Outback, I've been told so many times by the people living there, is the unexpected.

So I had to completely rethink my plans. Given that, to me, the Outback has always seemed such a tough and uncompromising place, full of dirt and dust and flies and snakes and danger and discomfort, it suddenly occured to me that I could fly over the stockroutes and see them from the air instead. And as soon as the thought came, I couldn't shake it.

Normally, I'd prefer to travel by land. I like to feel the earth beneath my feet, or a set of wheels at least. It's as if you haven't really travelled until you've felt the ruts of the road rattle in the small of your back, or walked 10 kilometres under a broiling sun in 40-degree temperatures in search of some stone or tree that someone swears is worth seeing. The years I spent travelling around the world – which lasted until I arrived and settled in Australia – helped to develop my fondness for overland travel. I'd always felt, almost snobbishly, that this sort of travel couldn't be beaten for discovering the *real* story behind a place.

But the downsides of a road trip were already causing me sleepless nights, and not purely because of the wet tracks. These were vast distances I was looking at traversing, and my tendency to daydream while driving has proved a touch dangerous in the past. Someone had also told me I might have to organise a convoy; driving alone in a single vehicle could be treacherous if something went wrong, and having a number of vehicles travelling together would make it much safer for us all. And then, of course, there was the know-how: at the very least, I'd need to be able to change a tyre – something I'd never done in my life.

The more I thought about it the more a charter flight looked like it'd be a fabulous adventure. Lake Eyre was now so full of water and birds that from the air it would be a splendid sight. I imagined being able to peer down at the entire landscape, and stop in at some of the most interesting places along the way. Of course, it felt as if I'd be cheating, but who knew when the rain and floods would stop to allow me through on land?

The good thing about arguing with yourself is that you usually win.

I eventually settled on a charter flight from Port Augusta, 300 kilometres north of Adelaide, and arranged it through Ian Fargher, the owner of the Angorichina Station in the Flinders Ranges. I'd met Ian a few years before while doing the book on

Outback women. I wasn't keen on travelling in a small plane, but people in the Outback don't seem to think twice before hopping aboard. So if I was going to see what it's really like to be in the Outback, then I would just have to man up, or er, woman up.

I'd arrived early that morning at Port Augusta and caught sight of the little plane on the tarmac as soon my comparatively giant one from Adelaide landed. It was a 1978 Cessna 172, which, although a four-seater, looked tiny. But the look of the pilot striding alongside it reassured me. Dressed in jeans, one of those navy-coloured jumpers with leather elbow patches, and wearing sensible work boots, he was obviously a man who didn't like to take unnecessary risks with fashion or, hopefully, anything else, either. He had silver hair – something that all pilots should have to indicate experience and wisdom – yet was probably only in his mid-40s. He introduced himself as Matt.

Matt'd been flying for over ten years, he told me, and always carried a good supply of Jatz biscuits on the back seat in case of emergencies. He was incredibly jolly. Even if we were to crash and run out of water, I suspected he'd probably still be wandering around, admiring the scenery and saying how lucky we were to see it so close up before we died.

I mentioned that his plane seemed a bit small. 'No, these planes are wonderful,' he said with a smile. Good teeth, I noted – excellent. He must brush twice a day, so he's conscientious too. 'They're referred to as "the camels of the air" for their reliability and dependability. They're very safe.'

I asked him casually about previous flights he'd done. He related the story of a group who once tried to come on board with seven slabs of beer. He told them the maximum was five. With seven, he wouldn't be able to get the plane off the ground.

They had said, OK, and got back in their car. I beamed at him. This was exactly the kind of story I liked to hear.

I clambered in and we took off, rising steeply above the rosy-pink sand dunes of the Spencer Gulf, past pools of blue, grey and silver water, and up over the chimneys of the power stations driven by the coal from the Leigh Creek fields further north. It was so bright the whole world glittered.

Over the dashboard, I can now see the curve of the earth, and out the window to the side I spot occasional little huddles of houses and sheds scattered across the wide green mottled landscape, full of native plants springing to life with the rains: bluebush, saltbush, porcupine grass and spear grass. Quickly, we draw level with the start of the South Flinders Range, its gorges and burnished red-tiered ridges dominating the landscape. To our left are the still waters of Lake Torrens.

We pass over the railway line that brings the coal down from Leigh Creek and I realise that Matt's actually talking into his headset and looking at me. All I can hear is static, but I smile encouragingly. He could be saying anything. 'Get ready to eject! We have to make an emergency landing! I forgot to put in the fuel! Assume the crash position!' Who knows? I just keep on smiling. There's not much I can do about anything, really, so I simply hope for the best while imagining the worst.

Another tiny plane darts past us, making me jump in my seat. Matt looks at me curiously. Oh, so he was probably warning me about that. Too late now. We pass over Quorn and Hawker and approach Wilpena Pound, a bowl-like depression in the earth, surrounded by massive jagged ridges. A couple of years ago, I stayed a few nights there at Rawnsley Park Station, in one of their eco villas, with a skylight over the bed through which you could watch the stars as you drifted off to sleep. During the days we went walking but, like everything in the Outback, I'd found things are never completely perfect. The scenery was stunning, the trails were magnificent, but I'd picked the wrong two weeks of the year. I've never been dive-bombed by so many flies in my life. They'd kamikaze down my throat, up my nose and into my eyes.

We sail past the station, and then towards the Northern Flinders. This part is more rugged still; apparently it's some of the wildest mountain ranges in the whole of Australia. It's a craggy landscape of gorges, ravines and weathered peaks and the site of the discovery of the world's oldest known vertebrate fossil, at a mere 560 million years. The granite at the top of the ridges weathers much more slowly than the sedimentary rock below and ends up looking like a series of fortresses built on the peaks. At one point, along the Trezona Range, we glimpse the *other* Great Wall of China, a bluff along the top of the mountain peaks that weaves around looking, for all the world, like its distant namesake.

Suddenly, we drop down, and I look over at Matt. There'd been lots more crackling on my headset but I hadn't really taken much notice. We must be near Blinman, where we're going to be landing. I strain to look for a landing strip but see nothing. Yet we're descending faster and faster. A few minutes later, we hit the ground with a soft jolt and careen along before the brakes roar into action and slow us down. I still can't see anything that resembles a landing strip. But apparently this stretch of bumpy grass is it. 'Tarmac?' Matt says, when I ask him about it. '*Tarmac?*' He gives the question a ridiculous air. 'Only one in 50 landing strips here is bitumen.'

We're met by Ross Fargher, brother of Ian, and the co-owner

of one of Australia's three 'hip hotels', the 1870s Prairie Hotel at nearby Parachilna. He wears an electric-blue R. M. Williams cotton shirt, jeans and a cowboy hat that appears an extension of his body. With his chiselled jaw and twinkly eyes, he could be Australia's answer to the Marlboro man. *Ladies, forget the man-drought in the cities; the Outback is where it's at. The men are smokin'.* Well, some of them. We jump into his 4WD and are given a tour of the area.

First stop, Angorichina, a 520-square-kilometre sheep station with a beautiful 1860s stone homestead, now owned by Ian and his wife, Di. This land was first taken up by Ross and Ian's great-grandfather John Fargher and has been in the family for four generations. It once carried around 7000 sheep, but with the drought and the bottom falling out of the wool market, the number has halved. Neither Ian nor Di was prepared to give up and leave the land, however. Instead, they diversified. Ian runs charter flights for tourists all around the state and beyond, and the couple offer 4WD tours, camping on their property and luxury guest accommodation in modern quarters, steeped in antique bush charm.

To adapt in this way was a smart decision by people who've become good at rolling with the punches the Outback has doled out over the years. After having one of their big windmills blow over no fewer than three times in wild weather, Ian and Di now plan on using solar power to pump water up from the ground.

We sit on rattan chairs at the stone table on their veran-dah, looking over the newly green lawns and the trees, drinking freshly squeezed orange juice and eating muesli with yoghurt and a compote of stewed prunes, figs and sultanas. This, I think to myself, is how the Outback should be. There's a soft creamy quality to the midmorning light, leaves are gently falling around us, there's the chirrup of birdsong and even the decaf coffee is good and strong. If only it was all like this.

But, of course, even as the Outback is putting on its best face, with twice the average rainfall here this year, it's still playing tricks on people behind their backs.

'Now coming out of nearly ten years of drought, there are record prices for sheep and wool, but we've all been destocking for years because of the drought,' Di says. 'So there's currently a real shortage of stock, but we can't afford to buy more at those prices.' The number of visiting tourists, however, is on the rise, with many people keen to fly over Lake Eyre in flood.

Di, softly spoken and funny, is a great ambassador for the Outback. Yet she feels it's almost the end of an era, with a lot of kids who've grown up there going away to school and not coming back. Young men who used to come to work the land are now being lured away to the mines, and their big wages. Girls once worked here as governesses, but not many people can afford to hire them any more. That's a shame in some ways: Outback life is so much easier now, with better roads, access to the internet and online social networking. There's no longer the aching loneliness of isolation that previous generations were forced to endure.

We take a walk around the homestead. Di puts a hand on my arm just as I'm about to walk into a massive web between branches of a tree, and I recognise my old cattle drive foe lying in wait: the golden orb spider. I tell her how I was terrified one would roll down my shirt if I brushed past on horseback.

'Yes, they can be a real problem for riders,' she says. I suddenly feel itchy and excuse myself and go to the toilet. There, I check my shirt and find nothing, but then notice a burr in my knickers. How did that get there? Even when the Outback looks pleasant, it's out to get you.

We carry on to the nearby township of Blinman – population 22, down from over 500 when the copper mine was operating in the 1860s. These days it comprises little more than the derelict mine, a few cottages, the highest post office in Australia at 2600 feet above sea level, a hotel and a startlingly good café-cum-gallery named Wild Lime after its speciality tart. We share a piece while talking to the owner, Robyn. She's originally from Melbourne but after 15 years in the same job with child- and community-care programs, she decided she wanted a complete change, and a chance to develop her creative side as a gold and silversmith.

'As soon as I saw this place, I loved it,' she says. 'It's a magnificent Outback landscape and people's connection with nature is wonderful. There's something really special about this place; it feels so creative.' She and her partner came out here eight years ago, and set up the café to support her jewellery making. Her partner, however, didn't adjust as well and returned to Victoria. The café has since become so successful, though, that Robyn has had less and less time to work on her art.

'But I've never regretted the move,' she says. 'It's been amazing in so many ways. A sense of place and that connection is really important to me – that's the beauty of the Outback. We moved here at a time of drought, when it was extremely bleak. It can get so hot and desolate in the summer, you can think, what a Godforsaken place! But then it varies so much from season to season, and the birds and reptiles are fascinating and the ecosystem out there is totally different to anything you've ever seen before. It can be a challenge living in a small town where everyone knows your business, but people pull together and that's great.'

Around town there's a huge amount of energy devoted to

drawing visitors in. Nearby, Ross shows us the old mine manager's cottage, made from hand-sawn cypress pine, with mud filling the gaps. He's slowly renovating it, and plans to one day host lunches here, which will include a trip to the mine that yielded, in its day, 10 000 tonnes of copper.

We then drive over to Parachilna, the northern head of the famed Heysen walking trail, to the Prairie Hotel for lunch. Ross owns the place with his wife, Jane. She's Di's sister – the two brothers married two sisters. The hotel is famed for its 'Flinders feral food', which includes an antipasto plate with kangaroo, camel, emu and goat.

Of course, I have a vegetarian option, but there are still a lot of special elements, like locally grown native limes and bush tomatoes, and homemade muntries chutney. 'Muntries', what a great word. They're the fruit of a native plant in the region that was a major part of the local Aborigines' traditional diet. Like many bush foods, they're now being increasingly marketed widely across Australia.

Towards the end of the afternoon, we take a trip out to Ross and Jane's station, Nilpena, a 870-square-kilometre cattle property on the edge of Lake Torrens. It's all rugged creek beds, salt plains, claypans and red sand dunes. A sign hangs on the gate to the homestead: 'Bugger the gardening. Gone to the pub'. Many of their stone buildings date back to the 1870s and are beautifully preserved. With some of them, there's been little choice. The old stone tanks that hold 150 000 litres of water have walls over 1.2 metres thick at the bottom and three-quarters of a metre thick at the top. We sit and watch two galahs smooching on the blades of the windmill above it.

We drive on and reach some of the reddest sand dunes I've ever seen. We clamber up and I just stare in amazement at the untouched expanse. It's like a postcard version of the Outback. This evening, with the sun lazily going down over the land and Ross producing wine, mineral water and cheese and biscuits from his car, things feel perfect. Soon you can't tell where the red of the dunes ends and the red of the sky starts.

'You never get sick of these views,' says Ross, crouching down in the sand. 'They say if you cross the Parachilna eight times, you'll never go back.' With my sense of direction, I'd only need to cross it once before I'd never be able to find my way back. But I still can't imagine ever *not* wanting to leave. When you think about the heat of the summer, the bitter winters, the drought and even things like the 240-kilometre-a-day school run – Ross's kids were at school in Leigh Creek – well, you start to appreciate the effort it must take to live in a place like this.

We return to the Prairie Hotel and I have a long, lazy bath in the huge spa, looking out into the darkness.

One of the biggest problems in talking about the Outback is trying to define it. Most city slickers would say it's anywhere west of them if they're on the east coast, anything north of Adelaide and pretty much everywhere in WA and the Northern Territory, whereas I've met people in some of the remotest parts of the western deserts who say, 'No, this isn't the *real* Outback. Look, we've even got air conditioning!' Once, when I referred on radio to a wild area of Victoria as the Outback, I was chastised by dozens of callers. And another time, on a late-night radio interview, when I dared to suggest Tasmania had no real Outback, the switchboard lit up with enraged locals who said I should never be allowed near a microphone again: they had some of the biggest Outback areas in Australia.

I head down from my room for dinner. Ross, who's come over for a drink, smiles as I ask him his opinion on the matter. 'Some say it's where the bitumen road ends and the dirt begins,' he says. 'Others say it's more of a feeling in yourself, in your own heart.'

I think to myself that it's more about dust up your nose and flies and vast, empty stretches of nothingness. But it would sound churlish to say that in such pleasant surroundings and when he's gone to so much effort to show me nice places.

Ross, in any case, is on a different wavelength. The best definition he's ever heard comes from his brother, Ian. 'He said it's where the handshake gets a little stronger and the smile lingers longer,' Ross says, with his big, lazy grin. 'It's pretty good, isn't it?'

7

'JUST CLOSE YOUR EYES AND STICK YOUR HAND UP.' A PREGNANCY TEST IN THE MIDDLE OF NOWHERE

The next morning, there's a surprise passenger in the plane: a vet who needs to be dropped off at Cordillo Downs Station to work with the cattle. Is it all right if Jack hitches a lift? And would I be able to lend him a hand?

I'm pleased. Cordillo Downs is one of the most remote properties in Australia, and I've always wanted to see it. Once upon a time, it was Australia's largest sheep station with more than 85000 sheep and, in the late 1800s, it had enough people living there to run its own post office, as well as a police station during shearing time and a polling box for elections, carted up by camels from Farina, just south of Marree where the Birdsville Track begins. Today it's still vast, at close to 8000 square kilometres of stony tablelands, gibber plains, red sandhills and spinifex, but now just a single family run 6000 head of cattle, together with a workforce of around eight.

This family is slap bang in the middle of the Sturt Stony Desert, in the far north-eastern corner of South Australia, and they're a long, long way from anywhere. I've often wondered how a family might manage being so isolated, especially with kids. But the major difficulty of finding that out firsthand is . . . they're always too hard to get to. This station, owned by Birdsville couple David and Nell Brook, and run by their son Anthony together with his wife, Janet, sounds as if it's an incredible place to live. Now, happily, I get to go there, and with a vet, the kind of person everyone's always pleased to see. Even better, he needs my help. He must be such a sensitive person; he intuitively knows what a great animal-lover I am.

Jack is tall and lean, with glasses, and dressed in jeans and a battered hat. He folds himself into a back seat and we set off early, the cockpit buzzing with a dozen flies. 'It'll be fine in a minute,' Matt says. 'They'll go to sleep soon. They breathe through their skin and so can't aspirate under air pressure.'

'That's a bit sad,' I say. 'Do they die?'

Jack shakes his head. 'No. They just have some peaceful time out and, as a result, they end up living longer when they get out the other end.'

That sounded nice. 'Really?' I ask.

Jack laughs. 'No, I'm just good at making shit up.'

We fly away from the ranges. The earth beneath us is a mottled orange and green, with bright flashes of water everywhere. We fly over Leigh Creek, the coalmines and Lyndhurst. Finally we pass Marree, the start of the Birdsville Track. I've flown here once before, with the flying doctors. Back then, three years ago, the landscape was red, dry and dusty. Today, it's so lush it's almost unrecognisable. The track snakes away northwards from the town, while the Oodnadatta Track heads westwards towards the southern shores of Lake Eyre.

'You see the dog fence down there?' Matt asks. I peer down.

At 5600 kilometres, it's the world's longest fence, stretching from Queensland's Darling Downs to the South Australian coast in the Nullarbor; its role is to keep dingos away from the sheep flocks. But I can't see it. I feel stupid not being able to make it out. 'Where?' I say.

Jack glances up from his crossword. 'It's the only thing around here that's a straight line,' he says. 'That should be pretty easy to spot.'

I can just make it out before we start approaching the flat lands of Lake Eyre, and the part of the trip I've been looking forward to most. It's a spectacular sight. The basin drains one-sixth of Australia – a 1.3 million-square-kilometre area, the size of France, Germany and Italy combined – and now, instead of the normal brilliant white salt crust, it's about 75 per cent full and is a pale blue, a pearly white and a glimmering grey in places. Explorer Charles Sturt's great legendary inland sea has finally really come into being, and today is alive with myriad birds clustering on the banks or flying in great flocks across the surface.

We duck down lower for a better look, and start lurching along the thermals. I feel sick, and hang on tight to the sides of my seat. We hover around, looking at clouds of pelicans, which are in such huge numbers they've been causing problems at the local airstrips. Matt asks if I'd like to go lower for a closer view of what's happening on the surface.

'Isn't that dangerous with all those pelicans?' I ask, failing completely to hide the tremor in my voice.

'No, we'll stay above them,' he replies cheerfully. 'They don't fly very high.' As we descend, we're kicked around by the air currents more and more violently. No one else seems bothered but my stomach is lurching.

Jack looks over at me, and I assume he's able to sense my

anxiety. I get ready for some soothing, comforting words. 'It's good for you,' he finally says. 'It tightens the sphincter wonderfully.'

The little plane continues to be thrown around until I just can't stand it any more. 'That's fine,' I say, after a few more minutes. 'I actually preferred it higher up. I'm not so keen on this . . .' Great. One of the most amazing, once-in-a-lifetime sights the continent's Outback can offer, and I'm wishing heartily that we can just move on.

We climb steadily and finally fly off east, back over the Tirari Desert and into the Strzelecki Desert, where the flame above the vast Moomba gas field burns day and night, sending a spiral of black smoke into the air. Just by it is the Strzelecki Track. When you can see it – which isn't often, I find out – it looks barely more than a thin ribbon over and around some of the harshest countryside in Australia.

The track, post Harry Redford, became a popular route down to the coast, but it was always so hard-going that not everyone made it. Looking down from on high, I feel happy to be flying over it rather than struggling to get through it on land.

We pass over Innamincka, where we'll be staying that night, and go on to Cordillo Downs. Jack will be pregnancy testing the cattle there.

I'm sure the cows will like me. After all, how many vegetarians do they get the chance to meet out here? I wonder if Jack will ask me to cow-whisper to the cattle while he encourages them to pee in a jar. Or maybe he simply takes their temperature? I like the idea of giving Jack a hand, then nipping into the homestead for a cup of tea and perhaps even a scone with jam and cream afterwards.

I feel certain that Anthony and Janet, who run the station, together with their four small children, will enjoy some company.

Pilot Matt's voice cuts into my reverie. 'Can you see the airstrip?' he's asking casually. 'I can't seem to find it.' I look out the window but can't see anything.

'No!' I say. It comes out as more of a squeak. 'Can't you?'

Jack glances out. 'I think it's over there maybe,' he says.

'I'll have a look out that way and see if we can find it,' Matt replies, sounding completely unfazed. 'It'll probably be covered in grass now with all this rain.'

We fly in the direction Jack suggested. It feels like hours before Matt finally says, 'Oh, yeah, got it!' and starts his descent. He sounds as unconcerned as if he'd been unable to locate a missing sock.

I feel my palms sweating as we eventually pull up on another grassy knoll. When I climb out of the plane's door, my legs nearly give way. But there's a ute waiting to take us straight to the cattle. No time to muck around. The driver nods as we pile in. He probably thought he'd be the one helping out the vet until I came along. This is where I'll come into my own.

We drive for a couple of minutes until we reach a clearing. There's a fire going, and five people in battered old hats sit around on fold-out chairs, crates and boxes. On the fire, there's a black billy can. Nearby, there are four swags set up under trees, and there's a truck, more of a chuck wagon really, with a table rigged up next to it. This looks like a classic painting of a stock camp, or a photo from the Outback archives. I'm spellbound. Stupid as it seems, it hadn't occurred to me that people still lived and worked like this.

They give us some tea from the billy and I notice that one of the people dressed in what looks like the regulation pink shirt and jeans is a woman. I go and sit down beside her. She's Jess from Dalby, just 19, who's working as a ringer, helping round up the cattle for the vet's visit. She was working as a nanny but decided to give station work a go. 'I like it here,' she says. 'It's good.'

Jess is a woman of few words, but I persist. She's been here just a few weeks but the outdoor life suits her. She sleeps for up to four nights in a row in a swag while they're working the cattle before going back to her lodgings at the station. No, she doesn't find it hard. No, there are no showers, but sometimes she gets a wash in a bowl of water, and she changes her clothes most days. After a while, she gets up and wanders away. Too late I realise that part of the lure of station life is probably not having to talk much, and especially to outsiders who don't have a clue about your life.

When the tea's been drunk, the whole group around the fire, plus Jack and Matt, head off somewhere. I trot along behind. This must be where we'll be checking out the cattle. I wonder how many we'll test today – ten, 20, 25? We go over the brow of a slope and before us stands a series of steel-barred intercon-nected cattle yards, some easily a quarter-acre, with interlocking gates all around a central elevated platform. This is apparently called the crow's nest and a person can use the levers to open and close all the gates in order to divide the herd into bulls, cows and calves, channelling the cattle wherever they need to go. But what catches my eye is the number of cattle inside: probably around 400. I don't believe it. How on earth can they be expect-ing to test that many? It's impossible.

Jack doesn't look at all daunted, however. He's been carry-ing a little case, which he now puts down on a bench and flips open. He pulls out a big blue apron, and puts it on over his head. Then he dons two regular-sized plastic gloves before putting on another long plastic glove that runs up to his shoulder over the top. I don't like the look of this at all. Surely . . . surely not?

At a signal from one of the men, ten of the cows are herded into the laneway leading up to Jack. The first one shies as she comes up to him, but a man to her right side slaps her rump to keep her going. Then there's an enormous crash and a bellowing. To her front, the driver of the ute, Darren, has brought down a lever, which traps her head inside a gate, while a man behind her has slammed a half-door shut to protect himself from a stray kick. Jack stands to the cow's rear, flexing his fingers in the glove.

As I watch, he pushes his arm deep inside her, up to his shoulder. When he withdraws his arm it is covered in cow shit. He flicks it off and I dart out of its path just in time. 'Heifer,' he says. 'Six months. Wet.'

Matt jots something down on a pad, and I watch horrified as the cow's finally let free and another one is caught, has her head trapped, then has Jack's arm thrust up her. 'Heifer,' he says of this one. 'Empty. Dry.' The whole process seems so undignified. Surely there must be a better way? When I say so, Jack looks bemused. 'This is how it's done,' he says simply. 'What did you expect?' I'm too embarrassed to say. Will I have to put my hand up there too?

I stand around for half an hour, and then ask someone where the homestead is so I can nip in for a cup of tea. He looks at me with a puzzled expression. 'It's about 40 kilometres from here,' he says finally. 'It'll be a bit of a walk . . .'

On a property this big, why on earth did I assume that the cattle would be close to where the family lives? It seems I have even more to learn than I thought.

I go over and talk to one of the men ushering in the cows. He turns out to be the man in charge – Anthony Brook himself.

Blond, with pale-blue eyes and a neat beard, he's dressed in the same pink shirt as his workers. Softly spoken, he talks to me between driving the cows up the laneways towards Jack, and heroically rescuing my notebook, which I manage to drop into a yard among the stamping hooves of several more bovine. He loves this land and this life, he tells me. He doesn't mind at all that the nearest towns, Birdsville and Innamincka, are at least three-hour drives away, and would never choose a city over this.

'It's nice to go to a city for a holiday, but not much longer than that,' he says. 'You feel too claustrophobic. And it costs money just to be there. Wherever you drive, there's a toll to pay, and then you pay for parking. There's nothing to do for free.' By contrast, life on the land offers freedom. 'It's the openness and the lifestyle here,' he says. 'While we work hard, there's such a variety of work. Whenever you're mustering, no two days are ever the same. The country's never the same: look at it now. We're lucky to see it like this. These rainfall events probably only happen once every 30 years.'

But how about bringing children up here? Surely that's hard? His children are now two, five, six and nine – wouldn't they prefer the amenities of a city? He laughs at the very thought. 'It's a wonderful childhood, growing up in a place like this. It's great for kids. They ride motorbikes, the eldest comes out mustering, they can sleep out under the stars . . . It's magical for them.' When they're young, they do homeschooling and later on they'll go off to boarding school, just as Anthony and his siblings did.

The greatest challenge is finding good people to employ, whether that's a teacher for the kids or people to work with the stock. With the mines luring so many workers away, there's now a shortage. But Anthony, like so many others in the Outback, has been filling the gap with overseas workers, often backpackers.

On a year's working holiday visa in Australia, they're often willing to come to even the most isolated areas to work as that then entitles them to apply for a second year-long working visa.

'We've found the Irish are pretty good,' says Anthony. 'One couple who came to work here, though, when they got here, the first thing the guy said to his partner was, "Sorry!" He hadn't realised it was so remote – we're easily the most isolated station. Anna Creek is bigger but there are a lot more people there.'

Other overseas workers who came to Cordillo Downs haven't worked out quite so well. 'We had one guy here who only lasted three days and a Pommy guy who complained about everything,' Anthony says. 'He told us he'd worked on a dairy farm and could ride motorbikes, but I don't think he'd done either before. We had to get rid of him. He was a square peg in a round hole. He was hopeless.'

Talking of hopeless, at that point someone yells that Jack needs me. Here's my big chance, although I'm still worried he'll be handing me a big glove. I climb through a fence and make my way to where he's still testing the cattle. 'That was brave of you,' he says to me when I arrive by his side.

'Why's that?' I ask.

'You just crossed the yard where they put all the bulls.'

I really must pay more attention, but Jack's already moved on. 'You're a writer,' he says. 'Take over from Matt now. He has to get the plane ready.' Matt hands over his pad and clipboard. I feel relieved that's all there is to my role. Jack continues. Cow in, trapped, hand up, verdict and a flick of the wrist to get rid of the shit. I'm writing down the kind of cow, whether her udder is full – that is, wet or dry – whether she's pregnant or feeding a calf, and then I get out of the way of the spray of shit as Jack whips his arm clean.

Jack gets through a huge number of the cattle in a surprisingly short time, and we all then break for lunch. There's bread, margarine, slices of beef – doesn't that feel just a tad insensitive so close to the cows? – plastic cheese portions (to add insult to injury) and tomato sauce all laid out on the table for us to make up our own sandwiches.

I offer to make Jack a cheese sandwich, but he says he'll make his own beef one. I wonder how he proposes doing that; he's pretty much caked head to toe in cow dung. 'And I hope you don't think you're getting back in the plane with us?' I joke. No, he's all prepared. He vanishes with a bowl of hot water to get scrubbed up. Later, someone takes him a fresh bowl. And then another.

It's late afternoon by the time we return to the plane and take off for the tiny historic settlement of Innamincka, 140 kilometres south. One of the most remote settlements in the world, surrounded by the Strzelecki, Tirari and Sturt Stony deserts, Innamincka is home to the Dig Tree, the old coolibah on the banks of Cooper Creek, under which rations were buried for Burke and Wills by a search party who waited and waited but left the day the ill-fated pair arrived. Not far away are the memorials to each where they died, and a marker where the sole survivor of their doomed expedition, John King, was found after being befriended by Aborigines. There are also some great waterholes for swimming. Allegedly. When we arrive, every single road out of Innamincka is closed because of Cooper Creek being in flood.

Innamincka itself is a funny little place. There's not really much to it. With only four permanent residents in town, there's the hotel, a homestay set-up, a store, some fuel pumps and not really much else. The town itself was abandoned in the 1950s but then revived ten years later with the discovery of gas and oil in the area, and there was a surge in tourism with the growth in popularity of 4WD trips. Now it's a stop on the Outback Loop, a road route that starts there, goes past Cordillo Downs and finishes up in Queensland at Birdsville.

I don't hold out much hope that the Innamincka Hotel will be up to much, but it's actually a pleasant surprise. The accommodation is basic, but clean and comfortable. Even the frogs in the laundry are friendly. But it's the food that's the most unexpected element. It's served in a newly built, spacious, high-ceilinged dining room attached to the old hotel, described by one past visitor as the 'Taj Mahal of the Outback', and is both hearty and sophisticated.

During the meal, I ask Jack for his opinion on an issue that's back in the news again, mulesing – the process of slicing a piece of skin from the buttocks of the sheep to produce a wool-free scar that cuts down on flystrike. He becomes pretty fired up on the subject, something I put down to the vast quantities of red wine that have been drunk that evening. Unfairly, I realise later, when I discover Jack is actually the co-inventor of an injectable method of producing tighter skin that replicates, and so does away with, surgical mulesing.

There's no shortage of passion in Innamincka. Michelle Hoffman, who runs the hotel, has only been here for four years. She's originally from Adelaide but has fallen in love with the Outback. It's all about the people here, she says.

'Although we're in a remote part of the Outback, we see different people every day, with different stories and on different journeys. And they're always excited to be here, to have made it here from wherever they've come from. At the same time, everyone who lives and works here loves it. If they didn't, they wouldn't last. So you get a great vibe. You never know what's going to happen next. Yesterday we had a helicopter landing in the car park to pick up ten cartons of beer!'

Longer-term residents are just as enthusiastic too. Julie and Geoff Matthews arrived in 1996 with their two daughters, after years of travelling around Australia. Originally from Geelong, where Geoff worked as a carpenter and joiner, and Julie trained as a primary school teacher, they'd been on the verge of a major Outback tour when they lost all their money in the late-1980s collapse of Pyramid, Victoria's biggest building society.

'We were devastated that we'd lost everything and our plans had gone up in smoke,' says Julie. 'But visiting different places, and then living and working in each community, gave us a completely different perspective on life. We really enjoyed it.'

Along the way, they homeschooled their kids, neither of whom has ever spent a single day in an actual school, until, eventually, they decided to settle down in one place. They looked for an Outback business to run and bought a tyre and auto-repair shop in Innamincka that they transformed into their Cooper Creek homestay.

'We'd often been through when we travelled around Australia and we liked the river and the scenery and the kind of aura the place has,' says Julie, now 59. 'It's an oasis in the middle of the desert. It can be really harsh but the creek never dries up completely, and it's usually four or five degrees cooler under the red river gums on the creek than on the gibber plains.'

Of course, it can be a tough place to live. In summer, the mercury can hit 55 degrees Celsius and in winter it can dip to minus four, while all year round the isolation brings its own difficulties. 'But what I really like about it is the challenge of doing everything for yourself, how you have to be self-reliant,' says Julie. 'We produce our own power, solar now, and if there's a water leak, you can't just phone for a plumber; you have to fix it yourself. I think that gives you a sense of your own worth. You prove to yourself that you're capable of looking after yourself and your family. You surprise yourself a few times too, with the things you can manage.'

And their children? Miranda's 25 now and she's doing her Master's degree in political science in Germany, and Ally has her own earth-moving contract business. It'd be hard to say they've suffered from spending so much time in the Outback.

As we take off the next day for our final destination, Birds-ville, before I have to catch the plane back to Brisbane and on to Sydney, something Geoff said while he was showing me around came back to me. Standing in his shorts and T-shirt, watching another brilliant sunset, he said he just couldn't imagine ever living anywhere else. Innamincka, for him, encapsulated so many values of the Australian Outback.

'People might travel a lot to Europe but that's all man-made history,' he said. 'But this is true wilderness, and it's the only area like that in the world that hasn't been overrun with people. This place hasn't changed since we first visited in 1979. It's timeless. There's still no water rates, no post office, no police, no crime. That's true Outback, and why so many of us love it.'

I wonder whether, at the end of my three months of travel, I'll ever understand that.

8

LIGHTNING RIDGE: THE PERFECT HIDING PLACE FOR BODIES

The surface is a deep luminous black, but underneath there's a glowing swirl of vibrant colour. I'm captivated as it catches the light, the blues wink and merge, the greens glisten and a flaming orange glints strikingly.

The salesman in the Sydney shop looks bored. He's seen this sort of spellbound gaze a million times before. 'Yes,' he says, in a flat voice. 'That's black opal. Lovely, isn't it?' He pauses for a few seconds, and I know he's giving me the once-over. 'But how much were you thinking of spending? I think those in that case over there you might find a little more affordable . . .'

There's only one place in the world that produces opals like this, and that's the NSW Outback town of Lightning Ridge, 800 kilometres north-west of Sydney. I decide to go there next. I've heard it's still as much a wild-west town as it always was and, while there are no flights there, I can fly to Dubbo, rent a car and drive from there. It'll be nice to do a bit of driving after having travelled in tiny planes for the past week.

I have a few days before I'm booked to leave, so I decide to look up Fred Brophy, the Outback boxing man. I discover he's just been awarded the Medal of the Order of Australia for his services to the entertainment industry and his efforts raising money for charity. I delve a little deeper and the more I learn about him, the more I'm drawn to his story. He grew up touring the showgrounds of Outback Australia, where his mum, a former trapeze artist, ran various side-stalls. He'd loved the boxing tent ever since he could walk. At the age of six, he started dragging other kids inside the tent to fight before the real boxing began; and in exchange the crowd would throw a few coins on the mat for the boys to buy ice-creams.

The boxing tents had their heyday from the 1920s to the 1940s in the Australian Outback but now, most outfits, like Jim Sharman's, have shut up shop. It's a sport that's been out-lawed across most of the rest of the country and the world – it's considered far too dangerous, with fighters not wearing any headgear, no boxing-ring ropes to retreat to, no doctors standing by. But Fred still runs his original family tent in Queensland, billing it as the last boxing tent in the world, thanks to some arcane state act that gives him the right to keep going. Facing increasing threats of regulation on boxers and bouts, however, he brings out the tent for just six big nights a year, including in Mt Isa at the rodeo, and in Birdsville for the races.

It sounds as if he and his tent will offer a great perspective on bush life. The documentary grey nomad Michael told me about had shown on SBS TV a few months before, so I order it to have a look. And I phone Fred at his pub in Cracow, Queensland, to find when his tent will have its next outing.

He answers on the first ring. I explain who I am and ask if I can visit to have a chat the next time the tent is up.

'I suppose so,' he says, without much enthusiasm. 'We've got one in three weeks at Kilkivan.' I have no idea where that is, but say I'd be keen to come up and have a look. He's fine with that.

'But you know what'd be even better?' I muse. 'If I actually had a fight there too.' With sudden horror, I realise it's a thought I've voiced aloud. There's a long pause on the other end of the phone.

'You think so?' he finally asks. 'You're serious?'

I hesitate. Of course I'm not, but I can't help myself. 'Why not?' I say with a boldness I certainly don't feel, and wonder if he's noticed the quiver in my voice.

'Have you boxed before?' he asks.

'Yes,' I reply. 'Well, on pads at the gym, just as part of an exercise class . . .'

'Uh huh,' he says, obviously unimpressed. 'How old are you?'

'Fifty-one,' I tell him, and hear a sigh of disapproval in response. 'Fifty-one?' he says. '*Fifty-one?*' He's saying it with such horror, it sounds more like a hundred and fifty-one. 'That's old,' he finally says. 'It's usually 20-year-olds we have. That's old.'

Evidently, at my age, I should barely even consider getting out of bed each day, let alone leaving the house.

'It's not that old at all!' I say curtly, making a mental note not to tell him that the night of the fight is actually my birthday, so I'd in fact be fifty-two.

'Well, I suppose so —'

'Great!' I snap. 'That's settled.' As I put the phone down, I wonder what on earth I'd been thinking.

I decide not to ponder it too much at this stage. I've got another three weeks before I go to Kilkivan. Anything could happen in three weeks. Instead, I fly to Dubbo and rent a car. 'Where are you off to?' asks the woman in the car-hire office.

Lightning Ridge, I tell her. 'Oh, you will be careful, won't you?' she urges. 'There're some pretty rough roads out there.'

'No worries,' I reply. 'I'll be right.'

'I wasn't thinking of you,' she says bluntly. 'I meant the car.'

I drive off, as the green of the rolling hills steadily bleeds out into the grey flat landscape beyond, interrupted only by dry clumps of bush grass and lonely fences. This is the land of towns like Coombogolong, Come By Chance, Goangra and Dungalear, all one-horse places, with weatherboard houses, tin roofs and the occasional pub, serving, I'd imagine, exactly the same clientele every single day.

Gradually, I can tell I'm getting closer to my destination. All along the road there are piles of grey dirt scratched up from the earth, and heaped in human-sized pyramids. Often, the twisted wreckage of a rusty old truck stands beside them. Occasionally, there's a little shack of corrugated iron hastily erected nearby. But I can see no one. It's mid afternoon, a blistering 38 degrees Celsius in the shade, and everyone who's serious about finding opal will be down in the cool of the mines, chipping and scraping and hoping and dreaming of the one big find that will set them up for years to come.

I arrive in town past the huge sign announcing, 'Lightning Ridge, population ?' – a nod to the local joke about the number of people living in the area. The 2006 census put the population at 2602, but the membership of the town's bowling club alone is more than 2000. With a population swollen by runaways, desperates, fortune-seekers, hermits and those eager to get away from it all, it's no surprise that the majority of people have so little time for censuses, officialdom and everything remotely connected with it. Locals put the population, conservatively, at more like 7000.

Checking into a motel, I have a shower in foul-smelling bore water pumped up from the ground. By the time I've dried myself, I feel just as hot and sticky as when I'd arrived. 'Oh, you get used to it,' says the woman at reception, barely looking up from the game show she's watching on a little TV below the counter. 'You'll get to like it before too long, I guarantee you.'

The town is quiet by the time I go for a wander, but in its centre a jewellery store is still open. It sits in the middle of a mock-miner's cave and is fitted out in cheerful, garish style. Owner Herman Kreller, a big jovial German, shows me his range of opals while lazily chatting about the town. He caught the mining bug on his first foray underground. An elderly Aboriginal man had shown him down his mine and, as the two lay chipping away by the light of a candle, the man struck a shining seam of precious opal.

'It was the most beautiful opal I have ever seen,' says Herman, his eyes glistening at the memory. 'But he admired it a couple of times and just left it there. I couldn't understand it. When I asked him why, he said that while it's down the mine, it's beautiful opal. As soon as you dig it out, it changes. You can no longer enjoy it for what it is. It becomes a question of what it's worth, who can I trust to tell, what can I do with the money. It loses its beauty.' That experience changed Herman's life.

These days, he's wedded to his shop and his occasional jaunts back mining, and wouldn't dream of ever leaving Lightning Ridge. It's both the mining and the gamble on the chance of untold riches tomorrow that get into the blood. So many people arrive intent on giving it a try for a year, and then simply never leave. 'How can I describe it?' he says. 'I suppose the mining fever is a bit like herpes, you can never get rid of it. You sit down there all alone in the dark and silence, chipping away. Sometimes you go, "Pick, pick, pick". Sometimes you vary it and go, "Pick, pick, pick . . . pick". But when you see that opal looking up at you, there's no feeling in the world like it.' He shrugs good-naturedly when I decide not to buy anything. 'Hey! There's plenty of time,' he says, smiling. 'I will still be here tomorrow and the next day and the next.'

Back out on the main road running through town, a well-dressed older man is standing, leaning against a campervan. He looks like a tourist, but he's not. He's lived in Lightning Ridge for over 30 years now and has never tired of digging for his dreams. He shakes his head when he thinks of the new people in the outpost town, all hoping to make a quick buck with a lucky find.

'People often come here thinking it's easy to make a lot of money,' he says. 'In fact, it's as hard today as it was 20 years ago. But attitudes have changed. We used to sit in the beer garden in the evening and show each other what we'd found. Nobody would do that these days.'

I look around. It's a stretch to imagine this place has changed much over the years. It still feels like a real frontier town, with a dusty main street and an air of neglect and indifference. The real action is just outside town, at the main opal fields. The town itself is merely a handy watering hole, a place to come in and shop, drink, eat, sell opal finds, swap gossip and talk to the tourists.

The man frowns. 'No, it *has* changed,' he says. 'Nothing stays as it is but it still has the same charm. The past here has no importance. It is the future, today and tomorrow, we are thinking of. Who cares about yesterday?'

That's one of the reasons I'm finding the place so fascinating: people often come here to lose themselves, to start all over again, to forget what's been and just concentrate on what could be. It's a whole bunch of people living in the now, not asking each other questions about where they've come from and why, but just accepting each other and moving on. That would rarely happen in a city, I'm forced to admit. But here, in the Outback, it seems people are far readier to accept strangers, take them at face value and just get on with living life.

The next day, I drive just outside town to a nearby field pitted with holes and dotted with mullock heaps of fossicked limestone. It's hot and the sun is pounding down on the pale-grey lunar landscape. The dust makes every breath a rasp. It's hard to believe anyone would actually choose to live in a place like this, but they do. What's more, it's becoming an increasingly attractive choice for not only hardy young men out to seek their fortune the old-fashioned way but also for an increasing number of families, battling to keep their heads above water.

There are a couple of small children here, bare-chested and in ragged shorts, picking over little shards of stone left in piles near the mines, then throwing them at each other. A woman, presumably their mother, is tiredly pegging out terry-towelling nappies and tiny T-shirts onto a line stretching between a tin hut and a post nearby. We exchange greetings as I wander past. I think I might go over for a word but, at that moment, one of the children starts screaming and the woman rushes off to blot a bright-red gash on his arm. A shard has obviously found its mark.

These new arrivals are easy to spot: they include women and kids for one thing. All of them look poor and a bit desperate, living in huts and lean-tos and caravans next to their claims. Appearances can be deceptive, though. Someone tells me that Lightning Ridge is home to the highest concentration of millionaires in Australia – and you'd never be able to spot one of them.

With all the miners closely guarding their claims and never wanting to publicise their finds, the millionaires drive beaten-up old jalopies, wear tattered clothing and often dig by pick and shovel or jackhammer just like everyone else. Indeed, that seems to be one of the main attractions of the place. The man who's just made his fortune with some fabulous seam of opal carries on working side by side with the one eking out a living just below the poverty line. A local Aboriginal miner would form a partnership with an Italian blow-in if it suited them both. Few pay tax or have ever thought to register their vehicles. Egalitarianism? Multiculturalism? Freedom? Anarchy? Lightning Ridge, at best, seems to offer something to suit everyone.

'It is a great life,' says Donna Hewlett, who came here with her husband, Bob, for a few months . . . and ended up staying 23 years. After arriving the couple immediately struck opal and made a couple of thousand dollars. 'Then we were hooked,' she says. 'We started out in a caravan, then put a roof over it, closed in the roof and put up some walls. Unfortunately, we've never made much money from opal since.'

Bob earns an income when he's not mining by helping wheat farmers at harvest time or doing fencing jobs, while Donna works in the office of the local school. 'But you can get trapped here,' she says. 'It's taken us 20 years to build our camp, and it's beautiful in the bush, next to a dam, and among the trees, but we'd be lucky to get $100 000 for it. So when we want to leave, where do we go? You can't get anything for that somewhere else.'

It's certainly cheap to set up at Lightning Ridge. Individual claims are limited to a 50-by-50-metre plot, meaning people can come in and set up for a minimal investment of $100 to register a claim with a $250 bond, but there's $5000 or so worth of equipment they need to get started properly. And opal is easy to spot, even for novices. In 1974 the government also agreed to allow down-on-their-luck miners to claim social security, which suddenly freed them from having to leave town when finds were too few or far between to finance food.

Now, as well as the traditional Lightning Ridge inhabitants – the old-time miners, the adventurers, the eccentrics, the loners, the drifters and those on the run from shady pasts – plenty more have opal fever: families who find they can no longer afford to live in the big cities; farmers with their lands devastated by drought or flood; bankrupt graziers; the unemployed and unemployable; and people who've just hit a run of bad luck.

I decide to drive out to one of the more distant opal fields, Sheepyard Flats, about 70 kilometres out of town. I start out bumping over the rough dried-mud road, coated in the same thick grey dust as seems to cover everything. Even the eucalypts are caked in it. Everything is so dry it's hard to believe it ever rains. But then it does. Without any warning, the heavens open and the rain gushes down in torrents, turning the road into a squelching brown slick, as slippery as an icerink. I slow down as I struggle with the steering wheel. I'm sliding all over the place and it seems to be getting worse.

Then, out of the corner of my eye, I see an emu mince over from the bushes. It runs onto the middle of the road in front of me and stops still. I pump the brakes and swerve to avoid it – at precisely the same moment it decides to exit in the same direction. Horrified, I slide straight into it.

When finally I come to a halt, I leap out of the car to see if the bird has survived. It's lying still on its side but, as I approach, wondering what the hell to do, it jumps to its feet, shakes itself and races off, completely intact, across the great fields by the side of the road. I breathe a sigh of relief and wave it farewell before trudging back to the car. It has fared appreciably less well. The front passenger side has completely caved in.

There's nothing I can do but continue, driving slowly and carefully and keeping a wary eye out for anything on the sides of the road. As the rain stops and the sun comes back out, I wonder how the woman in the car-rental place will react.

Finally, at a little cluster of tin shacks and caravans, I stop and wander through. I've been warned to be careful of my footing, and I am. With more than 300 000 mining holes in the earth around the area, some of them up to 12 metres deep and many of them left uncovered, it's a dangerous place for a casual stroll.

There's a man sitting on the step of a small caravan in a battered leather hat, an open denim waistcoat and faded denim shorts, cradling a mug of tea and watching a young girl kicking over stones. I go over to say hello.

'Had a bit of trouble on the road, did you?' he asks, looking at the car. I grimace. Still, it seems to help break the ice and since all the miners' vehicles are pretty battered, I no longer stand out from the crowd.

This man has been working down his mine since early morning and he's ready for a chat. His name is John and he and his wife, Carol, both 34, left their home on the NSW central coast ten years ago to start anew here. They'd both got fed up with city living and struggling to make ends meet, he explains, and longed for a simpler life. And in Lightning Ridge there is always the chance, however slight, of getting rich quick. I look over his shoulder at the tiny caravan set in what looks like a battle-scarred wasteland. And now, any regrets? I ask cautiously. He smiles.

'It's paradise,' he says, without the slightest hesitation. 'It's wonderful. It's the perfect place to bring up kids.' I search his face for a sign he might be joking, but there's none. 'We came here mainly for the lifestyle and if we find opal it will be a bonus. It's the lifestyle we love.' Hearing voices, Carol emerges from the caravan. I'd been expecting a woman looking far older than her years, battered by the sun and hunched from the years of helping John shovel and push heavy wheelbarrows full of potch away each day, but she looks radiant. Hard though life must be here, it clearly suits some.

John tries to explain. 'In the cities there are just too many people, people everywhere,' he says, sweeping his arms wide. 'It's too busy. Everyone's always rushing around, stressed out. No one has time to talk to anyone else; they're burning themselves out. For kids in a city environment, there's drugs and all sorts of dangers. Here, they get the chance to learn what life's really all about. You buy a claim, make a home and get on with it.'

Carol's nodding by his side. 'I have to have a really good reason now to go back to the coast or to Sydney, they've got too crowded,' she says. 'We never used to see each other. John'd come home from work, eat and go to sleep. Now we can work together. We can be much more free here and if you hit opal, you hit it. It's like buying a lottery ticket. There's always a chance.'

It's that game of chance that has seen Lightning Ridge – named after an electrical storm in 1863 during which lightning is said to have killed a shepherd, his dog and 600 sheep – thrive for so many years. From the day opal was first discovered here in 1887 and the first parcel of gems sold for 30 pounds some 16 years later, it's always been the Australian equivalent of the gold-rush towns in the American west. Now, the stakes are even higher.

While a good find might still be one chance in thousands, fine-quality black opal can now fetch $8000–20 000 a carat. It's prices like those that have fed the millionaire dreams, even though for every person who strikes opal – often, sadly, of poor quality and in only a thin streak – dozens more toil away without ever finding anything. Some find solace in drink. Some, even when they hit paydirt, fall victim to the 'ratters', skilled thieves who creep down their mineshafts under the cover of darkness, with sophisticated night-vision goggles, to clean them out. Over the years thousands have ended up leaving the place broken-hearted and penniless. A few have gone in coffins: the victims of cave-ins, flash floods in their mines, explosions and fights to the death with rivals.

But the success stories are legendary too. There was the man living in a battered tin hut, it's said, who struck an $8-million sales deal; another in rags had a fortune safely secreted overseas; Ken Westbrook, 67, went into the record books two years ago for finding the largest black opal, worth $4 million; yet another was living in poverty, unable to bear parting with the glorious stones he'd uncovered. One man is reputed simply to have tossed an opal on the bar every time he found one, and asked the barman to let him keep drinking until his tab was up. A Polish-Australian was commonly believed to have lowered a bucket down his new mine a metre, and hauled it back up with $500000 worth of opal. When a Dubbo taxman came round one day to investigate the miners, he was said to have quit his job and joined them.

Another old-time miner squirreled away a $1 million fortune in banknotes from the proceeds of his opal discoveries, burying them in the ground because he didn't trust banks. When he finally dug them up, he found they'd been eaten by termites. But the most tragic story involved two miners who became millionaires, yet still couldn't resist chipping out the opal in the column holding up the roof of their cave. As a result, it eventually collapsed, killing them both.

As well as the daily hardships, that darker side never seems far away. Many miners will only accept help in digging their claim from their own families, as they regard everyone else with mistrust and suspicion. In the local drinking hall, the Sheepyard Inn, I'm regaled with tales, both true and no doubt tall, of well-known enmities. For instance, the two brothers who dug daily side by side until they struck opal. Then they started watching each other all the time to check the other wasn't smuggling opal out of the mine. In the end, they both cut the pockets out of their trousers to allay the other's suspicions.

There were also families broken up when the men found opal and disappeared to the coast on the proceeds, leaving long-suffering wives and kids far behind. Sometimes, disagreements even lead to murder. A few years ago, a miner was sentenced to two life terms for murdering an elderly woman and her son in a dispute over a claim. Indeed, Lightning Ridge is said to have the highest ratio of unsolved murders and missing bodies in the country. Deep unused mineshafts make the perfect hiding places for bodies, and they're still popularly believed to be the last resting place of many a man who'd mysteriously left town without a word.

I wonder if anyone will be trusting enough to give me a peek down their mine. I chat to a few miners, buy them a few drinks and then am struck by a brilliant idea. 'In a couple of weeks I'm off to see Fred Brophy,' I casually mention. 'Fred Brophy!' one of them exclaims. '*The* Fred Brophy? You know him?'

'Well, no, not exactly, but I'm off to have a fight at his tent.'

'*You? You're* having a fight at his tent?' The effect is electric and while I'm not sure I like the incredulity in their voices, it's too late now. I've played my trump card and I have to keep going. 'Yes,' I respond with the slightest note of indignation. 'In two and a half weeks. In Kilkivan.' I swallow. Two and a half weeks. I suddenly feel a bit faint; that's not much time to learn how to box. But I push the thought to the back of my mind. I'm in Lightning Ridge, and I have to concentrate on the here and now.

The miners, I can see, are now looking at me with renewed respect and interest. I might not look like a fighter, but appearances can always be deceptive. 'So, have you actually ever seen down an opal mine?' one of them is asking. I shake my head and one of the guys, Eric, immediately offers to show me his. 'It's impossible to understand the appeal of a place like Lightning Ridge without feeling the excitement of being down a mine,' he says, striding towards his claim. 'You have to be there, and know that any minute you might strike it rich.'

I scurry on behind him, trying hard to focus on what he's saying, rather than on what got me the entree. He bought his claim from a friend for a case of beer and found he adores being here, relishing both the thrill of the gamble and the simplicity of the lifestyle.

'You get up in the morning, have breakfast and do a bit of washing or whatever you have to do,' he says. 'Then you go down your mine and do a good eight hours' work. You work bloody hard. Sweat pours off you. Then you come up, have a good scrub and you feel like a million dollars. You have a meal and a couple of beers and go to bed around 11 p.m. It's the only place left in the world where you can live so simply. It's a bloody good life.'

He stops by a hole in the ground, next to a homemade pulley powered by a little electric motor strapped on the side. He slides aside the wooden cover and flicks a switch. I peer down. Good. At least he has electric light. In the dim glow of a bulb, I can see the first few steps of a metal ladder going down.

'I'll go first,' Eric says, brightly. 'You follow. Give me a couple of minutes head start.' He steps down onto the ladder and disappears completely from view. I count to ten, and then gingerly kneel on the ground and push my leg down onto the first step behind me. I can hear the sound of Eric's shoes clinking on steps way off in the distance. I venture another step down. The ladder feels as if it's swaying against the walls of the hole. I take a deep, slow breath and start climbing down.

It seems like forever until I hear Eric's voice in my ear and I realise I'm at the bottom of the shaft. It's cold here. We're about 15 metres down, he tells me. Eric immediately crouches down and starts edging along a tunnel. I follow, warily. A few minutes later, he's waving a torch around and telling me to look up. 'This is the part I'm digging out now,' he says. 'Isn't it a hell of a buzz?' I look but actually there's bog-all to see, just a hewn-out wall and ceiling of rough rock. He points out different colours in the rock but, to be honest, I can't see anything. 'Here, hold this!' He thrusts an electric drill into my hands and switches it on. Then he puts his hands around mine and guides the drill up to the ceiling. We drill for a minute or two until he turns it off again. 'How was that?' he asks.

'That was great,' I lie. 'It's fascinating. Thanks so much for letting me come down. Shall we go back up now? I don't want to take up too much of your time.' I'm feeling a bit queasy in such a small space so far down. I can't wait to get back up into the sunlight, even if it does mean I have to skid back to town on that terrible road, and face the car rental company in Dubbo.

I might not have hit black opal down there, but I've discovered something far more important: I'm just about as likely to make a miner at Lightning Ridge as I am to become a real boxer.

9

THE MOST BRUTAL SPORT OF ALL

Back in Sydney, with two weeks before my fight at Fred Brophy's, I tell my partner, Jimmy, what I've done, and he's horrified. He immediately tries to dissuade me but I dig in deep, and deeper still, and eventually he gives up trying. I then, in a very small voice, ask if he'll come with me to Kilkivan – wherever that happens to be. If I get knocked out in my fight, I'll need someone in my corner (isn't that the right expression?) to help me. Incredibly generously, all things considered, he agrees. I decide at that point, however, not to tell any of my family just in case they try to talk me out of it too. I'm already feeling spooked, and I don't want to hear anyone else telling me how stupid I'm being, and how badly hurt I could end up. I just have to learn in the next two weeks how to be a boxer. How hard can that be?

I look up the names of boxing gyms in my area of Sydney. One, the Police Citizens Youth Club at Woolloomooloo, catches my eye. I find the phone number of the boxing trainer there, Paul Isgro, and ring to explain my mission and ask if I can come in.

A long-time trainer of young boxers, with over 32 years' experience, he sounds dubious about the whole thing but says he'll be happy to give me a few pointers.

The next evening, I turn up early and climb so many stairs up to the boxing gym, I feel exhausted before I've even begun training. Inside, it's brightly lit and busy, with two guys slogging it out in a ring at one end, and everyone else sparring at the other. There are some men whacking boxing bags hanging from the ceiling and others shadow-boxing, watching themselves in full-length mirrors. By the benches along one side of the ring, there are piles of gear: bags, jumpers, boxing gloves, headgear and, worryingly, a wide array of bandages.

It looks as though I am the only woman there and, even worse, the only person in smart, matching gym gear – everyone else is dressed down in old T-shirts and baggy shorts. I make a mental note to do the same next time. And the room feels like a furnace: all the windows are clamped shut and there's no air conditioning I can detect. There is a pervasive scent of body odour with overtones of liniment. I begin sweating immediately.

I ask a couple of guys where I can find Paul. They point to a mountain of a man standing at the side of the ring, shouting instructions to the boxers inside. I hover uncertainly, trying to ignore how hard the men, both wearing padded headgear, are hitting each other. Another man is standing nearby, all padded up, waiting his turn. He's probably about 30, tall and lean with muscled shoulders bulging out of an off-white singlet. He doesn't look very approachable but, hell, I haven't come here to make new friends. I ask him how long he's been boxing.

'Ten years,' he says. I look a little more closely, and can see his face bears the tell-tale scars.

'Do you still get nervous before a fight?' I ask.

'Not at first I didn't,' he replies. 'But after you've lost a fight, that's when you get nervous. You know how much it can hurt, and you know what that feels like.' That isn't really what I want to hear, but he's warming to the theme. 'You never sleep the night before a fight. And then you don't sleep afterwards, either: you're usually too sore.' I tell him about my own upcoming bout. He steps back and looks me up and down.

'Who said you've got to do that?' he asks. 'Who's making you? I'd try to get out of it, if I was you. There's no way you'd catch me tent boxing. That's *really* dangerous stuff.'

I feel queasy and wonder if I should get out while the going is good, but at that moment Paul notices me and beckons me over. He's even taller and broader than he appeared from a distance, and he takes my hand in a bear-like grip, crushing my fingers so hard I wish I'd put some boxing gloves on first. I wince but smile through the pain. It wouldn't be right to start whingeing before I've even tried to fight someone.

'I don't know if it's such a good idea for you to box in a tent,' Paul says, obviously unimpressed by what he's seen – and felt. 'But we'll help you out as much as we can. Carl over there will do some pads with you.' He gestures towards a smaller, older man who hears his name and comes over. 'Carl, this is the one I mentioned. Could you give her a go?'

Carl Ehmsen smiles at me, and I warm to him immediately. No one else has smiled at this gym so far – they all seem intent on looking dangerous and moody – and I feel grateful. 'You'll be all right,' he says with a wink. 'We'll look after you.'

He finds me some gloves, holds up the pads and barks instructions at me.

'Jab! Cross! Uppercut! Uppercut! Left hook! Right hook! And again . . .' I struggle to keep up but, determined not to look stupid,

I hit his pads as hard as I can. He nods at me.

'Let me guess,' he says. 'You don't drink or smoke, do you?' I nod back. I have no breath left in my body, and dark patches of sweat are appearing all over my neat little outfit. 'You're fit, I'll give you that,' he says. I feel hugely grateful for that mild compliment. 'But you'll need to do a bit of work here. When you're hitting, always look into the other fighter's eyes. They'll tell you their intentions, when they're tired, when they're leaving a gap. Read my eyes.'

We start again. The harder I look into his eyes, the less accurate my punches. The more I try to read him, the softer my blows become, and the more hesitant.

'Don't worry, you're doing OK,' he tells me, gesturing at me to take a break. I sit on one of the benches and try to catch my breath, watching two more guys in the ring. Carl sits beside me. 'You should go along to the gym at Redfern too. They've got a couple of women boxers there.' Then Paul yells something towards me and I trot over. He tells me it's time for my first go in the ring.

Someone hands me a helmet and I turn it over in my hands, trying to work out which way it goes on. Carl saves me again. He comes over, puts it on my head and ties it up. 'Get yourself a mouthguard for next time,' he whispers to me as he helps me step up into the ring, holding the ropes open for me to clamber through. 'Good luck.'

Already standing, waiting in the ring, is a tall man who's about 25. He nods and holds out his gloves. I'm so wound up I immediately try to hit him. He steps back and I can hear laughter from behind me. Too late I realise he'd been offering his gloves to touch with mine – the international gesture of sportsmanship between boxers before they fight. Don't I know anything? Feeling crushed, I apologise, and hold out my gloves in contrition.

'Go again,' Paul says from the corner of the ring, looking amused. This time, we touch gloves, and I wait for my opponent to approach me again. As soon as he does, I start swinging wildly, missing him each time as he ducks and weaves his body out of my reach. I've soon exhausted myself and, at that point, he starts hitting me. He's absurdly gentle, however, and while I feel grateful, I'm also pretty humiliated.

'Break!' calls Paul, and we each back into our corners.

Carl is waiting for me there, and he hands me my water bottle.

'What's your date of birth?' he asks as I drink. I tell him, waiting to be told how geriatric I am. But he takes a completely unexpected tack. 'Ah, the Year of the Pig. That's good. You've got a big heart. When you're cornered, you'll come out fighting.' The thought I might have a latent boxer lurking somewhere deep inside who might eventually make an appearance and save the day cheers me immensely. 'But you should work on your combinations,' he adds. 'Go into every fight expecting to win. If you expect to lose, you will.' I try to imagine winning. Then I try harder, but I can't picture it.

After I catch my breath, it's time for the next round, and this time I try to aim a bit better. The first time I actually manage to hit his body I feel momentarily thrilled, but I'm then forced to retreat behind my gloves onto the ropes as he immediately takes advantage of the gaps in my defence. I know I'm being toyed with. I try to hit much harder, but succeed only in catching my own face as I pull back to hit his chest. I hope no one has noticed.

'OK,' says Paul. 'Break now. You've done well. How's the face?'

*

The next night I dress carefully in old shorts and a T-shirt, and drive to Redfern, to former boxing champion Tony Mundine's Elouera gym in Eveleigh Street. With a massive Aboriginal flag painted on the back of the building, it's a landmark of the Block, the once-notorious part of Sydney that became synonymous with ghetto housing, anger at the disadvantage faced by Aborigines, and police raids on drug dens.

Now much of it is being redeveloped, but a lot of the old houses are still occupied in between others that stand boarded up, derelict and ready to be bulldozed. The gym, although pretty tatty these days, remains a focal point, with its proud tradition of great boxers visiting and training there, including Tony's son, WBA super middleweight Anthony.

In my eagerness, I've arrived too early and the gym is still locked up. After 20 minutes of waiting on the step, the door creaks open. I walk up the steps, past the walls decorated with Aboriginal paintings and messages about believing in yourself. I smell the gym before I see it, the odour a mixture of sweat and dust. I can hear it too – loud hip-hop music blaring. At the top of the steps, the gym opens straight up and a steady stream of men make their way either towards the boxing ring in the far corner, to the bags dangling from the ceiling, or to the weights near the entrance.

The place has obviously seen better days; a number of panels in the ceiling bulge from damp and the strip lighting is buzzing. Most of the gym equipment looks old and torn, and the punching bags have obviously been patched and re-patched many times. Even so, it has the air of a gym where people are serious about their training. The walls are lined with black and white photos of old boxers – Muhammad Ali, Mike Tyson, George Foreman, Jeff Harding and Tony Mundine – and framed posters of old fights.

All the guys there are dressed casually, although this time some of the shorts are made of satin.

I pay my $5 – which seems ridiculously cheap – and say I'm waiting for the women to come in. 'They'll be another hour or so yet,' the guy at the desk tells me. 'Go over and warm up with the other boxers.'

I recognise a number of the faces from the previous night at Woolloomooloo, but no one smiles. They all look deadly serious. I put on my practice gloves and start hammering away at the nearest punching bag. It's hard, and it's hurting my hands.

'Hey, try this one!' an older man by a red bag calls out. He's evidently seen me flinch. 'It's softer.'

He introduces himself as Barry and asks what I'm doing there. I tell him, and he shakes his head. He's been boxing since he was 14, had turned pro at 16, and his career was only cut short because, apparently, he'd had a bloody bastard of a manager who'd put him in fights he could never win. But once a boxer, always a boxer.

In my case, however, he has some advice. 'Don't do it,' he says. 'In the Outback, they go into those tents with a bellyful of rum. It's dirty; it's a mess. One bloke I know had a fight in Sharman's tent, he got hit and fell back on the concrete and . . .'

I don't really want to hear the rest of the story. 'Would you do pads with me for a bit?' I interrupt. He looks suddenly trapped. 'I suppose so,' comes his begrudging answer. It's obvious he has better things to do with his time than help train a woman who's never fought before.

'How old are you?' he asks as I begin my routine. I tell him, waiting for the rebuke. I don't have long to wait. 'How can you expect to fight an 18-year-old pro?' he asks. 'You'll get smashed.'

I say nothing.

'How long have you got?'

'Just over a week and a half.'

He snorts. 'You don't stand a chance.' He calls out to a man standing outside the ring, padded from head to foot, who seems to be playing the role of a real-life punching bag in the ring. 'You hear what she's doing?' Just in case he hadn't, Barry drops the pads and goes over and tells him. The man looks at me disapprovingly.

'You shouldn't do that,' he says. 'If you were 18 or even 25, you'd be fine, but at your age, you can't recover from injury. You can get one hit and your nose will be splayed all over your face and it'll be like that for the rest of your life. No, you shouldn't fight.'

I smile as if he's the one being ridiculous. 'I'll be fine,' I say, feeling close to the verge of tears. 'It'll be fine.'

Barry comes back with his pads and holds them up for me. 'Well, you've got one thing going for you,' he says. I wonder if he's glimpsed my latent boxer within. But no. 'You obviously don't feel too much fear. I had a great young boxer once. He was really promising, had a great future. But he was always so scared whenever he went into the ring. He was defeated by his own fear. That comes from within; it's self-made. It's only when you learn how to control your fear – that's the gateway to boxing.'

I know it was meant to make me feel better, but it doesn't. When Barry leaves to hold the pads for another boxer, I return to the front desk. The guy who'd been there is now training a young man on the mats in front. In time with the music, they're both jerking their knees up in a high march, and pulling their arms down. It looks like a beautifully rhythmic hip-hop dance.

When they take a break to come over for some water, I ask them what they've been doing. Were they with a band? They look at me baffled. 'No, we're kickboxers,' says the older man, who turns out to have been a past champion.

'But those moves look like a dance, with your legs and arms . . .' I tail off uncertainly.

'We're practising grabbing our opponent's head and putting a knee in his face,' one says.

'Oh!' Yet again, I feel like the stupidest person in this parallel boxing universe. I hastily change the subject and ask what time the women are expected. He looks at me quizzically. 'They've been here for ages,' he says. 'Look, there.' I look in the direction he's pointing, and see two tall, lean, tattooed figures slogging each other hard. I'd noticed them before, but they were hitting with such force that, from a distance and in the dim light, I'd just assumed they were men. I take a deep breath and go over.

They're Elsie Banks and Carmen Zdroykowski, two boxers both training hard for their first fight under the keen eye of their trainer, Tony O'Loughlin. I introduce myself to the trio, tell them what I'm doing, and ask if I might train alongside them. They say they'll be happy for me to do so. None of them say they think I'm mad, or that I'm far too old. I feel a rush of warmth towards them.

After an hour or so, it's our turn to take over the boxing ring. Elsie and Carmen spar first, then it's my turn, with Carmen. I'm plainly hopeless. Tall and strong, with short blonde hair and a ready smile, she seems to have such long arms, I can't get near her. The first time she takes aim at my head, I stagger back with the weight of her punch. She stops immediately.

'I did it softly,' she insists. 'That wasn't hard.'

I'm embarrassed. 'Sorry,' I say. 'It's just that you caught me off balance. Really, I'm not hurt.' But I do notice she barely brushes me from that moment on. On the other hand, Tony is quick to admonish me. 'You look like you're trying to hit her shoulders!'

he says. 'Why? You're meant to be going for her face.'

It's true. I'm finding it hard even to try to hit someone in the face. 'Come on!' he says. 'This is what it's all about. They're going to hit you in the face; you've got to hit them first. And in the tent, you won't have any headgear on, so you've got to make sure it counts!' I try, and even manage to touch Carmen on the chin one time. Immediately, I apologise. 'Don't say sorry!' she says as she charges around the ring. 'That's what you're meant to be doing! Well done!'

After also practising fighting our way back from the ropes, Elsie, equally willowy with soft dark hair and a surprisingly gentle manner, offers me some quiet advice. 'You've got to keep your eyes open,' she advises. I hadn't realised, but I'd been shutting my eyes every time a fist came close. 'That's dangerous. You've got to see what's coming next and get out of the way of it, and work out how to get your opponent when they're exposed. When you're sitting at home at night, put on your gloves and practise hitting yourself in the face, while keeping your eyes open. That way you'll get more used to how it feels to be hit too.'

The next week and a half follows the same exhausting routine. Every night, I either go to Woolloomooloo and get hit a lot, or to Redfern to be hit some more. Before I go to bed, I hit myself around the face just in case it hasn't all already been enough. Along the way, at every stage, I learn a little more.

Carl tells me that for the fight, I'll have Vaseline smeared over my face. That sounds OK. I guess it'll mean I'll photograph better and my opponent's punches will just slip off me? He looks surprised. 'No,' he says. 'It's to make sure you don't get cut so much, or bleed so much, that they have to stop the fight early.'

Trying to get more of an idea about what I'm trying to do, I watch movies about fighting and study how real boxers box. *Fight Club, When We Were Kings, Million Dollar Baby, The Fighter* . . . I watch until I scare myself silly.

I even go along to watch Elsie in her first fight, at a fight night held at Bondi Junction RSL. The promoter, Maydad Ronen, the former ABA bantamweight boxing champion, and the owner of the Bondi Boxing Gym, trains women boxers himself and says they often make good fighters. 'Girls listen and pick up a lot more than guys,' he says. 'They don't have as much aggression as men, so they have to rely on their ability and be smarter.'

That's all very well, but as a girl with bugger-all ability, and not terribly street smart either, I'm at a disadvantage. The only damage I keep doing to my opponents is purely accidental. In the ring, I keep treading on their feet in my eagerness to get close enough to hit hard. Seeing how determined I am, and how hard I train, people seem to be softening in their attitudes towards me. I can well understand the initial hostility; they've been fighting all their lives, how presumptuous to try to become a boxer in just two weeks. But, gradually, even Barry starts offering me tips.

'Your best friend is your smother, not your mother,' he tells me, showing me how to get in close to a boxer so they can't hit me when I'm on the defence. 'Form a wedge with your fists, welded together like an iron bar.' This is how to protect my face from blows. 'Duck when they come at you with their left, and then bob up and use your momentum to hit them hard in the stomach.' Easier said than done. Even so, I spend every spare moment hitting out at an imaginary enemy.

Eventually, I build up the courage to watch that SBS documentary *Outback Fight Club* on Fred and his tent-boxing.

It shows Fred as the Outback hero, keeping everyone on the straight and narrow through the discipline of boxing, while providing entertainment for everyone else. While he'd planned to retire – the film was intended to be the story of his last ever tour – in the end, he decided to keep going. Naturally enough, however, the female fighters steal the show for me. In the doco, his troupe member, the Bitch, is soundly beaten by the challenger, the Beaver. *Great!* I think, hopefully, *the troupe member doesn't always win.*

But then comes the knockout blow. I find on the web that Fred's troupe now contains a woman who's a past Australian heavyweight champion boxer, nicknamed the Cracow Mauler. She weighs in at nearly double my weight: 110 kilos. My heart sinks. This really is serious. However hard I try, however much I learn, I realise for the first time that this is an Outback adventure that could actually get me killed.

10

THE MORE YOU SWEAT
THE LESS YOU BLEED

Three days before I'm due to leave for Kilkivan, 50 kilometres north-west of Gympie, I have a brainwave. Who better to ask for some advice than the past master himself? I manage to get hold of Tony Mundine senior's telephone number.

I'm getting increasingly anxious at the prospect of fighting a champion boxer but at the same time, I'm determined not to wimp out. City people can be as tough as those in the Outback, I tell myself sternly. And if we're not, at least we can give these things a try. It would be pathetic to drop out now, especially after taking up so many people's time in the boxing gyms. I couldn't face going back and telling them I'd chickened out. I've always believed in trying everything once – except the obvious stuff like crime and hard drugs – and I'd hate to live with the feeling of giving up on a challenge. Besides, I've already invested so many hours, and so much effort, in learning how to box . . . or an approximation of it.

But maybe it is now time to seek a little reassurance. And

Tony, a four-division Australian champion and the one-time challenger for the middleweight world title, is the one to ask. I tell Tony about my plan to fight up at Fred Brophy's. He sounds uncertain.

'Well, if you really want to be a boxer at some time in the future,' he says, 'maybe it's a good idea.' Happily, he asks me neither my age, nor my intentions.

'But if, say, you went into the ring, and were fighting someone who'd never fought before, you'd be gentle with them, wouldn't you?' I ask. This is a thought I've been cherishing. *Real* boxers wouldn't be interested in pummelling incompetent amateurs. They'd go soft on us.

Tony, however, is having none of that. 'Hell, no!' he roars. 'It's a very violent sport. Anyone who gets in the ring has to be ready for that. You're in there to win, whichever way you look at it. Your opponent might not be a good fighter, but it just takes one lucky punch and it's all over. So I go in there to knock their heads off – whoever I'm fighting. You can't afford to be gentle and nice. No way.'

I thank him and put the phone down. Right, so I have to prepare for the worst, and just hope like hell for the best. I'm still not convinced that my opponent will be as merciless with me as Tony Mundine might. I wonder if I'd be able to strike a bargain with her on the night not to hit me too hard. If I go soft, she might too? The danger in hitting her as hard as I'm able, might be that she'll wallop me with a knockout punch that has 110 kilos behind it.

Friends can't offer much consolation. None of them has any knowledge of boxing. A couple say it's a vicious sport and should be banned. It's impossible to appeal to a boxer's better nature; they don't have one. They're fighters, bruisers, loners. They don't care about others as long as they win. On YouTube, I watch Richard Pryor telling of the time he agreed to an exhibition fight with Muhammad Ali for charity. As Ali approached him in the ring, warming up with fists flying so fast he couldn't even see them, he suddenly wondered if the champ knew it was just for fun. Then Ali smiled, leaned over close and whispered in his ear, 'I'M GONNA KICK YOUR ASS.'

I start guessing the weight of anyone big I notice to work out what 110 kilograms looks like. Terrifying, that's what. I find a newspaper story about a woman who fought once in Fred's tent, and broke her left cheekbone, had bruises around her left eye and her right cheekbone and suffered mild concussion for three days afterwards. That night, I train twice as hard. The trouble is, I'm becoming more and more tired. I'm not sleeping well, going over my moves every night in my head, and then getting so uptight, I can't relax.

I'm spending all my time either at the gym, thinking or reading about boxers – I discover someone I vaguely know, Paul Upham, has written a couple of excellent books on boxing – or watching boxing moves on YouTube or actual fights on Foxtel. I'm getting behind with my work; boxing is completely taking over my life. I feel the enthusiasm for my debut Outback fight gradually drain out of me. Ironically, this is just as everyone else begins to take it more seriously.

'You'll be OK,' the women's trainer, Tony O'Loughlin, tells me the next evening at Redfern, while he watches me whacking a punching bag, and smiles as it swings back to hit me. *Easy for him to say*, I think, irritated. He's been fighting since the age of ten, has trained boxers for 22 years – apparently over 4000 of them – and had, I later discover, been NSW head coach for six years from 2001 and Australian coach in 2004. He can obviously read minds too: 'Concentrate,' he says. 'Focus. And just make sure you hit her in the face. Punching her in the stomach will only leave yourself open to being hit.' But what if she's so tall I can't even *reach* her face? Tony smiles. 'You'll be fine. The more you sweat, the less you bleed . . .'

I'm training as hard as I can, sure enough, but it doesn't feel as if I'm making it any less likely I'll get badly hurt. But I thank Tony for his encouragement. Carl has come along to Redfern too, and it's always great to see him since he's invariably so welcoming. He's started buying me bottles of water, and bringing in pieces of fruit to keep me going.

'You've improved so much,' he says, trying to keep my spirits up. 'It won't be that bad; you'll see.' A number of the other boxers are now agreeing to spar with me, or hold pads for me, or even give me tips and allow me to shadow-box behind them, which must be terribly irritating at times. Kind of like a fly buzzing around your head, or a bad smell that you can't get rid of.

In return, I'm starting to become fond of some of them too, despite the fact that a few are still cranky about being pestered by a woman, and one who isn't very good, to boot. I'm starting to understand why so many of them love boxing so much; it really is an incredible way to keep fit, it takes a huge amount of skill, concentration and command of tactics to fight someone successfully, and it's a great release hitting someone's pads, a bag or perhaps a person – although I've still not really experienced that as yet – as hard as you can. A lot of the older guys there obviously live for the sport, and to them coming to the gym every other day is a way of life, a passport to a social life as well as a way to keep active. They love training the younger ones, and generously donate their time.

Many of them have dark pasts that occasionally you can draw

them on. One had been a heroin addict for 25 years from the early 1960s, but he's been clean now for 25 more. Another had been an alcoholic. A few had done time in prison but are now back on the straight and narrow. The younger guys all treat them with respect, and do as they're told. Many of those seem to have struggled, or are perhaps still struggling, with their own demons too, but have found, in boxing, a way through. They all look out for each other and, increasingly, they're looking out for me too.

One well-meaning boxer climbs into the ring with me but, while he takes my punches, refuses to hit me back. 'Please,' I implore him. 'Hit me. I need to know what it's like to be hit.' And, of course, I need to practise not crying when it hurts, but I don't tell him that bit.

He shakes his head. 'No, I'd never hit a woman.'

'But I'm asking you to!'

'No, I couldn't.' Any other day, it strikes me I'd applaud his chivalry. It seems bizarre that my life has come to this: standing in a boxing ring, pleading with a man to hit me. The whole thing feels too absurd for words.

Even the padded-up guy who gave me the lecture about my nose being flattened is catching a little of the mounting enthusiasm. 'You can spar with me tonight,' he says. After a few minutes, he even begins hitting me back, and hard, which, in a strange kind of way, I take as a huge compliment.

All this time, I've been struggling with various off-the-shelf gum-shields I've bought from sports stores. The first one I tried was too big for my mouth. I nearly gagged when I tried to shove it in. The second I tried was for kids and was a bit too small. Every time I wore it, dribble ran down my chin, and I had trouble breathing. I ended up keeping my mouth open and panting all the time; neither a good look nor a safe one – Elsie said my mouth must be closed during a fight to protect my teeth. Finally, she suggests I get a proper one made by a dentist . . . if I haven't left it too late. I call around several, and only one says they'll be able to fit me and make one in two days.

I drive straight there, and endure – silently, since I have the mould in my mouth at the time – the disapproval of the dentist who doesn't feel it's a proper sport for a woman. *He knows nothing*, I think to myself, bravely.

On my last day at both gyms, everyone wishes me luck. Elsie, Carmen and Tony hug me warmly, and tell me to come back and let them know how I go – and, I think to myself, to reassure them that I have survived. Others punch me a little too hard for comfort on the shoulder. At Woolloomooloo, Carl also hugs me and says I'm going well. 'No, I don't think I'll ever be a boxer,' I say. 'I just don't seem to have enough anger.'

'You just have to learn to access it from somewhere,' he replies. 'Learn that, and you'll be fine.'

At the end of that night, Paul shakes my hand solemnly. I notice, not without some satisfaction, that it doesn't hurt as much this time. He doesn't offer me any false hope, though, that I'll fight all right on the night. Instead, he chooses another route.

'You've got a big heart,' he tells me. 'You've got courage. Good on ya.'

I grin back.

I catch a flight with Jimmy up to the Sunshine Coast, and then drive to Gympie. We've booked a place at the Royal Hotel, a nice pub with smart, comfortable rooms, in which I can picture myself recuperating. We check in and then head off to Kilkivan to meet Fred to say hello before the fight.

Kilkivan is a tiny old gold-rush town in the hills of the Great Dividing Range, showing little hint of its wild past. Fred bought the Kilkivan Hotel a few years ago, along with the Cracow pub west of Bundaberg, as a Plan B for when his boxing tent days finally ran out. With little education to speak of – he'd only ever gone to school when the showground stopped in a town for a few days – Fred could easily run a pub. With the amount of drinking he did, he thought that at least he'd be pouring some of his money into his own pocket.

Fred's plan for a quiet retirement, however, has gone awry. As in many places across the Outback, the resources boom and the soaring price of gold has seen the old goldmine at Cracow reopened, and the miners come flooding back. With Fred bringing in a few backpackers, usually good-looking sorts, to serve behind the bar, the sleepy former ghost-town pub has been transformed into one of the busiest drinking spots in the state.

The same hasn't happened (yet) to its Kilkivan cousin. Despite the area's history of gold- and copper-mining, the hotel, albeit with its own pretty Scandinavian backpackers to help, remains a great old-fashioned Outback-style pub, low-key with no pokies. The bar, though basic, is the homely sort where everyone tends to talk to everyone else.

We walk in on a Friday afternoon, and after an hour I feel I know nearly the whole bar. Fred, tall and ruddy-faced below his battered old Akubra, is holding court with languid, lazy banter before a big band of old mates who faithfully turn up every time he pitches the tent. They call themselves his 'tent groupies'. Some of them are ex-boxers themselves, with flattened noses, cauliflower ears and nasty-looking scars I try not to notice; others are just lovers of the tradition. They've come from far and wide too: former kangaroo shooters from the Outback, a bank manager from the Gold Coast, a couple of sheep farmers from Victoria, a bunch of ringers from South Australia and a few curious tourists from Tasmania.

'They all love the tent,' says Fred, 58, sitting back with a beer in the garden of the pub. 'They love it here too. It's not like drinking in the city. There, if someone talks to you, you think they're going to rob you.' In his pubs, like in any real Outback pub, he says, it's only if a stranger *doesn't* talk to you that you become suspicious. And if you don't have a drink, or any money left for a beer, someone is sure to shout you. It's his proud boast that you can leave money on the counter of his pub and it'll still be there the next morning.

But we're here for the tent, and that's Fred's favourite subject. 'It's a wonderful thing and I don't know how much longer it'll continue. You have all sorts of people coming here for a fight; it's a great Australian tradition. It's the way young boys prove themselves, and men can show they're men. We have men fighting here whose fathers once fought in the tent, and their grandfathers before them. They have a fight, they come out afterwards and their girlfriend gives them a kiss and their mates buy them a beer, and they're proud to have taken part. They've proved themselves to be true Australians.'

It's a mantra Fred lives by. He fell in love with the tents the first time he fought in one as a boy, and is now eager to keep the tradition going for as long as he physically can. From the 1920s, the tents travelled around Australia – and often the UK and US too – following bush fairs, carnivals and agricultural shows, usually in the Outback and mining towns. With his mum running side-stalls around tents, it was only to be expected that Fred would join the carnival life as soon as he was old enough. He loved everything about it and while the sideshows included attractions like the half-man half-woman, the bearded woman and the tattooed pig with the golden tooth, Fred introduced a few novelties of his own.

With that old Outback gift of the gab, his first stall had punters throwing darts at a board for money – except there were no darts 'for insurance reasons'. Instead, he persuaded customers to throw imaginary darts, and he'd decide where they landed. There were even some bullseyes, but he rarely paid out. 'It was a bullseye, but unfortunately the dart just fell out,' he'd say. 'But for that, you can have three more goes for free.'

Another act he introduced was the frozen woman. 'She'd be a woman in a bikini behind glass and we'd say we gave her ice blocks for dinner,' says Fred. 'It's all smoke and mirrors, but it was always good fun.' Favourites were also the amazing performing mice, with mice superglued to the carriages of a trainset, and the incredible dancing ducks, with ducks standing on a plate placed over gas burners – the faster the music, the hotter the plate to make them 'dance'. Later on, he bought his own tent, and went off travelling with it.

Since then, he hasn't looked back. He runs it in a style all his own. 'I like to give all my boxers names,' he says. 'We've had the Mauler, Kid Goanna, Kid Valentine, the Scotsman and the Duke of Earl – all the way from Buckingham Palace. It's always been a bit of fun. We always tell crowds about the Masked Marvel from Yugoslavia, a man so ugly, women weren't even able to look at him. He was a legionnaire and was driving a tank in the desert war when it was hit and caught alight. He leapt out, with his long red beard and hair on fire. The only way they could put the fire out was to hit him with a shovel. But funnily enough, no one's ever seen him . . .'

It's all good-humoured blarney but, beneath it, there are real stories of tragedy and triumph. A number of Fred's fighters had been going nowhere when he picked them up, trained them and brought them to his tent. Now, they're fiercely loyal and many say he's actually saved their lives. Big Joe Sweeney, for instance, nicknamed Butterbean, is a huge thickset bloke, almost as round as he is tall, who's always given the toughest, most drunken men to fight. He uses his whole body like a weapon, charging them like a bull and bouncing off them, while challengers often pummel him with their fists to little effect.

He says it was Fred who taught him to control and channel the anger that, at one stage, threatened to destroy his life. Scarred by terrible burns at 13, and watching his older brother first jailed for murder and then himself murdered, Joe thought he might well end up the same way. But after years brawling in pubs, being glassed and being hit – and hitting back – with whatever weapon happened to be at hand, he was asked by Fred to join his troupe. The older man quickly became Joe's mentor. These days Joe has his own cattle farm, a wife and four kids he adores, whose names are tattooed across his chest, but his regular tent outings are the perfect way of letting off steam. 'It's been great,' says Joe, 37, drinking tinnie after tinnie in the far corner of the garden. 'As you see, I've started my training already. I love the tent. It's all good fun, and it's been great for me. I feel so proud to be a part of it.'

A number of Fred's fighters are past champions too. Steve Aczel, the former 1971 and 1973 Australian amateur light-heavyweight champion, who won the Commonwealth title in London, is sitting on a high stool, drinking beside a trestle table at the pub. Now 56, and long retired, he still comes along to help out Fred from time to time – although no longer as a fighter. Tonight, he's had so much to drink I'm amazed he can still talk, but he does so at the top of his voice and with an infectious good humour that charms everyone around him.

Catching sight of someone who's sitting alone at a table nearby, Steve bellows, 'Come on, mate, come over here so we can take the piss out of ya.' The man looks up and smiles, and then dutifully trots over, happy to be included.

'Want a beer, mate?' Steve asks.

The man shakes his head. 'No, thanks,' he says quietly. 'I don't drink.'

'Why not?' Steve roars.

'I'm not good on drink,' the man replies.

Steve doesn't miss a beat. 'Fair enough, mate. Good on ya!'

Despite his imposing size – and voice – Steve always has plenty of sympathy for the underdog. He was born in Hungary at the time of the revolution against Soviet control. When he was an infant, his parents smuggled him in a suitcase across five European borders in order to escape the crackdown against the rebels. Having been warned that if he made a sound, the family would be shot, he didn't speak until he was five years old, by which time he was safely in Australia. As he himself says, he hasn't stopped talking since.

Steve later took up boxing after years of being beaten up at school by his classmates, both boys and girls. 'I had to get my older sister to rough them up afterwards for me,' he says. 'I used to go home every day depressed and suicidal.' It was then that he went along to his local boxing gym. After training for a few weeks, his confidence grew tenfold. 'I went back to school and punched the shit out of every bully who'd ever beaten me up. I got into real strife with the headmaster, who called my mum in to see him. She said she'd had years of me coming home beaten up with ripped shirts and blood on my jumpers and now that I could defend myself, he was whingeing? He ended up apologising! But by the age of 15, I'd become a boxer. Boxing was my saviour.'

It was also a way of earning money and helping out his family. He'd finish school every day, change out of his school clothes and go to work as a bouncer at one of the roughest pubs in Melbourne. No one would believe he was still just 15. But by 17, he'd won his first Australian title, knocking out the man who'd been its holder for the past six years. He won it again at 19.

'I was a boy fighting men,' Steve says, with a grin. 'I was pretty shit-hot. I'm not shy about that. I was brilliant.'

During his career Steve fought Tony Mundine three times (and, of course, I knew how tough Mundine would have been on him). The first two times he lost and in the third he was ahead on points when the fight was stopped because of a cut on his eye. He's still annoyed that he wasn't able to finish the fight.

At 20, he turned professional and was, at one stage, sixth in the world as a light-heavyweight. Later, he was ranked tenth in the world as a heavyweight, behind such legends as Muhammad Ali, Joe Frazier and George Foreman. He was also rated number two of the all-time best Australian heavyweights, after Ambrose Palmer. Steve eventually retired in 1982, and came back the year after. At 45, he met Fred at his boxing tent. A couple of the troupe's boxers hadn't turned up, and Fred asked him to have a go.

'I agreed and thought I'd have a couple of easy blokes to fight,' says Steve. 'But instead, I got two boys who'd trained under the boxer I won my first Australian title against. One of them was 21 and he threw about 300 punches at me in the first round alone. Being a coward, I went into a positive defence stance and just let him go. In the second round, I cracked and knocked him out.'

Today, inducted into the Australian Boxing Hall of Fame and

still a huge fan of the sport, he's also a great supporter of Fred's. 'Everyone loves Fred,' he says. 'He's incredible. He's helping keep the sport alive. I just wish I'd known him earlier. I would have travelled everywhere with him. It would have been heaven. And he's a born showman. He'll look you in the eye and tell you the best bullshit, but it'll always be entertaining. How he's survived is beyond me, but he's outlived them all. His is the only tent left now in the world.'

Steve tries to go along whenever he can for the Outback spectacle. 'Fred's been going to Birdsville now for 33 years and he'll get crowds of 600 to 700,' he says. 'They've all heard of the tent and Fred, and want to have a go. But there'll never be any trouble in town as people save their aggression for inside the tent. Fred doesn't make much money from it after paying his boxers and putting on the show, and most of what he collects goes to charity. He can lose a lot of money too. He pays out whenever one of his troupe loses, but that doesn't happen too often. He might have someone punching the shit out of one of his troupe and he'll say, "How about a draw?" Then the crowd will boo and he'll declare the challenger a winner. If you win, you can big-note yourself for the rest of your life. But you really have to have balls to go in and fight.' I nod solemnly.

Then, of course, there are the women fighters. Crystal Shannon was a loose cannon as a teenager who loved nothing more than a good street fight. Despairing, her stepdad – another of Fred's troupe, fighting under the name Kid Valentine – took her along to meet Fred. Today Crystal is another member of Fred's group, happy, settled and now a doting mother. Not that she shows that soft side in the ring, I'm told. She's better known as the Bitch. 'And you'd better believe it!' one of Fred's mates tells me cheerfully.

On that note, I go off to find Fred again. I think I'd better organise my fight before I hear any more and chicken out. He's over with his friends at the table again. I join them and, when there's a gap in the conversation, bring up the subject of my fight. He takes a long swig of his beer, places it carefully on the table before him and looks at me hard in the eyes. 'You sure about this?' he asks, cocking one eyebrow. 'You don't look like a fighter to me.'

I smile. 'I've been practising.'

'Yeah?' He couldn't look more unimpressed.

'Yep,' I say firmly. 'I'm ready.'

One of the women sitting nearby overhears. 'You're thinking of fighting tomorrow?' she calls over. 'Did I hear right?'

'Yes,' I say. 'I've come up here for a fight.'

She turns to her neighbour to pass on the message. He looks at me and laughs. This isn't going quite as well as I'd hoped.

But then a woman on the other side of the table calls over. 'Hey! Are you Sue Williams?' Taken aback, I nod dumbly. 'I've just bought Fred one of your books!' she laughs. 'Here, Fred, here it is. She dives into a bag and comes out with *Women of the Outback*. She holds it aloft for everyone to see. There are murmurs of interest. 'It's a great book. Remember, Fred, I told you you'd like it?' Fred looks blank, but everyone else suddenly seems attentive. Silently, I thank her. I couldn't have planned such a perfect introduction in my fondest dreams. But then it takes an unexpected turn.

'But surely you can't be serious wanting to fight?' she carries on. 'I wouldn't have thought you'd know how. You're a writer, not a fighter.' There are more murmurs, this time of agreement. I feel crushed.

'I've been training at gyms in Sydney,' I protest. It sounds

144

lame even to my ears. 'It'll be fine . . .'

A woman on the other side of the table stands up. 'Look at this,' she says, lifting up her long blonde fringe. Underneath is a long, ugly scar traversing a number of reddened bumps. 'I got this boxing. It's bloody dangerous. You shouldn't do it.' I try to laugh but it comes out more as a squeak.

Her husband puts a hand on her shoulder. 'Nah,' he says, looking at me. 'You go back home to your gym in Sydney. You'll be better off there.'

This isn't going well at all.

I look back at Fred. 'I'll be fine,' I reassure him, although I know this doesn't feel at all real. I'm just playing the role of a valiant hero and I'll try to keep going until it's simply too late to be anything else. 'I'm ready. I'll be OK, you'll see.' He looks back at me and holds my gaze. Then he rubs the side of his face.

'Well, we'll see tomorrow,' he says. 'You see how you feel then.'

'OK,' I say. It seems, in the circumstances, the best I can hope for. I turn back to the table. 'I'm off now. Got to get my sleep before tomorrow night. See you then.'

Then with a wave I hope looks nonchalant, confident and tough all at the same time, I walk across the courtyard, through the pub and into the night. Tomorrow is another day.

11

WHOSE BLOOD IS THAT?

I don't sleep much that night. In my dreams, I'm lying on the ground in front of a huge crowd of people with my nose splattered across my face, blood pumping out by the litre. An ambulance arrives and carts me off to hospital. It's a long, long ride. 'But it's my birthday,' I keep telling the ambos as we bump along the bush roads. 'Don't let me die on my birthday . . .'

I wake to the sound of driving rain outside. 'Happy birthday!' Jimmy says.

I struggle to open my eyes; I'm so tired. It may be my birthday, but I don't think it's going to be a happy one.

My mood stays grey all day. There are odd moments when I cheer up, wondering if the rain might mean the boxing will be cancelled. I wouldn't mind that at all: no show, no shame. But as the day wears on, I start feeling sick too. Why had this once felt like such a good idea? And why, exactly, am I putting myself through all this? Couldn't I have been happy to meet Fred, and write about the tent as a spectator instead?

By late afternoon, I feel exhausted from all the worry. 'Let's just go now,' I say to Jimmy. 'We might as well get it over with.'

When we arrive at the pub in Kilkivan, there's a party going on, and it's in full swing. The place is packed, with a huge assortment of cars, 4WDs, utes, vans, caravans and motorbikes parked outside. I wonder if we'll even be able to get in. I realise, however, with an increasingly heavy heart, that from the size of the crowd, it's unlikely the boxing has been cancelled.

We push our way to the bar and buy a couple of drinks: lemonade for me; light beer for Jimmy – in case I'm too badly injured to drive. We wander into the dining room, with its flying ducks on the wood-lined walls, a grandfather clock and lace curtains fluttering over the windows. Tonight it's packed with tables, chairs and diners.

I sit and drink my lemonade, and listen to the chatter all around. Apparently the 110-kg Cracow Mauler isn't with the troupe now. Hurrah! And the Bitch isn't fighting either because of an injury. Instead, the woman on tonight is the Beaver. The hairs on the back of my neck prickle. The Beaver! She's the woman who beat the Bitch in the documentary.

I pick up my drink and walk out to the beer garden. I can see Fred racing around, delivering drinks, chatting to friends, darting off to get more meals, organising the ticket sellers for the fight. I wave but he doesn't see me. I carry on out to the yard at the back where the massive tent stands. It looks kind of hokey with all its flags flying, but also quite magnificent at the same time. At the top is a huge canvas poster, declaring, 'FRED BROPHY'S FAMOUS BOXING TENT', along with a drawing of the man himself, albeit in his younger days. On either side, across the top of the whole tent are images of fighters who've fought in the tent, from Tony Mundine and Jeff Fenech, to Lester Ellis and Steve

Aczel. Around the bottom, there are other panels: THE LAST BOXING TENT. CHALLENGING ALL COMERS. WHERE CHAMPIONS ARE DISCOVERED. Hmmm . . . I don't think, somehow, I'll count.

Over the front flap, a long wooden horizontal plank serves as a platform, reached by two ladders from the ground. From the doco, I know that this is the makeshift stage on which Fred will stand, introduce his fighters and invite challengers to come forward for a bout. I shiver and continue into the tent. I may as well have a look while it's empty, to get an idea of what I'll be in for.

It smells damp and water is dripping through a few holes in the canvas from the earlier rain. But it's brightly lit, and there are a few people already inside, presumably the tent boxers. One stops me to ask who I am.

I tell him what I'm doing there. His eyes soften. He obviously feels sorry for me. 'I'm the Scotsman,' he says, holding out his hand.

I take it. 'You don't sound like a Scotsman,' I say with a smile.

'You're right there,' he says. 'That's just the name Fred gave me. He used to get me to fight in a kilt when I fought for him. I'm not a Scotsman, none of my ancestors were either and I've never even been to Scotland. These days, I'm retired and my son is fighting in the troupe.' He points him out, a young man with a six-pack busily warming up. He is, apparently, Young Jock, even though he's just as Scottish as his father. But from what little I've learnt about boxing in the last two weeks, from the way he holds his body, the smooth way he moves and the crispness with which he jabs his fists, I can tell he's technically very good. 'So, come onto the mat, and see what it's like,' his dad continues. 'It's very different to fighting in a ring.'

He leads me onto the mat, which I notice is rippled over the lumps and bumps in the grass below. I'll have to be careful to pick up my feet, not to trip.

'The important thing to remember is to keep moving,' he says. 'Sashay like this.' He demonstrates a series of swift sideways steps, barely lifting his feet from the ground, and I follow him. 'Sashay sidewards out of trouble and then try to get around their back if they're hitting you hard.' He switches direction sharply and, even without the distraction of being hit, I trip over my feet trying to follow him. I try a couple of times more, then give up. It's a bit late to be learning new moves now. I thank him, and go back outside.

The beer garden is getting even fuller and the steady clash of beer bottles being thrown into the barrels for the empties is deafening.

Through a thick cloud of cigarette smoke, I can see Butterbean in the corner with a big group of bikies, drinking steadily. He's been 'in training' like that since eight o'clock that morning, someone tells me admiringly. The bikies are a bunch of massive tattooed blokes in worn black-leather waistcoats with 'Rebels – Queensland Chapter' on their backs, and either with long hair tied back, or no hair at all. The biggest one must be easily six foot six, with huge shoulders and a shaven head covered in tatts. That must have hurt. I try not to stare. I feel like I'm wandering through a strange dream, an outsider among such an unfamiliar crowd, not really a part of the action.

I go to the toilet for the fourth time that evening and look at myself hard in the mirror. It's a warm night, but I look pale and a bit ghostly. My mascara has smudged and I have a black shadow under each eye. I dab at my face with a tissue and notice my hand is trembling. But that isn't the only part of me that is.

My legs feel decidedly wobbly and my knees are tight, always a sure sign I'm stressed.

I find Jimmy chatting to a dapper older man called Leo Beutel, a former boxer-turned-boxing writer and broadcaster. He shakes my hand. 'I hear you're still thinking of fighting,' he says. 'Good on you.' A little man in a huge hat brushes past us and says hello. He's probably around 70 years old and he's twitching, going through some old boxing moves as he walks. He used to be a fighter. 'And you don't see too many boxers in old people's homes,' someone quips.

'Look over there,' says Leo. 'That's the Beaver.' I'm not really sure if I want to see her, but I can't help but turn. She has a pink mohawk and broad shoulders that strain against a red XXXX singlet. The Beaver looks dangerous – or is that just my imagination? She's an accomplished Muay Thai boxer, I'm told, and is currently still undefeated in Thailand. That must mean she's really good. But with Muay Thai, don't they also kick and use elbows and even their heads as weapons? Leo tries to comfort me. 'She'll only kick you if you kick her first.' There won't be much chance of that. I have too much to concentrate on already with just my fists and all that sashaying. I wonder if I should go over and buy her lots of drinks to get her drunk before we face off in the ring.

I casually wander over towards her and see she's now deep in conversation with Fred. As I get close, I can hear him asking her something. She's shaking her head. 'No,' she's saying. 'No, Fred, you know that's not my style.'

It suddenly occurs to me that maybe he's asking her to go easy on me. She's evidently refusing. I turn on my heel and walk away. I wish I hadn't overheard that. Now she's probably riled. I go back to the toilet for a last pee.

By the time I come out, I can hear a drum booming in the background. *This is it.* The show has begun. We all file into the yard in front of the tent. On the way, I bump into the woman who'd shown me the scar under her fringe.

'Remember me?' she asks. I nod. How could I not? 'She pushes her hair aside. 'I have to take tablets every day for the pain,' she says. I smile and then dive into the crowd to get away from her.

Fred is already standing on the plank, looking down on us all, resplendent in a baggy red-silk shirt, and banging his drum: *boom, boom, boom.* 'My name's Fred Brophy,' he cries, 'and this is the only boxing tent in Australia and the world.' He stops speaking and bangs harder. 'I'm a fourth-generation showman. And this is . . . this is the Beaver!' The Beaver, now dressed in a yellow-silk boxer's dressing gown, joins him on the plank, and starts ringing a bell in time to the beating of the drum. She doesn't look at all nervous. I hate her.

'Is there anyone here from Victoria?' shouts Fred. A few people call out. 'And anyone from New South Wales?' A few more people respond. 'Well, welcome to Australia!' he says to raucous laughter from the crowd. 'Unfortunately, the Masked Marvel from Yugoslavia has been detained in London tonight, so he can't be here. But we've got plenty of other top fighters for you.' He introduces them, one at a time, as they climb up the ladders – six men and the Beaver. Some of the guys are huge, others look incredibly fit. They all seem to be spoiling for some action. Butterbean, up on stage, appears massive, like he's been pumped full of air and is fit to burst. But Fred isn't ready yet. He's spinning this out to gee up the crowd.

'First I want to welcome some celebrities in the audience,' he says. 'We have Rex Hunt and his wife!' Everyone turns towards an older man with a grey beard and cheers. The man does indeed look a lot like the former Aussie Rules player-turned-football commentator and TV fisherman, but he's actually just a doppelganger, I find out later. Half the crowd, however, believes Fred. He's been introducing his mate this way for years, and the mate's happy to go along with it, even when he's pestered continually for an autograph. His wife is one of the women who'd been trying to persuade me not to box.

But now, finally, we get to the crux of the matter. Challengers get $20 for any round they win against one of his boxers. 'Have we any challengers? When you get up that ladder, you're a fair dinkum Australian.' A few men's hands shoot up. Fred invites them up on stage via the ladders. Fred's interviewing the challengers one at a time, asking them their names and where they're from. Then he asks them if they've fought before. Some say yes, more say no. Those who say no, he looks at very hard.

'You didn't get that nose from sitting at a computer,' he scowls at one. 'I've seen you before,' he tells another. 'Didn't you fight once at Birdsville? Yes, I think you did.' The man looks shamefaced. He asks one likely looking lad if he's ever boxed before. 'Nope.' Ever done any boxing training? 'Nope.'

'Then we know one thing about you, son,' says Fred. 'You're a bloody liar.'

Leo's already told me that Fred can tell from their handshake, and how they hold themselves, whether they're fighters or not. Yet for the challengers, it's in their interests to feign being a first-time fighter so they're given an easier member of the troupe. But Fred matches up everyone with apparent ease, based on the challenger's size, experience, the feel of their grip, who knows?

He calls for more challengers for the rest of the male fighters. There's jostling from the crowd as people encourage their mates to volunteer, and there's arguments as sometimes their mates refuse. Finally, seven more men make the climb. One pair is put in a tag team – they'll both be fighting Butterbean.

And then, finally, comes the moment I've been waiting for. Fred gestures over at the Beaver. 'And now,' he says, 'have we got a woman who wants to fight?' This is my moment, and I seize it.

'Me, me, ME!' I shout as loudly as I can through the melee, pushing my way to the front of the crowd. I've suffered so much for this, worked so hard, endured the mental agony, it would be terrible if someone was now chosen over me. Much as I really don't want to fight, having come this far I can't bear the thought of now not following it through. 'Fred! FRED! OVER HERE!' I yell.

A man with a far louder voice than mine points at me and draws Fred's attention. 'Someone here!' he calls. 'She's up for it!' Fred looks at me and I swear he sighs. 'OK,' he says eventually.

I scramble up the ladder, hoping not to fall flat on my face before I've even got into the fight. 'What's your name and where are you from?' Fred asks. I walk up to his microphone, balancing precariously on the narrow plank. Up here, it's even skinnier than it looked down there. And it wobbles.

'I'm Sue from Sydney,' I say in a small voice.

'Ahhh, Sue from Sydney,' he repeats. 'And why do you want to fight?'

Should I say – or not? I look down at all the expectant faces, sizing me up, no doubt thinking I don't look much like a fighter. 'Well . . .' I start. 'I'm travelling around the Outback, and I wanted to meet Fred because he's such an Outback hero . . .' There are cheers from the crowd. 'But I thought I couldn't see his tent without coming and having a fight in it.' There are a few cries of 'Goodonya!', some cheers and a smattering of applause, and I make my way back to the ladder.

That hadn't been too bad; maybe I'll get a bit of sympathy from the audience when they load me into the ambulance. I see Leo hold out a guiding hand to help and then steer me into the tent along with the other challengers and boxers.

We're sat down on the ground at the edge of the mat as the boisterous 200-strong crowd in various stages of inebriation follows us in, sitting and standing in packed rows behind us. I look up and realise that this is really it. There's no escape now. Even if I wanted to flee, I doubt if I'd be able to force a way through the crowd. Besides, would they even let me?

I sit stunned at the spectacle before me. Four of Fred's boxers have taken the 'stage' in turn and the fighting has been fierce. Young Jock has meticulously taken apart a big skinny biker kid with a faultless display of boxing. Butterbean has overwhelmed his opponents with sheer brute force, the pair of them falling into the audience at various points, threatening to flatten everyone they come into contact with. Butterbean even drank beer between rounds, and smoked a cigarette. I admire his elan.

During the fight, one of Butterbean's opponents is knocked to the ground, and Fred holds up a hand to his face. 'How many fingers?' he asks, to check if the man is OK to fight on. He has to look twice – Fred's little finger is missing. I find out afterwards he tells people he chopped it off himself after a row with his partner, Sandy, as a show of his love. He thought he could have it stitched back on with microsurgery afterwards, no big deal, but then his mate's blue cattle dog ate it before he could pick it up. True story? Who can say?

The man finally shouts the right number – 'Four!' – and is allowed to continue. Another of Fred's fighters is then in a bloody brawl with a huge, tremendously fit and determined man, who insists on fighting without a shirt, presumably the better to show off his six-pack. And two other guys slug it out with a ferocity that makes me quiver with fear.

I'm mesmerised by everything around me, almost in a trance. I flinch every time I see a fist meet a jaw, or when I hear the dull *thwack* of a glove meeting flesh, every whimper of pain or fear from a challenger. This can't be real, I can't be here, this isn't happening. But suddenly, I feel my arm being grabbed as I'm hauled to my feet. I'm momentarily confused, and wonder what's happening. Then, with a thudding heart I realise: *it's my turn.*

I'm pushed onto a chair at one side of the mat, and someone asks me if I'm ready, if I'm really going to go through with this. I nod dumbly. I shove in my mouthguard and I feel someone's rough hands on my face, smearing Vaseline all over.

Fred comes over. 'No, put more on her,' he tells the Vaseline-wielder, who must be my cornerman. 'Especially around the eyes.' Then Fred turns to me. 'Are you *sure* you want to do this?' he asks. Of course not, but it's a bit bloody late now.

Someone straps gloves onto my hands that are shaking so hard, he has trouble getting them on straight. Down below, I can feel my legs trembling equally violently. I silently pray they won't give way before the first punch is swung. I feel faint; it's hot, it's sweaty and everyone around us is baying for blood. And I suspect it won't be long before they get it.

It's time, and I get to my feet and walk shakily to the centre of the mat. The Beaver's already there waiting for me, flexing her tattooed arm muscles, her mohawk standing stiff to attention. Fred introduces me to the crowd.

'In one corner, we have SUE FROM SYDNEY!' The crowd applauds but I don't look at them. It's taking all my concentration to keep standing there. 'And in the other, we have THE BEAVER!' She lifts up her arms to acknowledge the crowd. It hits me: that's what I was meant to do. Oh well, moment missed.

Fred gets us both to the middle, says some things, none of which I hear over the shouting of the crowd, something about fighting fairly, I guess, and about how we'll fight three rounds of a minute each. Then we touch gloves, and the whistle goes. We separate and I start sashaying around, hoping she'll just finish me quickly with one knockout blow, then I'll be able to go home.

She's eyeing me with a degree of malice that is, frankly, terrifying. I'm staring at her with more a kind of blind fear. I bob my fists up and down in front of my face and we circle each other for a few seconds. I can feel my shoes scraping on the canvas beneath them – the canvas, an old boxer at one of the gyms told me, is there to soak up the blood. I can hear the shouts from the crowd, some on her side, but most for me, plainly the underdog. I can smell beer, cigarette smoke, sweat and fear – my own.

And then, at last, we pounce. I go in first, planning to hurry up and get it over with. Someone's yelling in the crowd, 'Fight! Fight! Fight!' and it's a chant soon taken up by others. I jump towards her and give two big left jabs but she shies away from them easily, and I'm left off balance, open and vulnerable. I leap backwards but she advances, and I see a powerful fist in an enormous purple glove swinging upward. She punches, and punches hard. Her glove hits me square on the jaw and my head snaps back. And then suddenly . . . darkness. *Oh my God, I must have been knocked out. How wonderful! The fight will now be over.* But no such luck. It seems there's simply a problem with the lights. Fred shouts at us both to stop.

After just a few seconds, however, the lights flicker back on and, before I know it, Fred's got us back together, touching gloves and blowing his whistle and bringing his hand down. Here we go again.

I punch, she punches, and both of us connect to varying degrees; she much more often than I. If only she'd stand *still*! It feels like she's playing with me, taunting me, luring me in and then whacking me after I've gone for her and missed. I get in a few punches – to her face, to her shoulders, to her stomach, and the crowd cheers each time I make contact, but my gloves seem to keep bouncing off her without doing any real damage.

She's more restrained, in control and at one stage pushes me away with one glove and then holds it to my face so I can't get closer. In frustration, I step back, and hit her arm with both hands at once. I don't know if I'm allowed to do that, but anything seems to go here. The crowd laughs.

'Come on, Sue!' I can hear people shouting. 'Use your right! Hit her with your right!' I resist the temptation to turn and tell them, 'Bloody hell! Can't you see that's what I'm trying to do!' Then my opponent darts forward and boxes my ears with her two gloves at once. That's *definitely* not allowed, but I suppose I did leave myself open. Riled, I go for her again, this time managing to hit her head, her chest and her shoulders. She's doubled over, but I suspect she's just planning her next assault. And then the whistle.

I'm jostled back to the chair by my cornerman. Someone's flapping a towel in my face and someone else is spraying me with water. 'You're doing great,' the cornerman is saying, a man built like a brick shithouse who could, no doubt, have finished either of us off in seconds, probably with both hands tied behind his back. A half-used bottle of water is thrust into my mouth for a drink, but most of it goes down my front as I haven't yet mastered the art of drinking with a mouthguard in. I can feel the back of my neck being sprayed with water. 'Are you all right to keep going?' I'm asked. I nod. Of course I am. *I'm gonna get her this time.*

The whistle sounds again, and I'm back up and fighting. This time, first hit, I get in a good blow to her chin. Her head goes back and she has a look of surprise in her eyes. That felt good, and the audience cheers. But I pay for it. She seems now to be taking me marginally more seriously, and is working harder. At one point, she boxes me again around both ears – I find later that move is called 'the buffalo'. My ears are already ringing from the first time. Then she whacks me on the top of the head – 'the windmill'. I don't really know what to do, but I keep ploughing forward, hitting and being hit, and being hit again.

Once, out of the corner of my eye, I notice a speck of blood on my T-shirt. Is that mine, I wonder, or could it be hers? The thought it might be hers – even though that's pretty unlikely – cheers me immensely. Then finally the whistle sounds and I go back to my corner and sit down. The crowd laughs and, too late, I realise I'm so flustered, I've sat on my cornerman's stool rather than my own chair. Red-faced, I'm hustled off and into my own.

I have more water poured down my front, more water sprayed over my face and neck. It suddenly occurs to me that my mascara has probably now dribbled all down my face. But in boxing gloves, there's not much you can do about that. After a break, I stand up first and walk purposefully to the middle of the mat. Instinctively, I'm trying to psych her out, even though reason tells me that there's no way she'd be scared of me. But what the hell: I'll just chuck everything at her. I'm ready and willing. I've got my second wind. Now, I feel no fear. *Bring it on.*

The whistle goes for the third and final round and I leap at her with the biggest barrage of punches I can muster. I've taken her by surprise, and I even get a couple in. Her head jerks back. But then she fights back, hard. The crowd whoops and cheers. They like this display of mounting aggression. It feels like this round is lasting for hours. But I refuse to give up, even though I'm tiring while she looks as fresh as at the start. I hit her, she hits me. On and on. Until, at last, the whistle blows and I stand there, realising it's over, but not knowing what I'm meant to do next.

Then the Beaver comes over and hugs me. I hug her back. It's heartfelt. She completely outclassed me and could easily have done some real damage. I'm very grateful that she didn't.

Fred and the cornermen all descend on us. The men untie our gloves and Fred grabs one of my hands, and one of hers. He turns and holds our hands down by his sides. I realise this must be for the declaration of the result. For a split second – just a split second – I wonder if I might have won. The power of self-delusion. I don't have long to ponder. Fred lifts up the Beaver's hand in victory and the crowd cheers, then applauds long and hard.

Fred shakes my hand and puts his other hand on my shoulder. 'Well done!' he says. 'You did bloody well.' Then Leo races up. 'That was great! You're very fit. You kept moving.' I don't have the heart to admit I was too scared *not* to.

As I walk off the mat, the crowd parts to make way for me. People slap my back and say, 'Well done!' The huge bikie leader steps out into my path. 'I tell you what,' he growls. 'You've got balls, lady. You've got bigger balls than most of the blokes here.' He hits me on the back in a gesture I assume is meant to be one of congratulation but I'm so unsteady that, under the force of it,

I stumble and almost lose my balance. I continue out towards Jimmy, but I'm stopped all the time by people wanting to tell me how well I've done, and buy me drinks. Even the bar staff applaud me. For a few moments, I feel like Rocky – except I'm trembling so hard, it's an effort even to walk.

When I finally reach Jimmy, he takes me into his arms. 'I am so proud of you,' he says over the ringing in my ears. 'That was incredible.'

For the rest of the evening, I don't stop shaking, but I'm treated like a hero. I wonder what it would have been like if I'd actually won? I watch the rest of the fights, people who can really fight, or who get through out of pure aggression. Really, I wasn't very good at all, but I think people just appreciated that I was ready to go out there, put myself on the line, and give it everything I had. Even 'Rex's' wife comes to congratulate me afterwards.

I have a chat to the Beaver too, who turns out to be a very nice woman called Brettlyn Neal, a former jillaroo-turned-security officer from Toowoomba who dyes her hair pink before each fight to raise awareness of breast cancer. At 26 years of age, she's played for Australia in both rugby league and touch football and, during a spell in England, was selected for England's rugby union second team. She's been fighting for Fred for six months, and aspires to become the world Muay Thai champion. She'd only just missed out on the ISKA Queensland light-heavyweight title a few weeks before, losing her fight in a split-points decision. I'm extremely glad I hadn't spoken to her before I went into the match.

But when all the fighting finishes and everyone adjourns to the bar for some serious drinking, I suggest to Jimmy that we go. I can't handle too much more of this. Besides, I'm hungry and exhausted. I say goodbye to Leo and then find Fred to thank him for the fight. He kisses me on the cheek. 'Well done!' he says again. 'That took guts. Well done!'

We drive the hour back to Gympie and then look for somewhere to eat. It's nearly midnight and the only place still open, we're told, is the McDonald's by the highway. We go up there, order some food and sit down by a window. We're just hoeing into it when a young man approaches our table. 'Excuse me,' he says. 'Are you the woman who just fought at the boxing tent?' I look at him surprised, and nod.

'I just wanted to say, you were brilliant!'

I smile broadly at him.

Two weeks later, I return to the gym at Woolloomooloo to say thanks to the guys who helped me. When I walk in Carl bounds over, with a huge grin. 'How did you do?' he asks, hugging me. 'You survived!'

'Well, I didn't win,' I tell him, 'but I didn't get hurt, so that was a big plus. Just a few cuts and bruises, but nothing much. I was pretty lucky. She went easy on me.' I give him the Fred Brophy T-shirt I'd bought for him, and he beams and propels me over to Paul.

He too looks relieved to see me, and shakes my hand. 'What was it like?' he asks me and listens carefully, curiously, as I recount my experience. He looks almost as if he'd loved to have been there. 'You did good,' he says finally. 'I knew you would. Congratulations!' As I go to leave, Carl hugs me again, and gives me an orange.

The next day, I drive to Mundine's gym at Redfern. As I enter, a few of the people there see me and start clapping.

I smile and wave. The one who told me I'd get my nose broken walks over and touches his gloves to my hands. I'm moved by the gesture. Then I head for Tony, Elsie and Carmen in their corner. They're so pleased to see me, I feel almost tearful. We all hug each other, and I tell them each how grateful I am for their help. We swap phone numbers and promise to stay in touch. I'll enjoy watching them box in future now I know I don't have to go up against them.

But Tony has something he wants to say. 'You know, if you came here every night for the next six months, I reckon we could make a boxer of you.' I look at him in astonishment. 'You've got the heart,' he says. 'You just need the technique.'

I thank him, but politely decline his offer. My one fight in the Outback boxing tent was both my debut and my retirement – I consider myself lucky just to have survived. The Outback was proving a more dangerous place than I'd ever imagined.

12

THE LONGEST BUS RIDE IN THE WORLD – AND THE TRAIN BACK

I'm tucking into egg and hot chips at a roadhouse somewhere in the middle of Australia, feeling happy. My big fight's behind me and it's sometimes the simplest things in life that bring the most pleasure. A good meal when you're hungry, a soft seat on a bus when you want to get somewhere and a full bottle of water to carry with you . . . They're sometimes all you need to really appreciate the Outback.

I've been travelling for hours now on the longest bus ride in the world, stretching south to north across an entire continent, and things are going remarkably well. While it's one thing to buy a bus ticket for a trip that's going to take you 3030 kilometres, from Adelaide to Darwin, once you're on board you can only sit back and hope it's going to be a trip as memorable for its comfort and excitement as the vast distance you're covering.

'New to this are you?' asks another passenger with a smile, as he glances at the book, magazines, maps and muesli bars in a neat pile at my elbow. 'It's a breeze. You'll love it!'

I'm still not so sure. Ordinarily, if I have to travel from Adelaide to Darwin, it's a simple case of flying direct for three hours and 40 minutes. But this time, I'd decided to try out my old mate, the Greyhound bus, and to return in luxury via the Ghan.

The two trips make perfect sense. For a start, on the way there, I can stop off to explore anywhere I want along the route. With ten days or so to spare, it will also offer a way of taking a quick look at some of those Outback destinations it often costs a small fortune to visit individually.

Also, it's an environmentally friendly way of touring Australia, with one full coach emitting five times less CO_2 per passenger, per kilometre, than a jet aircraft on the same route, taking 16 cars off the road and the company even allows you to offset your carbon emissions for $1 per booking. It's much less hassle being driven and gazing at the scenery through the window, high up above the traffic, than driving yourself.

And last but not least, it's extraordinarily cheap. My total fare, with a combination of specials and booking in advance is, for a trip totalling 97 hours and 20 minutes, just over $600. That price even includes one night's accommodation in Katherine. Surely there must be a catch I haven't yet thought of?

The bus leaves Adelaide at 6 p.m. on the dot and already I'm feeling relaxed.

Although I've done a fair few bus trips in Queensland, I've never been on one that's been longer than five hours. But this bus looks pretty new; it's clean and comfortable, with air con, overhead reading lights, reclining seats and plenty of leg room with a footrest too. There's cold water on board, a toilet, big windows and even movies. My fellow travellers seem a cheerful bunch too, a mix of people visiting relatives, backpackers and one family group on a cheap holiday.

Twelve hours later, I eventually arrive in Coober Pedy. The journey really hasn't been too bad at all, with regular stops to drink coffee, visit non-moving toilets, buy snacks and eat ice-cream – yes, I didn't need to be quite as prepared as I'd imagined. But it's actually nice to arrive somewhere, even if it is at the god-awful time of 5.50 a.m. Happily, the underground hotel where I've booked a room, since most homes here are under the earth to keep them cool, has agreed to let me check in early.

I have a nap, and then go out to explore. Without doubt, Coober Pedy is one of the most fascinating and eccentric towns in Australia. With its eerie pockmarked landscape of opal mine-shafts, warning signs not to fall down the holes, the quirky opal museum and the numerous gem sellers, as well as a drive-in cinema and a Serbian Orthodox Church drilled out of solid rock with an incredibly intricate interior, it has an atmosphere all its own. It's about half the size of rival opal town Lightning Ridge, and here the speciality is milky-white opals instead of the other's famous black ones. It feels as though it's an even crazier town somehow. There's all that weird Mad Max-style scenery, and on Friday and Saturday nights it seems to be almost taken over by hoons in revved-up cars driving round town.

I've arranged to go out on Country with a group of elderly Aboriginal women while I'm here. When I go to meet them, they surprise me with a Troopy – a Toyota Landcruiser Troop Carrier – that they've organised for our trip.

I go to climb in the back but no, none of them apparently has a driving licence. I drive for only five minutes before one of the women, through the interpreter, politely asks how much experience I have driving over such rough road. Not so much,

I admit. One of them, despite having no licence, takes over.

'She says with you driving it will take us forever where we need to go,' the interpreter explains apologetically. This is to be by no means the last time I'm embarrassed. At lunchtime, the ladies are plainly appalled by what I produce for them to eat: a selection of salad sandwiches. They'd, apparently, been expecting kangaroo tails to roast on the roaring fire they've built.

But it's not my only misstep in Coober Pedy. Later that day, I go for a walk, trip over and fall heavily. I knock on a nearby door to ask for help and am 'invited' in for chops and a beer – until I turn both down. It doesn't go well.

The next morning I get up early to catch the 5.50 a.m. bus to Alice Springs, eight hours away. I catch up on sleep as we drive, and then get off for a tea break at each of our roadhouse stops. In between, I doze, read my book and swap magazines with the other passengers. Kathy, a young Aboriginal lawyer going to visit family further north, is my nearest neighbour three seats away. 'If I'm in a rush I fly,' she says, 'but if I have the time, I love to do the journey like this. I don't like driving on my own, but this is the best of both worlds. You get to see all the scenery with none of the hassle.' I couldn't agree more.

We arrive in Alice Springs after lunch, and my spirits soar. I've always liked Alice. It's an atmospheric little town almost at the geographic dead centre of Australia; rugged, remote and with the kind of frontier-town boisterousness that comes from being 1500 kilometres away from the nearest city. The Todd River stretches through the centre – although it's mostly dry – while the town itself is set in what feels like an amphitheatre, with the red sandstone walls of the MacDonnell Ranges to the south and spurs to the north and east. There are some stunning Aboriginal art galleries and the Desert Park just outside town is a fabulous showcase of the types of landscapes, flora and fauna of the area.

The next day I pick up a hire car and make my way to Uluru. It's a stunning sight and the awe and wonder still hits, however many times you visit.

A group of Aboriginal women sit on the ground under the shade of a leafy bough shelter in the red wilderness four hours north-east of Alice. All around them, little kids dance and play. The women sing out to them from time to time, but don't stop what they're doing: painting a series of the most intricate designs. They work freehand and yet with an unswerving, unhesitating accuracy.

'That's beautiful, Gladdy!' exclaims Sonja Chalmers, looking over her shoulder. 'Really stunning.' Gladdy Kemarre looks up and beams. She's been working on this painting for a few days now, surrounded by pots of vivid colour, and is pleased at how well it's turning out. Beside her, the Ngala sisters – Kathleen, Angeline and Polly – call over, giggle and then lean back over their own canvasses.

I feel I'm getting a rare glimpse into the lives of some of Australia's most gifted Indigenous artists, working on their traditional lands in their own time-honoured way. I've come out here to visit Sonja who, together with her partner, Charlie, lives on the MacDonald Downs cattle station, which neighbours the remote Utopia Aboriginal community and runs a gallery exhibiting their work.

'The quality of their art is just amazing,' she says. 'The delicacy and finesse is awe-inspiring.'

I try to copy one of the patterns later, freehand, and there's no way I can replicate anything like the astonishing accuracy of their work. Their canvasses have all the tremulous fragility of butterflies. Mine looks like one that's been squashed under a road train.

Charlie's grandfather Charles arrived on this land in the 1920s after a seven-year trek from NSW across some of the harshest country in Australia. He had in tow his wife and small children, 300 sheep, a dozen horses and a small herd of goats. He immediately befriended the local traditional owners, a bond that continues to this day. Charles junior grew up on the property, while Sonja, his cousin, lived at the neighbouring station. While Charlie stayed, building a reputation as one of the area's pre-eminent pastoralists, Sonja moved at the age of 15 to Adelaide, and then travelled the world, marrying twice and living for a period in England. When she returned to visit Alice Springs, Charlie arranged to meet her and fly her out to the station. It was the first time she'd been back since she'd been a teenager.

'That was an extraordinary moment in my life,' says Sonja. 'I'd never wanted to go back to the Outback again. But when Charlie flew me back, it felt so right. The vast openness hit me; England had been suffocating. It was an amazing feeling.' At the same time, the two suddenly realised they'd always loved each other. Soon after that, they set up a home together.

Charlie was one of the first pastoralists in Australia to give a piece of land, 470 hectares on which the stunning ochre granite boulder outcrop Tower Rock stands, to the National Parks and Wildlife Services in order to preserve its wide range of native plant species and fauna. In addition, the couple are opening up their home to visitors so they can experience for themselves what it's like to live and work in an area rich with both Aboriginal culture and pioneer heritage.

As well as staying in the modern homestead, decorated with Aboriginal paintings and sculpture, visitors are able to see how the 2067-square-kilometre cattle station runs with the use of helicopter-mustering for their 5500 cattle. They can also meet local Aboriginal artists, like Gladdy Kemarre, whose paintings are held in private and public collections all over the world, and watch them work, while learning from Sonja about eastern desert art.

The painters themselves love the relaxed feel of these sessions. 'We come to Sonnie's and sit and talk and paint, it is good for us, this meeting,' says Susan Pitjara Hunter in her local Alyawarr language. Mary Kemarre Morton, who's always accompanied by between five to eight children at any one time, some of them her grandchildren, agrees. 'We paint here so we can make money for the family, for tucker and for clothes,' she says. Being able to work with their children close is extremely important to many. 'We want the family involved,' says another of the regular painters, Natalie Pula Holmes. 'It's important for us to be together and work.'

Having such ready access to canvasses and paint is also something many of the women cherish. Sally Kemara Perkins smiles as she bows her head over the complex coloured and patterned design before her. 'It makes me feel good to paint,' she says. 'I feel proud of the paintings.'

The women have today brought along witchetty grubs to share. I'm offered one, but feign fullness. One of Sonja's helpers looks trapped, and much more politely takes one and bites down on it. I can hear the squelch from where I'm standing. 'It's very good,' he says to the women. 'It tastes just like peanut butter.' I know myself I'd much rather eat the real thing.

Back in Alice, I go along to a didgeridoo show at the Sounds of Starlight Theatre on the mall. Andrew Langford is internationally recognised as one of the finest players of the instrument in the world. I watch his show, mesmerised by the sounds and images he evokes. Afterwards, however, when they call my name to go up on stage to join him, to play drums with his band, I ignore it. Musically, I'm hopeless. But they won't give up and, finally, I'm almost dragged to the front, where I'm given a kettle drum to play. They won't believe I don't have a musical bone in my body until I actually start to play. Then I think I manage to put nearly the whole band off its rhythm.

My next stop comes after the longest leg of my trip, ten and a half hours, but my destination, Katherine, is worth the journey. It's out of this world. I take a boat along the sapphire-blue waters of the gorge, between the rocky cliffs and escarpments, with the tour guide stopping to show us ancient rock paintings on the walls, talking about the lives of his ancestors in this part of the world, and pointing out the tracks in the sand on the banks of nesting crocodiles. We stay in a tented camp in the Nitmiluk National Park and I sleep soundly, undisturbed by the sound of the crocodiles that the others say they can hear.

From here, it's a mere two and a half hours to Adelaide River, the home of the famous 'jumping crocodiles'. It's touristy but tremendous fun cruising along, watching the giant crocs leap out of the river to tear at the meat they're being offered by the crew. After that, I move on to stunning Litchfield Park.

My final leg to Darwin is just two and a half hours. 'Come back soon!' calls the driver as I collect my bags at my destination. I smile back. Well, I enjoyed it, but my next trip's going to be at the absolute height of luxury. I just can't wait.

As the train pulls out of Darwin station, I lunge for the delicate flute of sparkling water – everyone else has chosen champagne – that sits quietly fizzing on the cabin table. With so many train trips in the past punctuated by spilt milk, stains from other people's red wine and, in one case, an almost full tureen of noodle soup upturned in my lap, I've learnt never to leave anything to chance.

But the Ghan is well on its way by the time I realise I hadn't needed to grab it at all. The most recent section of the track, Darwin to Alice Springs, feels smooth. I've now switched from the sublime to the ridiculous – or should that be the other way around? – travelling the 2979 kilometres back to Adelaide in the Ghan's top-of-the-market platinum class. And while it mightn't have quite the glamour, ritz and romance of the Orient Express, nor the technological wizardry and opulence of South Africa's famed Blue Train – which even has baths in some carriages – it's certainly now among the most comfortable trains in the world, and Australia's first of a truly international luxury class.

Whereas in the old premium gold-class section of the train beds are fold-down bunks and the bathrooms are small cubicles, in platinum, what are plush double chairs by day convert to a proper full-sized pull-down double bed, or side-by-side singles, by night. The bathroom, blissfully, is also a comfortable space, with a full shower, toilet, mirror and vanity basin over storage space.

It makes a world of difference on the two-night, three-day journey north to south across the continent. No longer is it a trip you undertake merely for the thrill of travelling through kilometre after kilometre of burnished red desert, dropping in on some of the world's most stunning Outback sights. It's now an extremely comfortable way to see the country roll on past, with breaks for stops in both Katherine and Alice, and glorious sunsets as the drinkers, at least, can sit back with glass after glass of – unspilled – champagne.

The little touches make it special. The five platinum-class carriages have a bigger than usual window to view the scenery, as well as a movable table, coffee table and two foot stools in each cabin. There are also dimmers on the lights for either night-reading or for best viewing the stars and moon over the quiet landscape outside. But the nicest touch? The call buttons for the 24-hour butler service, which turns out to be charming in a kind of informal knockabout Aussie way rather than anything too slick or pretentious.

The food's incredible too, particularly considering the size of the kitchen the chef works out of. That first evening, I'm served up a feast: grilled scallops and squid on egg noodle salad with a black bean dressing, followed by a steamed kingfish bouillabaisse and lemon myrtle dumplings, fennel, roasted cherry tomatoes and cheddar croutons. I think back to my roadhouse egg and chips of a week ago, at the start of this journey. I've come a long way in both kilometres and style. That's the thing about the Outback I learnt from the beginning: to expect the unexpected and savour whatever happens.

I settle back with an after-dinner decaf coffee and some chocolate mints, to watch another large sector of one of the most barren deserts on earth slide by outside, content in the knowledge that a proper bed with plumped pillows is waiting for me later. I need to make the most of such luxury, I tell myself. I won't have anything like this in the Outback again.

13

THE BIG THREE Bs: BIRDSVILLE, BETOOTA AND BEDOURIE

I'm standing on a fiery red sandhill outside Birdsville, watching the sun sink beneath the horizon in a blaze of crimson. It's casting a rosy hue over the vast panorama of ochre plains dotted with green spinifex, turning them a darker and darker burgundy. I'm lost in wonder.

Suddenly, there's a scream in my ear. I turn to see a young woman holding her head in her hands. 'Snake!' she's gasping. 'I was just about to stand on it when I saw it!' Her friend races to her side and I can hear the alarm in the voices of the people who brought us up here for a sunset supper.

'Get back!' one of them is shouting at us both. 'Get away! It's an inland taipan!'

The woman and I both leap back, almost into each other's arms, and stare at the fat brown-green snake, a lazy 1.5-metre long S-shape, lying motionless in the sand. The woman takes a step back towards it. 'Is it alive?' she asks. 'I don't think it's moving . . .'

The snake then rears its head and the woman jumps in fright. I back away even further.

And that's just as well. The inland taipan is not any old dangerous snake, it just happens to be The Most Deadly Snake in the World. *In the world!* It has the most toxic venom of any snake, with the maximum yield of poison ever recorded from one bite standing at 110 milligrams – enough to kill more than 100 people.

We all give it the widest berth possible and, while one person keeps watch to make sure it doesn't start slithering towards us, we pack up our gear hastily, pile into the car and head off back to Birdsville, where we'll sit in the hotel and tell the story of our narrow escape. Once again, I think to myself, just as you let your guard down and start thinking how pleasant the Outback can be, sitting up on that sandhill, drinking juice, eating biscuits and admiring a spectacular view, it delivers yet another nasty surprise.

I'd set off on another trip through the Outback, this time travelling to far-western Queensland, north and then east back to the coast.

I start out from Sydney, fly to Brisbane and then catch a Skytrans flight to Birdsville. How amazing to be able to fly directly from Brisbane to one of the most isolated towns in the world!

By halfway there, I've already decided that Skytrans is my favourite airline. Quite apart from its incredibly out-of-the-way routes, saving me several million hours of driving time, it must be the friendliest airline I've ever flown. I'd phoned the night before, in a panic, having forgotten to order vegetarian meals. Most airlines require at least 24 hours' notice and even then, in my experience, they still fail to load enough for all the passengers who've requested them. The response this time was a surprise. 'No problem!' the cheery voice on the phone line assured me. 'We'll make sure you have those meals. You won't go hungry with us, never fear.' Now, sitting on the plane, I'm surrounded by enough food to keep me going for my entire six-week trip. And how could they possibly have known that my favourite foods in the world are potato chips, peanuts and lamingtons?

There's plenty of entertainment on board too, although not of the type you might expect. The stewardess, on her routine safety briefing as we pass over some of the biggest dry landmasses in the world, isn't able to suppress a smile when she talks about what to do '*in the unlikely event* that we land on water . . .'

Meanwhile, the passengers on the 36-seater plane all chat with each other as if they're long-lost friends, and some at the top of their voices from opposite ends of the cabin. It has the air of a Sunday school or a rugby-club outing. While they mightn't have known each other before, many turn out to be friends of friends of a second cousin of an old boyfriend of an in-law of the next person, and everyone seems to be bonding over our shared journey into the Outback.

'The Outback's a big place,' a voice informs me from under a huge old hat a seat away. 'But there's not so many people there. So if you don't know someone, you'll often know someone who knows them.' And the airline magazine, instead of being packed with glossy ads for $5000 Swiss watches, pink diamonds and perfume, tells breathlessly of the latest in tractor equipment, fertiliser and something called geared motor solutions – 'We're torqueing big!'

We also fly so low over the landscape that we have a constant view of all that untouched wilderness down there: the red dust, rivulets of green and sand dunes as evenly spaced as soldiers marching across a parade ground. In addition, there are so many stops on this route – Toowoomba, Charleville, Quilpie, Windorah – that every time we come down on the tarmac, we're reminded of how far we've come and how far we still have to go. It's the perfect combination, for me, of air and land travel. At a couple of places, we even disembark while they refuel. At Windorah, I go for a pee in the 'terminal', a posh word really for an air conditioned shed, and jump nearly a metre in the air when a couple of frogs climb out from under the toilet rim to say hello.

Mind you, Windorah's never been a favourite place of mine. The one time I went there – to interview a rural area nurse, Anne Kidd – the town had been hemmed in by floods and there was no way out, or in, by road. The pub where I was staying had run out of food, with not even a packet of peanuts left to keep me going, and I remember sitting for hours on the step of the lone shop, waiting for it to open to see if they had anything to eat. The only non-meat thing they could offer, in the end, was a fried egg, and I'd never seen such a black egg in my life. It tasted foul, but when you're hungry . . .

In addition, the water had brought a tide of insects to the area, including mozzies, march flies and grasshoppers, and you couldn't stand outside without being covered in them and bitten half to death. At night, I couldn't sleep for insects crawling over me and when I had to get up in the pitch-blackness to go to the outside toilet and turn on a light . . . I still shudder today to think of the hungry swarms that descended from far and wide.

I'm yanked from such memories, however, by someone tapping me on the shoulder as I sit, waiting to be allowed back on the plane. 'Sue?' I'm asked. 'SUE?!' It turns out to be one of Anne's daughters, who fills me in on the family news. Gosh, the Outback's a small place. 'Aren't you stopping in Windorah to stay a while?' she asks.

'Not this time. I would have loved to,' I tell her, trying to look sad and feeling dreadful about lying, 'but I just don't have time.'

'That's such a shame!' she says, looking genuinely sorry, which makes me feel even worse. 'Oh, well, come back soon!' she says as I finally join the queue to get back on the plane. I smile and nod, but keep my fingers firmly crossed behind my back.

Safely on the plane again, the stewardess prepares to deliver her fifth security briefing of the trip. With so many of us having heard it all before – four times in the past few hours alone – this time, she does it as a quiz. 'Let's see if you've been paying attention,' she says. 'People in the emergency exits, when do you open the door?' There are a few muttered replies. 'Yes,' she responds crisply, 'when I tell you to; that's right. Where are the life jackets kept?' People point down to below their seats. 'Where's your nearest exit?' they point forward. 'And where's the oxygen?' they point up to the bulkhead above. 'No!' she says in triumph. 'The oxygen's from an oxygen cylinder that I'll distribute round . . .'

As we fly further towards Birdsville, I start watching for any sign of the tiny town of Betoota, 180 kilometres to its east. It was once known as Australia's smallest town, with a population of just one, the local publican. Today, the Betoota Hotel is the only building in the town, in fact it's the only building on the 400-kilometre dirt road between Windorah and Birdsville but, sadly, it's now all closed up. Its teetotal Polish owner Simon 'Ziggy' Remienko shut the doors for the last time in 1997 after 40 years behind the bar and, when no one stepped in to buy it, eventually moved away. He died at the age of 88 in a nursing home in Charleville in 2004.

After failing to spot the town, despite the fact that it's the only thing on that vast gibber plain, I sit and read a local newspaper, and come across a story about 108-year-old Edith McFarlane's secret to staying alive. A beautiful old lady with a soft cloud of white hair, she says it's fresh Outback air and the fact that, on her Cooper Creek cattle station, she had to walk 30 miles just to get to the front gate. I feel suddenly more optimistic about this Outback trip. On previous forays, I'd invariably arrive back in Sydney at least 4 kilos heavier from all the stodgy pies, chips and bakery items on the menu for every meal, and from never doing any exercise. But this time will be different, I tell myself. I'll go for a run every evening and seek out the salad that must be on offer somewhere in each town and station. I doze gently until I'm woken. Time to tuck in to the next round of chips and lamingtons.

Birdsville looks, at first sight, like a ghost town. Most of the roads both in and out are closed due to flooding, so there's a distinct shortage of tourists, which makes its old moniker as Australia's most isolated town even more fitting. On the edges of the Simpson Desert with its sand dunes to the west, the great gibber plains of Sturt's Stony Desert to the south and the Channel Country to the north, the town is closer to the South Australian and Northern Territory borders than anywhere else, which accurately places it pretty much in the middle of nowhere. It's not hard to believe that it once took six weeks to get here along the Birdsville Track from Marree, with Afghan traders leading their trains of over 100 camels from bore to bore.

These days, Birdsville is perhaps best known for its famous races, held almost every September since 1882. During this time the regular population of just 100 swells to more than 7000. But it's the town's permanent population that's the most amazing thing; they're simply an incredible mix of people.

I check into the iconic Birdsville Hotel and start exploring. The town is spread out around the edge of a billabong not far from the shores of the Diamantina River. It has everything you'd need in a small town, but only one of each thing – one hotel, one clinic, one shop, one bakery, one gallery, one museum, one police officer. That might well be the one reason people seem to get on so well too. In a town this small and this remote, with so few alternatives, you just can't risk upsetting any of your neighbours.

A lone tour group on an Outback safari has hit town and, at the bakery, owner Dusty Miller is doing a roaring trade in his trademark homemade curried camel pies, as well as rabbit pies, kangaroo and claret pies, and his Ringer's Regret – a hot vindaloo beef pie. Nowhere to be seen, however, are the XXXX and oxtail pies he once assumed would set the world on fire . . . until no one bought them. He's also selling a fair few caps swathed in mosquito netting, which look rather like a Middle Eastern head-dress, to keep away the flies. 'From Bagdad [sic] to Birdsvillle' proclaims the poster. But the rush is short-lived. The group moves on and, behind one of the town's two coffee machines (the other is in the pub), Dusty sighs. 'There're just no tourists at the moment,' complains the big, bluff man with the handlebar moustache. As well as the water on the roads, the strength of the Aussie dollar is luring people overseas, away from exploring their own backyard.

That's especially hard to stomach when Dusty, a radar technician by trade, has invested so much money in automating his bakery equipment, with machines capable of making 700 pies a day, mixing the dough for 20 loaves of bread at once and, so he tells me, mincing a man in two minutes. *But how does he know that?* I ask myself.

Dusty used to come up regularly from Adelaide for the races until someone casually mentioned that what the town really needed was a bakery.

'I thought, Stuff it, I'll do it!' he says. 'I've always had an affinity with the bush, and the Outback has such a romantic notion attached to it. It can be isolated and desolate, but I thought Birdsville was a real tourist destination and a place where you can have a go. I've always had a bit of a passion for food and I'm not sure that a real baker with proper skills would have survived. When your machinery breaks down, you can't get some bastard in to fix it, so my electro-mechanical background has been very useful.' It also helps that Dusty is so entrepreneurial. During the races each year, he sets up a bed in the storage container behind the bakery for visitors – making sure he gives them a cordless phone so they can call whenever they need to be let out.

Birdsville sometimes seems to be a town almost completely made up of outsiders who moved there wanting to make a new life for themselves. Across town at the Blue Poles Gallery, for instance, owner Wolfgang John arrived in Australia in the 1960s from his native Germany, fell in love with the Outback and moved to Birdsville 17 years ago. Aged 72, with long hair, square-framed glasses and a gentle manner, he looks more like 40, and says all the credit belongs to the town.

'It's the air here; it's very good,' he says. 'And every morning I go out and walk to the horizon or to the next sand dune or along the airport.' But like Dusty, he too is having a tough time economically. People usually love to buy his vividly coloured pictures of the rich red earth around the Cooper, but the trouble is, now it's green. And no one wants those pictures.

For John Menzies who founded and runs Birdsville's Working Museum, it's also feast or famine. Sometimes there are too many tourists wanting to look around his vast warehouse stacked with displays of everything Outback – including the kitchen sink. The 65-year-old, with long silver hair, a cowboy hat and a natty red kerchief, runs himself ragged giving them tours and demonstrations of many of his treasures, including an early record player made of cardboard, the first model of food mixer, old carbide lights, homemade mule packsaddles, a 1923 ammonia fridge, an 1890s washing machine, horsedrawn buggies, wagons . . . everything and anything you could ever imagine. But at other times, it's so quiet, it hardly seems worth opening.

'I love it here, though,' he says. 'It feels like being back where I belong. The isolation doesn't bother me. I was born in Sydney but I was always a bush boy in the city. As a kid, I went out to Bourke, then I worked on stations and for drovers and then in the rodeo.' He rode all around Australia, New Zealand, the US and Canada, then 18 years ago came to Birdsville, opening the museum as his own privately funded enterprise in 1993. These days, he's thinking of selling it and retiring further east in Queensland. Although he's received offers for various parts of his collections, so determined is he to see the museum keep going in its entirety, he may well never sell any of it.

There are locals to be found around town too. David Brook, the owner of a number of stations near Birdsville, including Cordillo Downs, grew up here. He's always doing his best to introduce new people to the place. He had success with those Irish backpackers who answered the ad for workers at Cordillo Downs in order to extend their Australian holiday. Olivia O'Neill applied to be a ringer – even though she had no idea what that was – and her husband, Padraic, a mechanic. They drove out to the station in an old Ford Vermont and, as the road became narrower and narrower and rougher and rougher, Olivia grew more apprehensive. At Innamincka, they stopped for a break.

'Haven't seen one of them for a while,' a passer-by commented, gesturing at their vehicle. 'What, a Ford Vermont?' Olivia asked. 'No,' he replied. 'A car.' By the time they arrived at the station, she was appalled by how isolated it was. 'You looked out of the window, and there was absolutely nothing.'

But gradually the pair became used to the way of life, and started really enjoying it. When it came time to head back to Ireland, they bade station managers Anthony and Janet Brook a sad farewell. Yet in Ireland, Olivia and Padraic found they just couldn't settle. The economy was bad, and they yearned for those wide open spaces of the Australian Outback. New job offers came – this time from David and Nell – Padraic to be the mechanic for all their stations and Olivia to work in the office at Birdsville. They eagerly snapped them up, even though the pair had just had a baby son, Patrick. The three arrived in Birdsville in April 2011.

'After two or three weeks here, it felt as if we'd never been away,' says Olivia, now 29. 'It's brilliant. I think the beauty of the Outback is in the simplicity. You realise how little you need to live well. You don't need to worry about much in a place like this. There's so little stress and anxiety. It's a very healthy way of life.'

Another local is Aboriginal elder Don Rowlands, a descendant of the Wangkangurru people of the Simpson Desert, who's today a national park ranger. When he was two, his father drowned in Cooper Creek while swimming a mob of cattle across and, 12 months later, his mum fell ill, and was taken by the flying doctors to hospital in Charleville. She never came back. To this day, Don still doesn't know the cause of her death. Suddenly orphaned, he was brought up by his grandparents and, by the age of eight, was working as a ringer on a nearby station.

Even as he grew older, life was pretty tough for him. He was often picked on because of the colour of his skin, and when he fought back he was labelled a troublemaker. Despite the long hours he worked, he was paid only in meat and damper. Under Queensland's Aboriginal Protection Act, his wages were supposedly paid directly to the government or police authorities for them to look after. Like most others, he never saw a cent of it.

'I thought I'd have a nice nest egg when I finally got permission to leave my job,' says Don, today a gently spoken 63-year-old man with silver hair and a dapper Errol Flynn-style moustache. 'But there was nothing. I think I had more money before I went to work than when I left! But you can't be bitter.' He laughs, a touch ruefully. 'Life goes on. And this is a much better place now than it used to be. I'm happy with how I've gone through life, and what I've done. I've been a ranger now for 17 years, and that's been a good job. I also have a real link to the land, thanks to my upbringing and learning about our traditional stories. I've always been vigilant about the conservation of sites and the importance of dissemination, rather than the hoarding, of traditional knowledge. I understand and know my way across the country.'

History and understanding have also driven a much more recent migrant to Birdsville. Rick Avery has only been in town six months, but already he's doing tours for visitors, with commentary covering everything you could ever want to know about Birdsville's past, present and future. Rick and his partner, Barb, had been travelling for three years before they decided to settle here to run the town's caravan park for a spell. Barb, originally from Dubbo, and Rick, a court officer from Sydney, met in Parkes and are now in love with Birdsville.

'With modern communications, you don't feel so isolated,' says Barb. 'And there's great community spirit here; it's very special. We all look after each other.'

I'd considered stopping off in Bedourie, 166 kilometres north of Birdsville, on the way to Boulia, but I'm impatient to get some miles under my belt. Bedourie is the administrative centre of the Diamantina Shire, which covers 95 000 square kilometres – twice the size of Tasmania or Denmark – yet has a population of just 322. But Rick tells me that it's pretty wet around there, so even if I did stop, I wouldn't be able to get around. So I don't.

Instead, I stay in Birdsville a day longer and Rick and Barb invite me along to watch the sunset from a sandhill outside Birds-ville. I'm lucky they're quick thinking too, with the appearance of that inland taipan just after the sun's slipped below the horizon.

'You never know what's going to happen next in a place like this,' laughs Rick, as we later sit safely at the bar at the Birdsville Hotel. 'That's part of the charm of the place.'

I can think of many words to describe the experience of having a lethal snake sneaking up when your back is turned and the light is low, and charm would certainly be nowhere near the top. But I let it go. I'm fast discovering that the Outback perspective on life, and death, is very different from the city point of view. And making the best of what you've got is a true Outback trait – a thought with which I console myself as I head off to a place that sounds, for a city girl like me, one of the most dangerous places in Australia.

ABOVE: Three of the best at the old drovers' reunion in Longreach, QLD. Jack 'Goldie' Goldsmith, Bruce Stratford and Goldie's old enemy, Gordon Storer, relive their memories. *Photo by Amy Naef*

BELOW: The sensational scenery you take in after a long day in the saddle on the Harry Redford Cattle Drive in Aramac, QLD. *Photo by Bruce Hutchison*

ABOVE: Boss drover David 'Chook' Hay in his element, pushing the herd through the scrub.

BELOW: Tucker time – the highlight of my days during the drive.

IT'S A DROVER'S LIFE

RIGHT: Me, with sneaky Stutter, who looks deceptively calm.

BELOW: This is the life – a much more civilised sort of ride.

Photo of Stutter by Jan D'Auria; other photos by Bruce Hutchison

ABOVE: Do I have what it takes to be a champion goat-racer? I can't bring myself to twist the poor goat's tail 'to make it go faster', so maybe not.

LEFT: Desert land at Nilpena, near Parachilna, SA. Goanna tracks prove there's life in the harshest terrain.

ABOVE: Cut off by floods, the red heart turns green around Innamincka.

BELOW: Jack the vet getting 'stuck in', pregnancy testing cattle at Cordillo Downs Station.

FLOAT LIKE A BUTTERFLY

ABOVE: Fred Brophy's boxing tent, the last of its kind in Australia.

LEFT: After it's all over, with the man himself – can you see the relief in my eyes?

OPPOSITE: Here's me putting up a fair fight with the Beaver.

Photos by George Fetting

ABOVE: Boulia, QLD, home to the mysterious min min, and a long, long way from anywhere.
Photo by Jan Norton

BELOW: 'Dinosaur' Dick Suter and one of the area's earliest residents – a fossil – at Boulia, the town set on what was once an inland sea.

Residents in Boulia make their own fun with camp-drafting competitions (LEFT) and the most dangerous sport on earth – bull riding (BELOW). *Photos by Jan Norton*

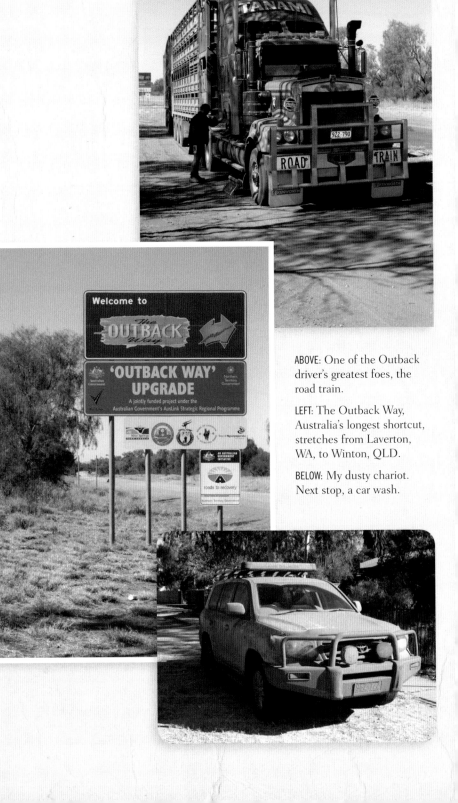

ABOVE: One of the Outback driver's greatest foes, the road train.

LEFT: The Outback Way, Australia's longest shortcut, stretches from Laverton, WA, to Winton, QLD.

BELOW: My dusty chariot. Next stop, a car wash.

ABOVE: Alyawarr women of the Eastern Desert region, NT, part of the Utopia Aboriginal Artistic Community, painting at the MacDonald Downs cattle station.

BELOW: Camels have a long history in the Outback, proving a near-perfect transport solution in the desert. Other uses for the cranky beasts include racing them and, if you're a Birdsville baker, making them into pies.

CATCHING THE MINING FEVER

ABOVE: The brilliant turquoise, and deathly silence, of the old uranium pit at Mary Kathleen, QLD.

LEFT: An iron-ore reclaimer in action at BHP Billiton's mine at Port Hedland, WA.

OPPOSITE: The massive super pit in Kalgoorlie, WA, where huge dump-trucks, at over seven metres high and with a capacity of 345 tonnes, look like tiny toys.

ALL THINGS WEIRD AND WONDERFUL IN THE OUTBACK

OPPOSITE: Madame Carmel's establishment, keeping the men of Kalgoorlie entertained since 1904; despite this counsel, a few brave souls still choose to tough it out in Wittenoom.

LEFT: Property protection in Cook, SA, population four and one of the most isolated towns in Australia – you've been warned.

BELOW: One of Antony Gormley's spindly figures watching over Lake Ballard.

ABOVE: First light at Mt Sonder, the highest point of the Larapinta Trail.
Sometimes the hardest effort yields the best rewards.

BELOW: Me, at the end of my journey.

14

DANCING IN THE DIRT

My next stop, Boulia, 200 kilometres further north on the way to Mt Isa, has always sounded like an interesting town. For a start, it's home to the mysterious min min, a weird ghostly orb of light that's appeared before numerous drovers, farmers and travellers in the district over the years, and could well have lured some to their deaths.

As well as chasing the min min, the people of Boulia seem particularly keen on finding ways to kill themselves. It's famed for its annual camel races, its rodeo and its campdraft – an event in which a rider on horseback 'cuts out' a cow from a mob of cattle and then steers it, galloping, around a course – and Boulia has even spawned an Australian champion in the most dangerous sport on earth: bull riding. In that activity, even if you don't break your back whenever you're thrown off, you stand a decent chance of being gored or stomped on by 800-odd kilos of enraged animal afterwards.

I've timed my trip to witness that local appetite for danger firsthand. The annual rodeo and campdraft is about to take place, to be followed by an open-air dance. Although I planned to skip the dance, I've never seen either a rodeo or a campdraft, and I'm keen to put that right. After all, both are massive events on the Outback calendar.

Not so massive, however, that they don't broadcast it far and wide when they decide to change the date. As soon as I arrive, I discover that while the campdrafting is still on, the rodeo has been shifted to later in the year. I'm disappointed, but also a touch relieved. I'd planned to enter on the day and try my hand at riding a bucking bronco or a bull or whatever else I might be allowed to have a go at. Now I was off the hook.

But even doing nothing in Boulia is not without its challenges, I soon discover. On arrival, I'm warned about the swarm of bush rats around that can chew out the electrical wiring on cars, turning them into lethal weapons. Then, after checking in to the local pub, the Australian Hotel, I'm shown to my motel room out the back, where I have a shower to freshen up. As I do, the bathroom floods, presumably from the volume of insects caught in the plughole. I take a deep breath and ferret around to free the flow. Then I change and get ready to have a look around town. The impulse seems innocuous enough, but I soon run into trouble.

There's a shrill chirruping in the room, probably the battery needing to be replaced in the smoke alarm, so I'm in a rush to get out and away from the sound. I twist the doorhandle to let out the button on the lock, but nothing happens. I try again. And again. And again. By now, the squeal of the battery is drilling into my brain, and I can taste the sweat on my upper lip. I stand closer to the door and try lifting up the handle before pushing it down, and then I jiggle it sideways, but still nothing happens.

I go to the window and pull open the curtain but there's no one in sight. This is ridiculous! It's all very well not coping with the heat of the Outback, its snakes and its insects, but I should be up to opening its motel doors! But after ten minutes more of trying to get out, I'm finally reduced to phoning the front bar to ask for help.

'Hello, I've just checked in and I'm in room three,' I tell the barman.

'Oh, yeah?' he says, with a total lack of interest.

'Well, the thing is, I'm stuck in my room and can't get out.'

'Come again?'

'The lock seems to have jammed.'

'Oh, yeah?'

'Yes, I can't budge it.'

'You're meant to twist it and the little button comes out and unlocks it,' he explains patiently.

He obviously thinks I'm even more of a moron than I am. 'Yes,' I say sweetly. 'I've tried that, but it won't come out and unlock. I've tried everything. I just wondered, could you come and let me out?'

'I suppose so.' He sighs. 'I'll be there in ten.'

Ten minutes? It seems a long time to wait when he's just 30 seconds away, but I don't have too much choice. I can't risk upsetting him. 'Thanks very much,' I say meekly.

Fifteen minutes later, just as I've discovered that if I lean against the wall, I can keep two pillows wrapped around my ears, almost cutting off the noise, the door flies open. A young man's standing there, looking at me quizzically. I hadn't heard him unlocking the door from the outside.

'Great! Thanks!' I splutter, pulling the pilllows away. 'Did you have trouble?'

'No, not at all,' he says. 'I just put the key in and it opened.' He comes in and shuts the door behind him, then pushes in the button to lock it.

'No!' I cry, but too late. 'We'll both be locked in now.'

He looks at me blankly, twists the handle and the button pops brightly out. 'That's what you do,' he says reproachfully.

'No, that's what I was doing and it didn't work,' I say lamely. He repeats the process three more times, each without a glitch.

'Well, it didn't work before,' I protest. 'But thanks. And is there any chance the battery could be changed on the smoke alarm?'

'Why's that?' he asks warily, obviously thinking by now that I'm a madwoman.

'Can't you hear that?' I say, a tad incredulously, pointing up at the alarm.

He looks up and squints as he listens intently. 'Oh, *that*,' he finally says. 'Yeah, I'll get it done.'

'Thanks,' I say, picking up my bag. 'I'm off now to check out the bright lights.'

He stares back at me. I'm certain he now thinks I should be certified. *Wonderful.*

I wander out into the street and look around. To be honest, there really isn't all that much there. Boulia feels like a fly perched on a very large tabletop. It's a tiny town of just six wide dusty streets running north to south and another four running east to west, with the odd building scattered along them, hunched in the middle of incredibly red, incredibly flat and incredibly vast treeless plains. The whole shire covers an expanse of 61 000 square kilometres, yet has a population of just 440. Beyond the giant windmill at one end of the town, the dusty endlessness of it all continues as far as the eye can see. Where are all the people, and what the hell is there to do here?

Shelley Norton comes to my aid. A bright and bubbly young woman, she's the town's tourism officer and is seemingly dedicated to promoting her town as an absolute Mecca for, well, just about anything and anyone. She is a fourth-generation Boulian and, apart from a five-year stint at boarding school in Charters Towers, has been here her whole life. She simply can't imagine wanting to live anywhere else. 'I just love it,' she says cheerily. 'I love it for its lifestyle.'

'What lifestyle?' I ask. I don't mean to be rude; I'm genuinely curious.

She's the second person within ten minutes to look at me as if I'm two sheep short of a flock, or whatever else they might say around here to indicate sheer bloody stupidity. 'It's such a laidback lifestyle, so relaxed . . .' she begins.

'But isn't that,' I cut in, 'because there's not much to do?'

She shakes her head and her pert ponytail of thick copper hair bounces around her shoulders. 'There's everything you need here,' she says. 'There're great jobs, housing is not too expensive, everyone says hello when you walk down the street. In a city they'd think you're weird if you did that. And there's loads to do.'

Loads to do? *Really?* Shelley nods vigorously, her commitment to her cause unwavering. 'There are so many events all the time, here and in other places nearby. There are festivals. There's sport. There's the sports and aquatic centre. There's the camel races, the rodeo, the campdraft, horseracing. We have great facilities for the middle of nowhere. On big nights, they bring a portable stage and park it on the other side of the racetrack so you can dance on the track.'

'On the track?'

'Yes,' Shelley says firmly. 'Dancing in the dirt is what you do in the Outback.'

Later, I discover Shelley, 26, is indeed a mini-tornado. If there ever isn't enough to do in this town then, by God, she goes and organises something. In 2010, she won the Royal Flying Doctor Service's Spirit of Queensland Award after raising $43 000 for them from major events she put on around Boulia, Winton, Bedourie and Birdsville. They included a fancy-dress night, a golf day, a fishing competition and an old-time woolshed dance while she also, astonishingly, managed to inveigle country singer Anne Kirkpatrick to perform a concert at the Bedourie races.

Even Winton's rugby league players were no match for her. They undertook a charity bike ride for her fundraising, riding motor scooters from Winton to Boulia – a not inconsiderable trip of 370 kilometres. 'Most of the events are ongoing, so they're now added to the social calendar,' she says happily. It was, presumably, little surprise when she won the Boulia titles of Organiser of the Year and Citizen of the Year. No one else would have stood a chance.

But even when there's not much to do, the secret of success-ful living in the Outback seems to be about making your own entertainment. In the old days, everyone in the outlying districts used to ride a horse and buggy to weekly dances. Today, even the young people there go to extraordinary lengths for entertainment. Four young men, nicknamed the Boulia Boys – Trent, Jack, Mick and Shelley's brother Luke – actually travel the 740 kilometres to Winton and back nearly every weekend just to play a game of rugby league for the Winton Diamantina Devils. Some weeks, the matches are in Barcaldine (550 kilometres each way) and Blackall (another 214-kilometre round trip on top of that). That can mean a drive of as long as eight hours there and eight hours back again, all for the sake of an 80-minute game.

'It's worth it – when we win!' says Mick. 'We like the social side of the game as well.'

After a tour around the town, which doesn't take too long, Shelley guides me back to the pub. Sitting there is Julie Wood-house, the president of the annual camel races, billed, at least by locals, as the Melbourne Cup of the Outback camel-racing world. They were started in 1997 to help put Boulia on the map and, with around 40 camels being brought in from all around the country to take part every July and 2500 visitors arriving to watch, they succeeded.

Of course, there has been the odd setback. One year, there was such a bad dust storm that the camels could barely be seen racing around the track. Another time, a couple of camels went walkabout through a nearby campsite, and people woke up in their swags to find their tents either collapsed on top of them or missing completely.

'But generally, it's bigger and bigger every year,' says Julie, who sells raffle tickets all year round to raise money for the event. 'I love it. It does take up a lot of time in organisation, but I couldn't stand to see it end.'

After the cattle-droving, boxing and outwitting snakes, I feel I'm up for anything Outback, and ask if I'd maybe be able to ride a camel in the upcoming 2011 races. She hesitates. Camel-racing can be dangerous, and is often best left to people who know what they're doing, she obviously wants to say, but is far too polite actually to do so. In reality, I hated riding a horse so much that the thought of perching on the back of an even taller, less comfortable animal who's running as fast as it can around a track fills me with trepidation. But we go for the middle ground and agree that I'll get in touch again closer to the date. In the end, however, the camel races are cancelled altogether because the rain leaves the track under water. Secretly, I'm again relieved.

But certainly I'm not the only one in this pub looking out of my depth. Behind the bar are three young Irish female backpackers, dressed in what looks like a uniform of tiny hotpants and singlets. They arrived on the same plane as me, obviously doing their time working in the Outback to extend their visa and earn a bit of extra money.

'How's it going?' I ask the one who's serving me. She forces a smile.

'It's not what we were expecting,' she says carefully. 'But I'm sure it'll be all right.'

'What were you expecting?'

'Well, we had no idea the town would be this small,' she says. 'Or so far from anywhere. But at least we have each other.'

Yet it mightn't be too long before they have others to console them too. Outside the pub, a couple of young men are nipping in for lunch. 'There're new barmaids,' one yells out to another mate on the other side of the road. 'We're checking them out,' he explains to me. 'Apparently they're good sorts.'

Boulia's main attraction remains the infrequent appearances of the min min, that eerie light that suddenly appears and vanishes just as quickly. It's described variously by witnesses as a hovering white ball of light, a shimmering spectral light or, in the first written account in 1838, a 'jack-o-lantern' that appeared before a camped group of explorers, who followed it for over an hour before they gave up.

There's debate over what it might actually be: the sparks from geophysical elements in the ground . . . phosphorescence in marshes . . . lightning . . . UFOs . . . ghosts . . . evil spirits . . .

But whatever the cause, there's little doubt that Boulia is making good use of the spooky phenomenon, billing itself as the home of one of Australia's greatest supernatural mysteries.

The Min Min Encounter is a centre devoted to Boulia's favourite curiosity, and it's great theatre, with talking life-sized mannequins, animatronics and all sorts of high-tech effects. Now ten years old, there are parts that look a little clunky, but it's generally charming, and fascinating. During peak times, the centre is packed from 8 a.m. to 5 p.m., with every single 45-minute show full. 'People love it,' says Boulia mayor Rick Britton, an immensely personable, earnest man. 'It really helps keep the history, and the mystery, alive.'

Another of the town's major draws is the Stonehouse Museum. But while it's a beautifully preserved old home, dating back to 1888, it's not so much the building or the artefacts inside that are so interesting. It's the resident curator, 'Dinosaur Dick' Suter, a man known as a colossus in the fossil world, who is the drawcard.

Dick grew up in Sydney's beachside suburb of Manly with two lion cubs, which were kept in the spare bedroom upstairs as playmates. His father, George, was a circus lion tamer who bought Judo and Baby from Sydney's Taronga Zoo – £35 for the pair – and displayed them in a silver cage at the local library. But as the cubs grew, the neighbours started complaining about the smell, so the family moved out to follow the show circuit. George trained Judo for the 'head in the lion's mouth' act by putting his arm between his jaws, and punishing him with a clout if he got bitten and rewarding him with a piece of steak if he didn't.

Next, he started putting his head in. All went well – even on the night at the circus when George, with his head between Judo's teeth, accidentally trod on his tail. Luckily, the lion just gurgled a complaint. Baby wasn't quite so obedient, however. His job was simply to sit up and 'kiss' George on the cheek. One night, he bit him on the chin instead and there was so much blood a man in the audience fainted at the sight of it. Another night, a drunken tent-hand put his swag too close to the bars of the lions' cage. George arrived the next morning to find that Judo had pulled the boy's leg into the cage and was licking it, like an ice lolly. The lad never came back to work drunk again, nor slept so close. A plan to attract religious members of the audience by putting a lamb in the lions' cage came unstuck when they started eating the lambs as soon as George's back was turned.

Eventually, with the public losing interest in wild animal acts in circuses, and a single lion costing more to feed than his whole family, George got out of the business.

By this time, Dick was 13 and, being a bit of a wild spirit like his dad, he was constantly in trouble. He hated school and didn't understand why he had to go, especially since all he wanted to do with his life was ride horses. He kept running away – literally, or by catching trains, hitching lifts, riding horses and getting odd jobs on farms or in work gangs – before being caught and brought back home by the police. As he grew up, he did all sorts, including helping out at stations, fencing, droving, even cattleduffing, and eventually came to Boulia to work on a property in 1952. Forty years later, he started educating himself in paleontology and digging up fossils.

Boulia, so far from the ocean, is quite bizarrely a rich source of marine fossils. The town sits on the bed of what 100 million years ago was an ancient inland sea. Dick, today a spry 75-year-old, dressed in jeans, a T-shirt splashed with gravy from his daily steak-and-onion-pie breakfast, a chequered shirt and an old army hat, has been going out on regular fossil-hunting forays with mates for years.

In their hunt for Outback sea monsters, he's collected a tremendous store of fossils, including kronosaurus bones from a large marine reptile, a rare swordfish skull, and shark and turtle fossils. One type of turtle has even been named after him, while the skull of an adult icthyosaur – a kind of ancient dolphin – takes pride of place in his museum to the back of the Stonehouse. He shows me around his workshops too. There, Dick patiently chips away at giant rocks until they reveal their treasures. While he keeps up a friendly rivalry with museum and university paleontologists, who often bridle at some of his self-taught methods, he's earned a begrudging admiration from them over the years.

A documentary's now even being made about Dick and his mates. *Outback Fossil Hunters: an adventure 100 million years in the making* bills them as the 'foot soldiers of paleontology', the 'dinosaur hunters' and – Dick especially likes this one – the 'Indiana Joneses of paleontology'.

'This one, we reckon, is 600 million years old,' he says excitedly, carefully unwrapping from its layers of sackcloth what looks like an unremarkable lump of rock. 'This one has so far taken 455 hours of preparation.' Yet he never takes himself, and his passion, too seriously. 'How about this one!' he exclaims, touching another piece of rock with such tenderness and reverence that you'd swear it were made of burnished gold. 'Doesn't it look like Tony Abbott's ear?'

That night, as I sleep in the motel room with a chair wedged under the doorhandle so I don't need to use the lock, I dream of a massive sea monster rearing up from the ground and baring its teeth at me.

*

The next morning, I'm up early with the sun. It isn't my intention but I have little choice. I wake up with a start in the early hours of the morning to a deafening blast of snores. I lean over to touch my partner Jimmy's shoulder to ask him to roll onto his side. He isn't there. Then I remember where I am, and that I'm on my own, but the snoring is so loud, the whole room feels like it's reverberating. I switch on the light and realise it must be the snores of the man in the room next door, whose boasting of his travels to his girlfriend I could hear through the wall and which had kept me awake till 2 a.m.

I try to cover my ears with the pillows again but, at 6 a.m., his alarm goes off. Finally, I admit defeat and climb blearily out of bed. But on the bright side, I know I'll be nice and early for the gymkhana, races and campdrafting. And while I'm still sad to be missing the rodeo, I do manage to catch Grant Wells, the local bull-riding hero, for a chat.

The son of the owners of a local station, Grant went to a boarding school in Brisbane, which kept cattle out the back. When he noticed some of the students were trying to ride them, he jumped over the fence and had a go himself. And then another. And another. His dad, Adrian, tried to put him off by entering him in the Boulia rodeo at the age of 15. It had quite the opposite effect.

'I got absolutely smashed,' he says, laughing. 'But it just made me more determined. And the rest is history.'

Since that day, Grant has become one of Australia's most successful professional bull riders – where participants have to stay on a bull's back for eight seconds before falling or jumping off – ending up, at the age of just 17, the runner-up in the 1997 national championship, then winning the title of Australian Bull Riding Champion in both 1999 and 2002. After that he went to the US for five years to compete on the bull-riding circuit there, coming home to Boulia every year for the rodeo.

'It is the most dangerous sport in the world,' he admits. 'But it's also the biggest high you'll ever have in your life. It all happens in an explosion; my dad reckons it's like a car smash. I've had plenty of injuries but you can get injured in anything you do. I wrecked one of my knees playing football as a 12-year-old, and I hurt the other on a motorbike when I was mustering on the property. With bull riding, you just have to wait to heal up and then you go off again.'

Now 32, and still tall and lean with a chiselled face, Grant's currently recovering at home after a bull stepped on his chest in a rodeo, breaking two of the ribs over his heart. If he hadn't been wearing a padded protective vest (standard garb for all professional cowboys since world champion Lane Frost died from being whacked by a bull's horn in 1989) he'd be dead today, he believes. 'But no, that doesn't put me off at all,' he says. 'I just can't wait to get back going again. You can't be half-hearted about a sport that might finish you off one day. You just hang on like hell and give it your best.'

Hang on like hell? Jeez, they build them tough out here.

Later, I cadge a lift over to the campdrafting at the stadium just outside town. Everywhere there are people in cowboy hats sitting on horses, idly chatting to each other. Some of them have toddlers perched on the saddle in front of them. Elsewhere there are small kids on other horses, walking around and occasionally breaking into a trot.

Walking gingerly between them, I eventually reach a mini grandstand of banked wooden seats set alongside the ring, and

I climb up and squeeze onto the top bench for the best view. Below me, the arena is much bigger than I thought it would be, and I strain my eyes to try to work out what's happening.

There are a few poles here and there, driven into the dusty red earth, and occasionally a lone cow is let loose. Then someone on a horse gallops in and attempts to ride close to the cow to steer them from the outside, without touching them, around each of the poles along a predetermined course. The winner, presumably, is the one who guides them around the course in the shortest time. It all looks chaotic to me, but I assume the riders know what they're doing. Some do, but others don't. A few of the riders successfully get on the outside of the cows and weave them around the poles, racing behind them to zip over to the other side when they need to. Finally they reach the end together, with a whoop and a raise of the hand and a cheer from the crowd. For most of the others, the cow darts away and escapes to stand at a distance, looking at the frustrated rider with disdain and, I swear, a smile.

It looks incredibly difficult. Not only do you obviously have to be an excellent rider, managing to stay on the horse's back as it whips this way and that, leaning into the turns, you also have to be able to control the cow without ever bumping it, matching it almost stride for stride, while also navigating the course. It's as much as I can do to even capture it on my camera.

'You have to try and anticipate which way they're going to go,' a woman next to me says, obviously amused at my disappointment each time I look at the shot I've just taken – with the horse having disappeared from view, or the cow run out of frame. 'Take it as they turn, as they're riding towards us.' The woman turns out to be Shelley's mum, Jan. Just in front of us is mayor Rick's wife, Ann. Boulia's a small place.

198

Like everyone else here, Jan loves Boulia because the people are so friendly and like to do things for the community. It's a pretty go-ahead kind of place; its residents are proud of their town, and promote it with verve at every opportunity. I have to agree with her on that. In Winton a week or so later, I even see a sign erected by the Boulia Shire Council, urging people to drive to Mt Isa via Boulia – a route 200 kilometres longer than the direct trip – because it's simply too good to miss.

After the campdraft's finished, I meet up with a Mt Isa police officer, a friend of a friend of a friend, whom I'd called from Sydney. She was due to be in Boulia the same weekend as I was, and offered me a ride back to Mt Isa. Working for the Police Citizens Youth Club, she'd come to Boulia to put on a games afternoon and blue-light disco for kids.

I find her sitting in the dirt in a ring of tiny children, some Aboriginal and some white, playing games. She asks me to join in, and I race after the kids, following her lead, to squeals of excitement. As the sun sets and the lights blaze on, the music starts up and everyone begins dancing. I hold a couple of the smaller kids' hands and jump in time to the music until I realise that, just like they do in the Outback, I'm finally dancing in the dirt alongside the best of them.

15

GOING UNDERGROUND WITH GHOST TOWNS AND TOWN GHOSTS

'Happiness,' says the T-shirt in the shop window, 'is Mt Isa in the rear-view mirror.'

It's an odd memento for a souvenir shop in the mining town to be selling, but the sentiment, from a purely aesthetic point of view at least, is hard to argue with. The first sight of Mt Isa as you drive in comes as a shock, with the towering 270-metre tall stack from the lead smelter belching clouds of white smoke totally dominating the view. And from that point on, the jolts just keep on coming: the realisation of just how close the town is to the mine, how bad the air smells, how corroded so many of the bonnets of the otherwise gleaming-new vehicles parked along the streets are, and how the earth shudders at 8 a.m. and 8 p.m. each day with the blasting tremors from underground.

'You know that sign?' someone asks me on my first day in Mt Isa. I do. You can hardly miss it on the way into the town: a big wide signboard on the main road bearing the images of various celebrities, with 'Welcome to the Isa – Birth Place of Champions' in huge letters across the top. 'Well, think about those people,' he urges me. I do. There's tennis player Pat Rafter, golfer Greg Norman, actor Deborah Mailman, footballer Scott Prince, and William Barton, the internationally acclaimed didgeridoo player. 'Maybe they were all born in Mt Isa,' the man continues, 'but how many of them live here now?' He pauses for effect. 'None of 'em!' he says triumphantly. 'They're the town ghosts. They all live somewhere else now. And why would that be? What's here for them?'

The truth is that Mt Isa is such a long way from almost anywhere – 1829 kilometres from Brisbane, 1598 kilometres from Darwin, 2585 kilometres from Canberra and even 991 kilometres from the nearest big city, Townsville – that anyone seriously involved in the arts, cultural or sporting life of the nation needs to move somewhere a touch closer to the action. If you're involved with the mines, however, or any of its related industries, then there are probably few better places to be. This is a town absolutely thriving on the back of the resources boom, where people are paid big money to go about their business at one of the most productive single mines in world history. In turn, the city council and an admirably active local chamber of commerce, in partnership with the mine owner Xstrata, are doing their best to turn the Isa into a more pleasant place to live. New facilities, like a multimillion-dollar family water and activities park close to the city centre, are being built everywhere.

But it's always been a tough town. Even the man responsible for the town in the first place, John Campbell Milles, the prospector who first stumbled on the lead and silver in the rocks, never became rich. He sold his leases for shares and later traded those shares for a pittance in favour of continuing to look for gold up north. He never found it.

Yet despite Mt Isa's overwhelming ugliness, you can't deny it has an odd kind of quirky Outback charm. There are some who say anywhere that's voted for the mercurial Bob Katter to be its MP for the past eight years – and his dad, Bob Katter senior, for 24 years before him – would have to have a healthy sense of humour. Even the size of the place defies logic. Although it looks pretty small, with just 23 000 people, bizarrely it's in the top ten of the world's largest cities geographically, simply because the town of Camooweal to its north-west is considered an outer suburb, giving it a total land mass of 41 000 square kilometres. As a result, the 188-kilometre-long stretch of road between the two places is often billed as the longest main street in the world.

Mt Isa also boasts the world's most remote, and landlocked, life-saving club, formed when sand was dumped on the shores of the human-made Lake Moondarra, the town's main water supply, to create a beach for families. The place also remains a major service centre for the cattle properties around it, so the local newspaper sometimes reads more like that of a rural country town than that of a major industrial hub. And it's the home of the largest annual rodeo in the southern hemisphere, attracting over 10 000 visitors a year.

My new mate Fred Brophy, whose tent is a regular at the rodeo, calls it one of the toughest towns in Australia and if he thinks it's tough, Jeez, I thank my lucky stars I didn't end up fighting here. Men are men in the Isa, he says, and women often are too. But he still loves the town. 'You've got everyone here,' he says. 'You've got cowboys, you've got Indigenous people, you've got ringers and miners and you've got tourists. You've got every-thing, mate. I love it.'

*

But it's the mines that make the town, the very reason for its existence. Copper, zinc, lead and silver – without those, this area would still be little more than a set of tractless, hostile plains where the first Europeans wilted in the searing heat, battled to find food and often died of thirst. My first morning there, a public holiday, I almost know how they felt. Every shop is closed, and drinking the warm liquid left at the bottom of my water bottle while hunched over one of the tins of tuna I carry for emergencies, I gloomily look over the leaflets on what to do in Mt Isa. Of course! What better way to get to grips with the town than to go down a mine myself!

The Hard Times Mine located at the town's star tourist attraction, the Outback at Mt Isa centre, was never a real mine, but was purpose-built for $5 million to show visitors what a mine, and working in one, is like. And just like with the real thing, everything is taken very seriously. Everyone in our eight-strong group is instructed to take off their outer clothes and slip into something much less comfortable: bright-orange overalls, a helmet with cap lamp, a heavy belt for its battery pack and radio, earmuffs and gumboots.

'I'm not wearing these!' I hear a teenage boy tell his dad. 'They look dorky. What if someone sees me?' His father whispers angrily, 'It'll be dark down there anyway. We've paid now so either you get changed or you'll pay me back from your next three weeks' pocket money.' I emerge at the same time as father and son, both kitted out in orange, the kid looking daggers at everyone. I smile encouragingly at him. I feel pretty stupid myself and I'm already hot and sweaty and wondering if I should have stripped off further to my underwear. The kid scowls back.

But it's too late now. Leon, our guide, and a former miner himself, is off and running and we trudge in our boots as fast as we can as he leads us to the cage outside the centre, where we each have our photographs taken. 'Smile!' he urges. 'It's so we'll have dental records in case anything goes wrong.' I giggle at that. But the teenager just looks accusingly at his dad. Obviously Mum will be hearing all about this later. In the cage, we're lowered 25 metres from a headframe that once serviced a real mine.

It's dark, gloomy, hot and wet, and already I feel weighed down with equipment. It's bad enough just standing still; what would it be like to actually have to work in a place like this? Why would anyone want to do it? The money, I suppose. But when I ask Leon, he says that's not it at all.

'I used to work in the mines and if you were to ask me to go back, I would. Any time. Most of us would.'

'But why?' I ask. 'It's so hot and uncomfortable down here.'

'This?' he looks around him. 'This is nothing! The real thing is much deeper underground and with the machinery going, and the friction of the rocks, it's much hotter. Some days you might drink 10 litres of water in six hours. This is nice and cool.'

I try to imagine what it might be like at the bottom of the deepest bit of the copper mine in town, a world-beating 1.9 kilometres underground. It must be hell. 'But what's there to like?' I ask him. 'Apart from the money?'

He sighs. 'It's the culture, the ethos, the camaraderie. In a place like Mt Isa, there's miners, and then there's the rest of the population. It's special. Miners are special.'

I want to ask him why he's not working as a miner now if it's all so bloody wonderful, but instead I nod as if I understand completely, and then shut up. It's probably tourists and our stupid questions that make toiling in a hell hole seem so attractive. We all climb aboard a little train, which rattles through winding tunnels until we reach the 'crib room', an underground room with a long table and seats either side, where miners have their meal breaks. The room is named after the card game they used to play, and perhaps still do.

Leon talks about the history of the mine, the type of rock, the mining equipment, techniques and processes, how it all works. There's one man in the group who used to be a miner somewhere else, who keeps asking him enormously technical questions about things. Leon cheers up. I think he was afraid all he might get was dumb-arse questions like mine. He likes this bloke, you can tell. Like he said, there are miners, then there's the rest of us. I slip into a gentle snooze.

Eventually, we're told to each take a metal tag from the 'out' board and move it to the 'in' board, so the mine can be sure where its 'miners' all are. We then trudge down endless tunnels, with the light of our lamps to guide us, sloshing through the puddles. In truth, there's just 1.2 kilometres of tunnel down here, as against the nearly 1000 kilometres of tunnels in the real mines. Thank God I'm not a real miner, however special they might be.

Leon stops us to show how miners drill holes in the rock, place the explosives in and then set them off. He asks if anyone would like a go with an air leg-drill. I think it might wake me up, and so volunteer first. I put on the earmuffs and he hands me the drill, and holds one side as he turns it on. Immediately, my whole body starts vibrating, and my teeth chatter. I just can't stop. I'm dripping sweat and my arms feel so weak I can barely hold it. After about a minute, he turns it off and I almost collapse as I let go. He says something but I can't hear him. I seem to have gone deaf. He leans over and pulls off my earmuffs.

'I said,' he says, looking irritated, 'imagine what it'd be like working with that, especially overhead.' I try. Those miners deserve every cent of their pay packets, I decide.

We plod off further through tunnels, stopping to look at other old machinery on the way. There's a digger so dangerous it's called a 'widow-maker'. More drills. Carts. An underground workshop. The stores. Ventilation pumps. At every stage, the ex-miner of the party asks a stack of other questions. I shoot him hostile glances and wish I still had the drill. At this rate, we won't be back up on the surface before sunset. Eventually, we end up back in the crib room again for a cup of tea, a look at some bits of rock and a listen to what a detonation might sound like. Pretty bloody loud, I can tell you, even with earmuffs on. 'How about women?' I ask Leon. 'Are there many of those underground these days?' From his look, I can tell he's thinking, 'One too many.'

'Only the prettiest women,' he replies.

'Sorry?'

'Most of them you'll find are good-looking,' he explains. 'They're often chosen on their looks – and only sometimes if they have previous experience.'

I laugh, assuming he's joking, but he looks deadly serious. Maybe he is. After all, this is the town where Mayor John Molony created international headlines by suggesting a novel way of fixing its woman shortage: encourage ugly women to move there. 'May I suggest if there are five blokes to every girl, we should find out where there are beauty-disadvantaged women and ask them to proceed to Mt Isa,' he so famously said, before being drowned out by a chorus of women who said men like him were reason enough not to want to live there. But I can't quite believe Leon is cut from the same cloth, and meant what he said, and say so. 'It's true,' he insists. 'It's still very much a man's world down here.'

I make a mental note to ask someone else about that later. I can't be bothered to argue now since he's telling us to put our tags back on the out board. Finally, it must be time to go.

We climb back into the train to be taken to the exit. I can hear someone coughing; we turn round. 'Just one more question,' the old miner asks Leon. This time, even the teenager groans.

Back up top, we climb out of our mining clothes and back into our real ones, and I rush through the rest of the centre. I need to get out into the fresh air.

I call up my new pal Gina, the police officer who gave me the lift from Boulia. She's proved to be an absolute delight, one of the funniest people I've ever met, with a quick, self-deprecating wit. And yet she's completely dedicated to her job. She suggests driving over to Lake Moondarra, 20 kilometres north of the city and I happily agree. She picks me up and we wend our way through the brilliant ochre landscape of the Selwyn Ranges, along the Leichhardt River.

The lake is actually very pretty and there are a few people walking along its shores, sitting fishing for barramundi, and having barbecues. I can imagine these kinds of places just outside town make it a bearable place to live, with miners in particular relishing being out here in the fresh air, camping for weekends with their families. I start to soften towards Mt Isa, although I still can't see it as quite the oasis that the tourist brochures promise, nor do I like the boorish claim, 'Remember: You're not a real Aussie till you've been to the Isa.'

Naturally, it has its issues. The air frequently stinks like rotten eggs from the levels of sulfur dioxide being pumped into the sky, while soil testing in the town started after an astounding 11 per cent of its children were found to have lead poisoning. One five-year-old boy tested had a blood level three times the international safety limit. Queensland's chief medical officer blames emissions from the mine, but Xstrata argues that the poisoning is caused by the natural occurrence of lead in the land.

Some say that the mine company doesn't do enough for the community, while others say it's doing a huge amount for locals. Quite apart from employing 20 per cent of the town's population and providing work in connected industries for most of the rest, there's also a lot being done for kids and teenagers. Kerry Brisbane, for instance, the electrical apprentice team leader at the Xstrata Skills Centre, is passionate about creating satisfying careers, including for young Aboriginal people and for women of all ethnicities.

She's incredulous when I mention the notion that only attractive women are recruited to the mining industry. 'That's ridiculous,' she says. 'This year we have 18 apprentices and three are girls. We've had five some years, and they are doing very, very well. I have the opportunity to mentor, encourage and promote women every day, and we're also starting up an Indigenous training program.'

On Indigenous issues, there's little doubt that some of the kids aren't doing so well in patchier parts of town, but there are people working hard to help. Gina lends a hand to one program, providing breakfast every day before school for a group of Aboriginal kids. Auntie Marge Body, 72, a gorgeous local Aboriginal lady, does it every day, often waking up the kids, getting them washed and changed, and feeding them before taking them to school.

'It's so rewarding; I like working with the kids,' she tells me. 'I'll walk around the reserve from house to house and get them to the centre, where we'll look after them and give them cereal and orange juice and egg and toast.' In Mt Isa, they like to look after each other like that, she says. She looks at me and smiles. 'Now, can I give you a hug?'

The Isa also has great sporting facilities and everyone talks about the community spirit and camaraderie that flourishes in a place that's so isolated from everywhere else. There's a great mix of nationalities: families have come from all over the world to work the mines here, Gina tells me. As if on cue, we walk up to one of the picnic areas around the lake and stumble on a cluster of Fijian families. They invite us to join them, then one man starts playing a guitar as the others sing in beautiful soft voices. I look over the deep blue of the lake, framed by red cliffs and green gums, watching the slow setting of the sun and listening to the lilting music. Yes, the place is growing on me.

On the way back, we drive to the top of Telstra Hill, the lookout about 7 kilometres from the town. By the time we get to the top, the night is pitch-black. Mt Isa, however, is ablaze with lights, a small glowing ridge with three high stacks – from the lead smelter, the copper smelter and the acid plant – belching smoke in the middle of vast black plains, with lots of small flickers of lights from people's houses all around the mines. 'Town planning wasn't so big in those days,' Gina remarks wryly. 'I doubt today if you'd ever be able to build houses so close.'

We gaze at the sight. 'But it is quite beautiful in a strange kind of way,' she adds. 'It looks just like an ocean liner in full steam.' Indeed it does, with the stacks the funnels on the ship and the small lights those from cabins. Some people even dub it the Titanic, but only in jest.

Both the town and its mines have weathered a lot in their time, from the early rough years of even just surviving in such a Godforsaken spot, to miners' strikes – including a beer strike in protest against rising prices, amazing for a town that once held the record for the biggest beer consumption of any similar-sized place in the Commonwealth. Besides the allegations people are being poisoned by lead fumes and dust, there's also the wildly fluctuating prices of natural resources. But the locals, as well as the mine's current owners, have always seemed to cope. They're now even looking at developing a large all-in-one open zinc-lead-copper pit mine to extend the life of the industry beyond 2060, necessity being the mother of invention and all that . . .

Gina suddenly shrieks in my ear. She's spied a snake. We both peer into the darkness and see it disappear under a bush. We scramble to her car, but on the way driving back down the hill we spot two more, this time on the road. With the first, we get out for a look and I pull out my fabulous new miniature solar-powered torch I bought for the trip. It emits a beam of light so weak and thin that Gina tells me to hurry up and turn it on. I make a mental note to buy a big old-fashioned torch at the earliest chance I can.

As we arrive back into town, Gina suggests going to look at a copper pour at the mine. This is a sight, she says, all visitors to Mt Isa should see. We drive around the maze of roads outside the mine, staring into the mass of machinery for any glimpse of glowing yellow that could signify a copper pour about to happen. Gina finally sees what she's looking for and we race to a different spot on the road, pull over and press our noses against the metal fence. There's a line of massive mine dump-trucks, each carrying 150–340 tonnes of ore, waste or rock, thundering along the road inside but, behind them, there's a flash of yellow. We stand and stare as molten copper matte is poured in to a converter. The glimmering sheet of golden light casts a glow over everything around it as it roars into its new home. 'Things to do in Mt Isa when you're bored,' Gina says with a laugh.

*

The next day we head out for a drive to explore some of the old ghost towns, deserted when their mines were either exhausted or closed down. Kuridala, once a thriving copper and gold town of 1500 people, is now just a sad industrial dump, littered with the debris from its proud past. Another extremely good road doesn't seem to lead anywhere. But it once did, Gina assures me. This was the road into another busy mining town of nearly 1000 people, called Mary Kathleen, with its own hospital, cinema, library, pool, store, police station, bank and market gardens.

We stop the car, and trudge through the high grass. Sure enough, every so often we come across the foundations of an old house, a cracked tiled floor that used to be someone's kitchen, the lines painted on a scrap of ground that made up part of a former car park. Gina, who grew up in the tiny town of Gunpowder, 120 kilometres north of Mt Isa, which was built after the discovery of copper in the 1920s, seems to knows this place well. 'Oh, I do,' she says. 'I used to come here a lot when I was a kid. We used to get *so* excited at the sight of a bitumen road. We'd ride bikes here to see what it was like to cycle on a bitumen road. This was once a really impressive town.'

Mary Kathleen was founded in 1954, after two prospector mates broke down in their truck, switched on their Geiger counter and watched the needle go berserk at all the uranium in the ground. The production of uranium began in earnest from 1956. A glut led to the mine's closure seven years later, but new international contracts saw it reopen in 1975 and continue up until 1983. When the mine closed for the final time, the town also closed and the plant and all the buildings were auctioned off to the highest bidders, who physically removed them and set them up elsewhere. Some of those houses are still being lived in at Cloncurry, 60 kilometres to the east.

We continue on to the old open uranium pit, past the big *Danger!* sign that warns of the perils of radiation, falling rocks and unstable edges. It's spectacular. The stepped rockfaces down to the mine are streaked in red, white and green from the oxidisation of all the minerals in the earth, while the water at the bottom of the pit has formed a stunning lake of the most vivid electric turquoise. It's a colour you might see at Hamilton Island on the barrier reef, not this far inland in the middle of such a dry, desolate stretch of the Outback.

It's a blistering hot day, and there's little I'd like to do more than race down and have a dip. Gina smiles. She puts her finger to her lips and tells me to listen. I hunker down on the ground and do as she says. It's strange; I can hear nothing. There are no birds, no cicadas, no calls of wildlife, not even the sound of wind through trees. I stare at the lake. There's no sign of any life there either – no birds swirling around the cavern, no bats, no fish breaking the surface, no insects buzzing. There's just an eerie, deathly silence. Even though the sun is burning, I shiver.

'I came here a couple of years ago with a friend and he insisted on going down for a swim,' says Gina. 'I did everything I could to stop him. But he wouldn't listen. He went in, then he came out really quickly, saying he didn't like it at all.

'I phoned a friend, a doctor, to ask if he'd be all right. He said he'd been so quick, he'd probably be fine. But I told the friend that I was sure he'd look good bald, and immediately he found a loose hair and became convinced it was all falling out. He's never been back.' I suddenly realise how much I'll miss that Outback wit.

16

WHERE HAVE ALL
THE YOUNG MEN GONE?

Nothing prepares you for your first sight of Port Hedland.

The largest town in Western Australia's Pilbara region, which the resources boom has turned into the world's biggest iron-ore port, is busier, noisier, dirtier, smellier, richer and more horrible than any other place you've ever seen.

'It's a f…ing cesspit,' says Ron, a man in his late 50s with dyed jet-black hair and too-tight clothes. He'd found me wandering around the dusty red streets of Port Hedland at nightfall, looking for somewhere to eat, and shown me the way to the Pier Hotel, apparently the only food source on a Sunday night. 'Look at this pub. It's a f…ing shithole.'

Obediently, I cast my eyes around. It's a big drinking barn with the reputation of being the most dangerous pub in Australia, I'm later told by a tour guide. It holds the dubious record of the greatest number of murders in one night on a licensed premises – seven. And, allegedly, 16 stabbings. Tonight, thankfully, all seems peaceful on the western front; it has only around 30 customers, mostly dressed in orange high-visibility jackets and grouped in little rowdy knots, each drinking steadily and heavily, with stacks of dirty glasses piling up on the wooden benches before them. I peer through the gloom. Strange – every single person here is male. I feel suddenly even more uncomfortable than I did when I first walked in.

There's a sudden burst of laughter from one side of the room and I turn round and see my first woman. Her stilettos are perched on the rung of a bar stool and she's leaning over, wiggling her rear end, covered only by the thin black lace strip of a G-string. She stands up, catches me looking at her and laughs, then climbs down from the stool and heads straight for me. *Oh, God, no!* I pray for her to turn away but she just keeps on strutting towards me, wearing little more than that G-string, a tiny wisp of a skirt that barely grazes her thighs, a matching lacy black bra and a big red-lipsticked smile.

As she draws level, Ron and his mates notice her too. 'Jasmine!' one of them calls. 'How the f...ing hell are you tonight?' Ron turns round to greet her, and slaps her on the bottom. I silently will her to slap him right back, but she doesn't.

'I'm all right,' she says in a voice that could scrape paint off a car. 'And wot about you boys? Anuvva drink?' Ron tosses a hundred dollar note on her tray. 'Five more beers and . . . what about you?' he asks me.

'Thanks,' I say. 'I'll have a lemonade.'

He scowls. 'For Christ's sake, have a proper bleedin' drink. I'll be the laughing stock of all the f...ing c...s around here.' I shake my head, and try to keep a polite smile glued on my face. 'Oh, all right,' he says. 'You heard that, Jas?'

Jasmine nods, smiles and turns on her heel, coming back five minutes later with the drinks and some notes in change that, for a moment, I fear one of the blokes will try to stuff down the

214

front of her G-string. 'Keep it,' says Ron, waving her away.

Thank goodness for small mercies. 'I'll pay for the next round,' I say in a pathetic little voice.

'Will you f…!' barks Ron. The perfect gentleman.

I order a vegetarian nachos from another room out the back to be delivered to the table, then try to make polite conversation while I wait. Ron and two of his mates work on the dredgers in the harbour that go out every day to keep the harbour from silting up and stopping those massive ships – which if you apparently stood them on their end, would be taller than the Eiffel Tower – running aground.

'You should see the f…ing stuff we dredge up,' says one of them, slurring his words drunkenly and spitting as he talks. 'F… knows how many f…ing fossils millions of years old we smash up. We're f…ing the environment to feed China.'

'Shouldn't be allowed,' his mate agrees, burping loudly and sending the stench of stale beer towards me. 'If the greenies could see us! But what do those c…s at the port authority care?'

They both go on and on, the fs and cs getting more frequent by the sip, and the others join in. They drive forklifts and trucks around the port and, while they all say they hate their jobs, they love the giant machinery and the pay packets that go with them. They're from across the country, but fly up here for two months' work, fly home for a week, then return. They're keeping the whole f…in' country afloat, they say. WA should run the whole country, they say. The rest of Australia should kiss their ….s.

In the meantime, they seem to be competing against each other to see who can stuff the most profanities into a single sentence, using them not only as adjectives and verbs but also, even more offensively, as adverbs. While I've never really minded swearing, the sheer frequency creates a really nasty, intimidating

215

and aggressive atmosphere.

When my slurry of corn chips, cheese and tomato finally arrives, I wolf it down as quickly as I can – if only I could have gulped down that ironwoman damper at half the speed – so I can get the hell out of here. Ron, however, doesn't want to have seen the last of me. 'Why don't you come out with us tomorrow out on the dredger to see what it's like?' he asks. 'We'll show you a bloody good time. We have a f…ing great feed and it'll be interesting for you to see what we do.'

I feel like a kangaroo caught in a dumper truck's headlights. Yes, I'm tempted for a flicker of a second to see such a horrendously big and busy port from the water, but I really don't want to go out on a boat alone for a day with these men.

'Let me think about it,' I say eventually. 'I might have something on tomorrow.'

'Like bloody what?' asks Ron. 'You've only just f…ing arrived. What can you have on?'

I quail before his hard stare. 'Well, give me your mobile number,' I say. 'And I'll give you a call tomorrow.'

Ron thinks about that a moment. 'OK,' he says. I scribble his number in my notepad. 'Now you give me your number. Then I can call you too.'

I hesitate. I really don't want to, and consider giving him a false one but then, at the last minute, think better of it. I tell him my number, having to repeat it three times for him to punch it successfully into his phone. Then he immediately presses the call button. My phone rings in reply.

'Good!' he says. 'I don't like being f…ed around, and you might have given me the wrong number.'

I die a little inside. 'But I must go now,' I say. 'Sorry, I'm really tired. Great to meet you all,' I wave to all the flushed, boozy faces sitting around. 'See you later.'

'Yeah,' says Ron. 'See you tomorrow.'

I walk outside and the dank warm dark quickly swallows me up. I seem to be in a shadowy industrial site, and there's no one around, but lights flash distantly in what I hope is the direction of where I'm staying. Out of the corner of my eye, I see a big man slip out of the hotel and eye me over. He looks as though he's following me. If he catches up, Fred Brophy veteran or not, I won't stand much of a chance. I quicken my pace and look back. I'm sweating.

I can still see him, but he's now standing by a tree, doubled over, loudly vomiting. It's a wonderful sight.

I knew Port Hedland might prove a touch tricky from the outset. I've never been to the Pilbara before and, thinking the port might be a good place to start, booked a flight from Perth. But when I called the visitors centre from Sydney, I got the distinct impression it might not have been my smartest move.

'I hope you've booked your accommodation,' were the woman's first words. 'Because there isn't any. And even if you find some, it's very pricey.'

'Oh, well,' I said, trying to rally all the positivity I could possibly muster, 'I can always sleep in the car . . .'

'That's good,' she said briskly. 'So you've managed to find a hire car?' My heart sank.

It hadn't occurred to me that finding both would prove such a trial, but they did. All the fly-in, fly-out workers, the port and the mining companies routinely book almost everything, I discovered. As a result, I finally ended up with a 2WD instead of the sturdy 4WD I'd planned to hire so I could later power along the dirt roads of the rugged Karijini National Park to the south. And I'm now sitting in the world's most expensive donga – a kind of portable shed – set on a stretch of concrete close to the harbourside, in place of a comfy hotel room. Still, there are worse things, I tell myself as I put down my rucksack in the bleak little room, than a Hyundai Getz and well-appointed donga. But not many. At 3 a.m. the couple next door decide to loudly make up after having argued at the top of their voices for an hour.

The next day I get up early, say good morning to the much quieter man on the other side, who's sitting on his step gutting fish (Ah, *that* explains the smell!), and have a wander around town. It's a strange sensation. Nearly every person I see is male; I feel like almost the last woman on earth. What's more, everyone is dressed in orange, yellow or blue overalls, with either work boots or thongs on their feet. No one seems to wear their own clothes, even when they're obviously not working. It's like they just can't be bothered. This town is where they work. They go somewhere else to live.

The actual centre of town is pretty small, just a higgledy-pig-gledly selection of a few shops, some takeaway places, a couple of uninspiring cafés and the visitors centre. Most of the nice old buildings, I later discover, have been blown away by cyclones, undermined by tidal surges, eaten by white ants, burnt down, bombed by the Japanese looking for the secret airbase out of Marble Bar to the south or bulldozed to make way for something else. It's a dangerous old place, Port Hedland.

At the airport in place of the usual 'Welcome' signs, there's an incredible wealth of information about the different kinds of snakes commonly found in the area: three main species of python as well as the desert death adder, the orange-naped snake, the common mulga or king brown, and the western brown snake.

Outside, along the roads, there are plenty more warning signs about things to take heed of, including long road trains, flood-plains, cyclone alert levels, and cows and kangaroos wandering across the road. Even in town, your thoughts are constantly punctuated by the *beep, beep, beep* warnings of reversing vehicles, while there's also the glee with which everyone recounts the sightings of big saltwater crocodiles in the harbour. Although everything here is tinged with the red dust of the iron-rich earth, even the pigeons, there's no room at all for rose-tinting the realities of life.

I take a visitors-centre tour of BHP Billiton Iron Ore to try to get to grips with the guts of the place – to see why, since it was first developed in the 1960s, it's become known as the engine room of Australia. In a minibus, we bump along to the processing site for a glimpse of what I imagine Hades' underworld might look like on a bad day. There's billowing smoke, massive great churning machinery, gigantic dump-trucks thundering around filled with iron ore, engines, 78 kilometres of conveyor belts and orange-clad men everywhere.

The statistics of the operation are mind-boggling. It takes around a tonne and a half of iron ore to make one tonne of steel and every year 150 million tonnes of iron ore pass through this harbour – a volume projected to double by 2015 – from the company's seven mines around the Pilbara. These include Mt Whaleback, the biggest single-pit open-cut mine in the world at 5.5 kilometres long and nearly 2 kilometres wide. The crushed ore is transported here from Newman via the world's longest private-owned railway, at 426 kilometres, a feat of engineering undertaken with the help of nearly 400 gallons of beer drunk by the rail workers for every mile of track laid.

Pulled by some of the most powerful diesel engines in the

world, a number of the trains are around 2.5 kilometres long, an absolute bugger of a wait when you're caught at the rail crossing, I later find out. But that's still nothing compared to the one that ran in 2001 straight into Guinness World Records, which was 7.35 kilometres long, carried 82 262 tonnes of iron ore, and was operated by just one rail technician. From here, the iron ore is loaded into giant ships, mostly bound for China, Japan and Korea.

But it's not only iron ore that Port Hedland is famed for. There's also salt. Great pyramids of it. Pumped from the sea into ponds, evaporated, harvested, washed and dried, around three million tonnes of the stuff is exported every year, mostly for industrial and chemical uses. But before it goes, it sits prettily in big stockpiles at the Rio Tinto-owned Dampier Salt site near the Port Hedland deep-water berth and at sunset glows pink against the darkening sky as you try to take a photo while the road trains blast their horns and threaten to squash you to a pulp.

In the final interests of increasingly fashionable 'industrial tourism', I decide to go along that evening to the mining camp Port Haven, which houses 1200 fly-in, fly-out BHP Billiton workers. Visitors can go along for dinner but, first, the women at the visitors centre have some advice for me. 'Don't wear anything low cut,' says one. 'And don't wear a short skirt,' says the other. 'And wear long sleeves.'

I'm bemused. 'How about I wear a burqa?' I ask. They look at me icily.

'These men are in single men's quarters and a lot of them haven't seen a woman for weeks,' the first one admonishes. 'We're only telling you for your own protection.'

Later, driving round and round the darkened suburbs past the airport, I wish they'd given me better directions for my protection. Eventually, however, I find it, park and buy an all-you-can-eat ticket at the front office for the bargain price of $22. As I walk into a big building, not unlike a shopping centre food hall, with stalls of different offerings around the edges – roasts, pizza, Asian, Italian, flame-grills, sweets, ice-cream – I realise how overdressed I am, in my long trousers, T-shirt, scarf, billowing long-sleeved, buttoned-to-the-chin shirt and shapeless jumper. It's sweltering in there and everyone else is in singlets and shorts.

I wonder how I can strike up a conversation with anyone, but I don't have to wonder for long. I help myself to some food and sit down at a table. The man two seats away to my right immediately leans over.

'Hello,' he says. 'Are you all right? You look a bit flushed.'

I smile. 'I'm fine, just a bit hot,' I say.

'I'm not surprised,' he laughs. 'You look like you're dressed for a northern winter.'

He's Darren, a 42-year-old who works here four weeks on, and one week off. He lives most of the time in Brisbane with his partner and their three kids, but is doing this to try to pay off their mortgage a bit quicker. On his $3000-a-week wage, he's quadrupled the repayments. He's planning to stay just two years, before going home for good.

'But will you be able to leave?' I ask. He grins.

'Possibly not, but I'll try. I've seen a lot of blokes stay too long and have their marriages break up in their absence.'

When he goes, Michael, Pete and Kerry take his place. It seems I'm a bit of a novelty, and not only for the way I'm dressed. They ask me why I'm there, and then tell me how the trio, school-friends from Melbourne, made a pact together to come for a year. This is their third. 'It's just too easy,' says Michael, the elder of the group at 28. 'We work, we go to the gym here, we have our food made for us, our rooms get cleaned every three days with clean towels and sheets. We have a laugh together. There're just no hassles. We go into town and have a drink, sometimes with a woman called Jasmine, who works in one of the hotels. And the money is great. We can't earn anything like that outside.'

Where have all the young men gone? Gone for mining – every one.

Over dessert, feeling a bit like a speed-dater, I meet Sydney-sider Damien. He's appreciably gloomier. 'So many of the blokes around here get institutionalised,' he tells me. 'They ask to do eight weeks on and one week off, then ask for 12 weeks on. Eventually they never go home at all. They work hard, but then spend all their money on drink, cigarettes and prostitutes. They never end up saving any of it. It's a bloody trap, that's what it is.'

So is he trapped? 'Oh no, not me,' he insists. 'I'm smarter than that. I don't drink, I don't smoke and I don't pay for sex. Aren't you hot in all those clothes? Would you like to see my room?'

For me, that's my cue to make my excuses and leave.

Am I being fair to Port Hedland? There must be more to it than this, I tell myself.

'No, there isn't,' says young mum Hazel. 'It's a shocker. There's nothing to do here for families. We're responsible for keeping Australia afloat, but there's not even a cinema or bowling alley here. It's just about getting rich quick, and then getting out.'

The fish-gutter next door feels similarly. He bought land a year ago and has been trying to develop it ever since. The trouble is, he can't find any labour; everyone's working for high wages elsewhere. He's been living in a donga now for a month, fishing for his supper to stretch out his rapidly diminishing savings.

A couple of backpackers I bump into around town aren't fans

of the place, either. They're sleeping in their car and cooking on a barbecue at one of the parks every night as they can't afford accommodation. 'It's the pits,' they say as one.

Then I meet a chef at one of the other hotels around town. He's got both a place to stay and a paid job. What does he think? 'I handed in my notice last week,' he tells me. 'I can't stand the miners coming here every weekend, banging on all the doors, looking for hookers.'

I drive over to South Hedland, the big residential satellite suburb of town, 18 kilometres from the port. It's designed along the same lines as Canberra, all roundabouts and roads that curl in and around, so immediately I get lost and drive round and round and round again. I stop at the soulless shopping centre, with its stink of fried food. There is a gang of people clustering around a noticeboard advertising a room to rent in a house for $665 a week. I leave there to go and have a lemonade at the Last Chance Tavern, a pub with no windows.

Yet there are people who love the place. Or say they do. Peter, the manager of the visitors centre, is at pains to talk about Marapikurrinya Park, the outstretched fingers of the picturesque tidal creeks, the mangroves lining the natural harbour and the black swans, terns, ospreys, egrets, waterfowl, cormorants and sometimes the native stork jabirus that all reside happily cheek by jowl with industry. The woman in charge at Dalgety House Museum, a centre developed to show what life was like during colonial times, chats with pride about Red Dog, a travelling, hitch-hiking stray Kelpie–cattle dog cross, now immortalised in the movie of the same name.

And then out past the old detention centre in the council office there's the mayor, Kelly Howlett. She's a surprise on a number of fronts, including being a woman, a Melburnian, a former Greens candidate and, now 34, the youngest mayor to be elected in the state. Formerly in charge of the visitors centre, she is so incredibly enthusiastic about the joys of Port Hedland, she makes it feel un-Australian to be otherwise.

'I think every Australian has an investment in Port Hedland,' she points out, 'particularly through their superfunds. Everyone has. It's one of the rites of passage to come here, like when people go to Canberra to see Parliament House. *Everyone* should visit.'

But while it's certainly an important place, I say gently, even she has to admit that it's hardly pleasant. Kelly looks aghast at the very thought. It is industrial but it's also beautiful, she insists. 'I went fishing at the weekend and within two minutes I had two dolphins swimming past. Then there were juvenile green turtles popping up out of the water. The harbour is just so healthy.'

Yes, maybe so, but the town's still a bit of an eyesore. She won't budge an inch and I admire her iron will to stay on message.

'There are beautiful places to walk, there's so much to see and do, and it's a great place to bring up children,' she says. 'The only problem, really, is the housing shortage and, with the help of the state and federal governments, we're tackling that challenge too. A thousand more houses are being built every year.' In fact, soon the town, current population 20000, is going to become a city of 50000. I wonder how all those newcomers are going to feel about their new home.

Thanking Kelly, and taking my leave, I get in the car and drive back to my donga. Perhaps I have been a bit hard on Port Hedland. Perhaps it's not really as bad as I thought.

Just as I get to my door, my phone rings. 'G'day!' booms a voice. 'It's Ron here. Remember me from the Pier? I thought I might take you out for the night . . .'

17

SURVIVING OUTBACK HAZARDS, FROM SNAKES AND POISON TO SHARKS

I'm driving south through the eastern Pilbara, one of the most isolated and inhospitable regions of Outback Australia. In summer here, hot winds blow straight off the Great Sandy Desert and temperatures routinely hover around 40 degrees Celsius. But it is incredibly beautiful. Every time the road rises, a huge vista of ochre-stained plains unfolds, pale yellow in the early morning sun and sprinkled with green spinifex, framed by great rocky ranges whose colours constantly shift with the light, from orange to red, purple to mauve.

My heart lifts. Port Hedland's behind me and I'm on my way to Karijini, around 300 kilometres south. It's Western Australia's second largest national park and reputed to be one of the country's most stunning. I'll sniff the fresh air, I'll walk among the gorges, I'll rejuvenate. My only one nagging worry is that I don't have a 4WD for the dirt roads. Oh, yes, and a friend told me to take along plenty of gear for climbing down into the gorges, and I don't have that either. But in every other way I'm completely prepared for this latest Outback adventure. I've even written a note to myself to stop at the first service station I see to pick up all I'll need for the drive ahead: plenty of water, snacks and fruit.

And then I see the sign. Next Services 220 kilometres.

By the time I arrive at the Munjina Roadhouse, I'm gasping and feeling light-headed, and reminding myself how dangerous the Outback can be when you're not well enough prepared for it. The isolation, long distances and harsh conditions, as well as the vagaries of nature itself, can all prove hazardous, often when you're least expecting it. And that means pretty much all the time for those of us who live in cities. Still, I've got through this time, and I make a promise to myself to be more careful. I buy three of the biggest bottles of water they have – and drink half of one straight down – a couple of sad-looking apples, some chocolate bars, popcorn and an ice-cream.

Happily rehydrated, I drive on, munching on the popcorn, and feeling almost as if I'm sitting in a movie theatre. The highway passes directly between Mt George on my right and Mt Lockyer on my left and then close by the Munjina Gorge itself. It's a veritable wide-screen panorama of great craggy walls of crimson-hued rock, a dramatic contrast with the clear blue of the sky, wildflowers and silvery grasses.

Finally, I reach the turn-off to Karijini, the 627 000-hectare park set in the Hamersley Range, wedged between the massive mining towns of Newman to the south-east, and Tom Price on its western side. I drive another 35 kilometres to the entry station and then turn right towards the Dales Gorge. I'd printed a map from the internet and know I should stop off and look here before heading on to the visitors centre and the eco retreat where I've booked a bed for the night. I feel my spirits rise still further as I approach. This is an ancient landscape of massive mountains and escarpments cut by gorges more than 100 metres deep, and promises a series of spectacular sights, 'an adventure two billion years in the making', according to the publicity.

I park and look around, but can see nothing – just a flat red landscape overgrown with grass. I check my map again. Yes, I should be there. I look around for someone to ask, but there's no one. I start walking and then, suddenly, I see it. Instead of great gorges towering above me, they're deep ravines carved in the earth tumbling below. I wonder if any unsuspecting European explorers might have fallen to their deaths here.

I take the top trail walking around the rim of the gorge, peering down from the lookout above a fern-lined pool and the gushing Fortescue Falls far below. The walls of the gorge are banded in different shades of orange, red and pink, with snappy gums and bloodwoods clinging on to the sides. Up here, there's a timeless hush. I'm totally alone and can hear nothing but the whisper of a breeze rippling the grasses, and the soft whine of flies that are so languid, they don't move from your body until you physically knock them off. I could well be the last person left on earth.

After I've finished walking, I drive on the last stretch of sealed road to the modern visitors centre, built in the shape of a goanna. I wander around the displays, and then go to the desk to ask them about the conditions of the dirt roads ahead for a 2WD, and for recommendations of which gorges to visit. I want to be prepared for anything. The woman behind the desk shakes her head sadly. 'I don't know,' she says, and wanders away to the back office.

'Excuse me, excuse me,' I call out after her. She returns. 'What do you mean, "I don't know"?' I ask.

'What I said, I don't know,' she replies.

I'm stumped. 'But . . . but . . . how can I find out then?'

She thinks for a moment. 'You could phone Perth and see if anyone there knows.'

I look at her. Is she joking? Finally, she explains. 'I'm just helping out,' she says. 'All the regular staff are at a funeral.'

I have no idea why she didn't explain before, but I try a different tack. If she's from around here, she must at least have some local knowledge. 'Do you know what the road north to Hamersley Gorge is like? And do you know if I can get out of the park through that route?' I don't want to give up. I haven't yet realised I really am on a hiding to nothing.

She hesitates and rubs her nose. 'Maybe you can, maybe you can't,' she says. 'I wouldn't really have a clue.'

I bite my lip and drive back off towards the Karijini Eco Retreat, where I'm staying the night. The road's rough with lots of corrugations but I take it slowly, especially when another vehicle appears and sends a cloud of orange dust so thick, I momentarily lose all vision. The car's rattling, and I feel my teeth rattling with it, but as long as the road stays like this, I guess I'll be all right. Reaching the retreat, I leave my big bag there, take out my daypack, put in one of the enormous bottles of water, and head straight on to the Weano and Hancock Gorges. I don't have much time here, and I want to make the most of the daylight.

I park near the Oxer Lookout, and peer down at the floor 100 metres below where the gorges meet. I then start climbing down steps until they stop and a metal ladder bolted to the wall starts. I take a deep breath. I'm not sure if I should be doing this alone. What if I fall? I know there are a number of accidents here, and even deaths, every year among tourists. I don't want to be the next. But if I want to see this, I don't really have much choice. I start descending. It's actually not as bad as it looks, and soon I'm standing on flat stone at the bottom. Even better, I can hear voices. They sound as if they're coming from in front of me. Excellent! I can maybe tag along with them.

I quicken my pace along the trail until I see a group of five people standing in front. 'Hi!' I say casually, as if I'm disappointed not to have the whole place to myself. Nothing, of course, could be further from the truth. They greet me too. They look like proper hikers dressed in all the right gear. Even better.

But I think I overdo the disappointed tone. 'Do you want to go in front of us?' asks one of them. 'We're a bit slow.'

'No, it's fine,' I say. 'You go first.' Then I see what they're contemplating; the rock ledge disappears into a pool of water. Gawd. What do we do now?

'OK!' their leader says to me. 'Thanks!' I generously shrug off his gratitude, watch them each step in, then copy what they're doing. The water is waist-high and so cold, it takes my breath away. Ah, this is what I needed wet-weather gear for. I wonder if my boots will ever dry out, but I keep a fixed grin on my face as if I'd known about this all along.

We emerge from the other side and my companions change their shoes. I obviously don't have any to change into but, big-heartedly, insist I'm happy to hang on for them. We all then continue as the gorge narrows with the cleft walls, purple strata of shale and stone, allowing only enough room for people to slip through single file. We all carefully pick our way along, my squelches echoing throughout the cavern, until we finally end up at a second crystal-clear pool. It's even more stunning down here; it feels almost as if we're at the heart of the earth, surrounded by all this ancient weathered stone. Looking up, there are spots where I can see the bright sunshine flowing down the gaps between the walls, but down here, it's cool and quiet.

It seems my little group is going no further, so I go along behind them until we've climbed back out. I then breezily make for my car, gathering my own personal wad of thick orange Karijini earth caked onto my shoes as I go. I reach the retreat just before the setting sun, and slip into my room, a grand canvas tent with a king-sized bed set up on an elevated timber platform. I yank off my shoes, which now weigh a tonne, and sit on the cane chair on the verandah, eating one of my chocolate bars, and watching the sun set. What a beautiful place. It feels a world away from the frenetic mining hub of the Pilbara I've seen so far.

I take a leisurely solar-heated shower in the open-air bathroom, in which I also wash my shoes, and then wander up to the restaurant for a meal. I ask the staff there about the roads and they're infinitely more helpful. There's absolutely no way I should attempt the Hamersley Gorge in a 2WD, they say, as that steep stretch of road's still wet and slippery after recent rain. And no, I shouldn't try to exit there; I have to go out the way I came in. I sit and eat and make a few notes at the table until I'm almost asleep, then go back to my luxury tent and crawl between the crisp sheets, feeling relieved I'm not in a tent in the campground nearby. It has been a good day.

It's only the next morning, when I return to the visitors centre, that I notice the warnings to lone walkers to make sure they're carrying enough of the right gear, including a navigational device like a handheld GPS and something to communicate with in case of emergencies, such as a UHF radio. And the dictate that they should always, *always*, leave word with someone about where they're planning to go. It had been an even luckier day than I'd realised.

*

I sleep soundly in my luxury tent and, over breakfast, have a chat to the Perth-born manager of the retreat, Fiona Gordon, who came here four years ago after managing a spa company in Malaysia. She'd never camped in her life before, but was intrigued by the idea of an environmentally responsible Aboriginal-owned retreat set in the middle of the Pilbara gorges. She came to have a look for two weeks . . . and has been here ever since.

'My friends laughed when they heard about it,' she says. 'They used to say that my idea of roughing it was wrinkled sheets. But it's been an amazing experience. I've had to learn how to do everything myself out here, from looking after the poo farm and water-treatment plant to dealing with emergencies like backpackers getting lost, from losing power at 3 a.m. to first aid, from cars breaking down to rescues. That's the beauty of the Outback, it makes you so much more self-reliant.

'Now it's home. It's just so beautiful out here. Every time you drive around, it's different and the whole landscape changes from morning to the middle of the day, to night. Now there's all the tiny pink wildflowers out, or you might spot an acacia you've never noticed before. You learn to respect the environment, understand it and protect it.'

I can imagine how that happens. This part of the Outback is simply so magnificent, it would be hard to tear yourself away. From the tiny fraction of the gorges I've seen so far, I know how stunning they can be, with their splashes of colour from the marble, iron and silica, their crystal-clear pools, the ledges and the tunnel system that runs through them, and how bewitching it could all be. The flat plains above are beautiful enough with the yellow-flowering cassias, the wattles, Northern Blues and purple mulla mullas clustering around massive red termite mounds. Even the note in the tents to beware the family of frogs, who like to sit on the toilet float, preventing it from flushing, seems, in these surroundings, absolutely charming.

I reluctantly pack up and then drive towards Knox Gorge for a look from the rim. I wander around and look down the deep red slash in the earth. At the bottom there's water so clear I can see straight through it. There's a sign here, a warning to beware of high cliffs, undercut cliff edges, loose rocks, etc., etc., but as I sit down to read the detail, I see something move out of the corner of my eye. I leap to my feet; a small brown snake is curled less than a metre away – just about the only thing the sign didn't warn against, even though it's probably by far the most dangerous.

Shaky now, I walk on and, as I return, I give the area a wide berth. Of course, I hadn't told anyone I was coming here so if anything happened, I'd be stuffed. I wonder to myself just how many times I need to be told . . .

I'm not returning to Port Hedland just yet. First I want to visit Wittenoom, the legendary town that became the victim of one of our worst-ever industrial disasters, with all its lessons about mining gone wrong. Blue asbestos was mined and milled at Wittenoom Gorge from 1943, amid clouds of dust, by workers supplied with no protective clothing at all, and tailings were laid throughout the town. By 1962, the very first mesothelioma case in Australia was diagnosed in a local worker. From that point on, doctors were horrified by the number of new cases and other forms of asbestos-related diseases developing among employees.

By 1966, both the mine and the town that had once been the Pilbara's largest, with a population of 20 000, were closed down. Officially, at least 1000 people died as a result of their exposure, although the Asbestos Diseases Society of Australia puts that figure closer to 2000, and say there could be as many as 5000 more to come. Western Australia now has the grim boast of having the highest rate of mesothelioma and other asbestos-related cancers per capita in the world. Midnight Oil wrote 'Blue Sky Mine' about the place.

Today, a lot of effort has gone into expunging the memory of Wittenoom. The town has been largely evacuated, most of the buildings have been torn down or removed, it's been de-gazetted and deleted from most maps, and the road signs for the town have long been taken away or blanked out. I have to ask back at the roadhouse even to try to work out the way. Eventually, I end up on a road that's one of the widest, smoothest and most modern stretches of paved highways into any non-town in Australia. But I know it's the right one when I see a sign halfway along it. WARNING: BLUE ASBESTOS DUST PRESENT IN WITTENOOM AREA. INHALED ASBESTOS DUST MAY CAUSE CANCER.

I stop to look and then speed away. As I accelerate, I can feel the car sliding sideways across the road. A yellow light starts flashing on the dashboard and there's an urgent-sounding beeping. I pump the brakes gently and try to wrest back control. After a few seconds, it levels out and slows down, shuddering to a halt. I put my head on the steering wheel and take a deep breath. Shit! Careening off this road and ending up upside down in a ditch suffocated by airbags on the way to a place that no one ever goes to any more . . . That would be an awful way to die.

But perhaps that's what Fiona, and so many others, mean when they say one of the best things about the Outback is that it teaches you to be self-reliant. You have to take complete responsibility for your own actions. If I crashed a car in Sydney, I'd have a bevy of emergency vehicles, lots of passing motorists and half a dozen hospitals close by. Here, I'd have no one for days and days, perhaps weeks or months. I really need to take more care.

And while that's challenging, at the same time it's somehow liberating and grounding and *real* – you come to understand that you truly survive or perish on your own wits.

I pull away, more slowly now, and keep on driving. It's a fair few kilometres but the only other sign is a big one saying, halfway down, Tom Price and Nanutarra; there's a piece of metal hammered in to conceal whatever the top half said. No prizes for guessing. Finally, there's a turn on my left and I take it. This used to be one of the main streets, but today there's precious little left. It's all overgrown fields, loose bricks scattered around and some long-dumped pieces of old furniture. As I continue, I can now see a grid of roads, and the occasional house, usually completely boarded up, that's still standing.

Further up, though, I can see my first sign of life: a man working on his vehicle. He must be one of the eight people living here who still refuses to leave. I slow down and wave but when he looks up and sees me, he scurries indoors. He obviously doesn't want visitors.

I drive around and eventually spot a woman working on her garden. I pull up and say hello. She looks startled. But when we start talking, it becomes obvious that she's pretty lonely. She barely pauses for breath. A spritely 69, with a worn face, short grey hair and dressed in baggy trousers and an old T-shirt, Lorraine Thomas lives in her house alone, and is determined to stay here for the rest of her days.

She came here from Victoria when the town was already closing down, looking for warm weather and a rural area in which to bring up her three young daughters. She knew nothing about the asbestos.

'There was nothing on this house's title deed to stop me purchasing it,' she says, taking a seat on the verandah of her small fibro cottage. 'And I think the government is overstating the danger so they can take over the area and open more mines and put a railway in through here. There's no more airborne asbestos here than anywhere else.'

Already a widow when she arrived here, Lorraine married again, to a man called Les, who'd settled in Wittenoom in 1962 while the mine was still operational. He later died of cancer. His death certificate states the cause of death as mesothelioma but Lorraine thinks otherwise.

'I know that's a lie,' she says. 'He had lung cancer. I should know. We were married for 25 years.' Secretly, I wonder how being married to someone would make you any more capable of diagnosing their disease, but I stay silent. She's adamant that residents here face no greater risk than elsewhere, and that one day the government will be forced, by litigation being prepared by her and others, to admit it. 'It's a risk going to bed because people die in their sleep,' she says. 'But the government doesn't stop people going to bed. I have faith that the truth will out in the end.'

Next door, her neighbour Donna Howarth is a little less dismissive of the risks, but is philosophical. Growing up in Tom Price, 130 kilometres away, as a kid she visited Wittenoom regularly, playing in the tailings in the dam where her family brought her to camp and swim.

'If the asbestos was going to get me, it would have got me by now,' she says. 'But I've also had skin cancers and I've smoked for 30 years. You weigh it all up and take it as it comes.' She laughs, with a rasping, smoker's voice. The blonde 46-year-old, with four piercings in each ear and one in her nose, has been living here now for eight months with her two dogs, seeking a bit of time out from the rest of the world.

'I like the seclusion here,' she says. 'And I like the heat. I've always been an Outback person. The red dirt gets in your veins.' Just like the deadly blue asbestos dust, perhaps.

Their nearest neighbour is a few blocks away, Mario Hartmann, a short, chubby Austrian with a strong accent gained after learning his English while working in Scotland. He's been here 21 years now, and the place suits him just fine. The asbestos might have been dangerous while they were mining, but not any more, he believes. And although it did get a bit depressing when the government was demolishing so many of the buildings, he adores the lifestyle here, on a patch of earth that is, he says, with the magnificent Wittenoom Gorge just 10 kilometres away, truly God's own.

'I love the freedom here,' says Mario, who'd been having an afternoon nap when I knocked, and thrown on an orange safety vest, shorts and thongs to talk to me in his backyard. 'You can do what you want when you want, just do your own thing and no one ever bothers you. I have plenty of friends who visit, and family too, and they like it here as well. The gorge is really nice, the pools there are beautiful and I like the scenery and nature. The temperature in winter is 26–27 degrees. Where in Australia could be nicer?'

Mario, now 47, chanced on Wittenoom when he was travelling around Australia as a tourist in 1987, and three years later he returned here to settle. He now lives cheaply off his investments, pumps his own water from a bore, has a generator for electricity, grows his own vegetables, makes his own bread, shoots kangaroos to feed his dog and cat, and travels to town to shop – to Tom Price, 240 kilometres to Newman or 300 kilometres to Port Hedland – just three times a year. He doesn't even miss the pub. 'I have all my own drink here,' he says. 'I can drink at home whenever I want. I'm totally self-sufficient.'

I eventually say my farewells and drive away from the desolate town, wondering about the people I've met. Lorraine unleashed such a torrent of words, it's obvious she's terribly lonely but maybe even if she lived elsewhere, she still would be. Donna has obviously found a peaceful refuge for a while, but is already planning her getaway, with a dream of getting a job as a truck driver with one of the mines. Mario, however, seems simply a true loner, someone perfectly happy with his own company. And there'd be few other places in Australia where you could live for practically nothing in the middle of nowhere. The asbestos, to each of them, seems just about irrelevant to their lives, transformed almost into a convenience to keep others away.

It's a slice of the Outback that, for some, provides real isolation. Too bad that, for others in Australia's most toxic town, it became a last stand that proved the death of them.

'Auntie Doris,' the small Aboriginal woman says, holding out her hand. 'Pleased to meet you. You're trying to get out of this filthy horrible place too, are you?'

I've just climbed aboard a Greyhound bus back in Port Hedland, ready for the ten-hour ride to Coral Bay on the Ningaloo Reef. I'm still on my trawl of Outback nature and this time I've opted to go for a swim with sharks. Not any old sharks, mind you. My preferred predators are the largest sharks, and fish, in the world: whale sharks that can grow to an astonishing 18 metres in length. And Coral Bay is the place in Outback Australia between April and June to join them for a swim.

Auntie Doris doesn't think it's such a good idea, and invites me to get off the bus with her in Roebourne instead and stay a while with her family. I thank her, but explain I really must get going. But when we do stop in Roebourne, I can't help feeling a little wistful waving her goodbye. Karratha, just beyond it, looks a pleasant-enough place too. We stop here for an hour to grab some dinner – travelling by bus can be so civilised! – and it has a friendly air.

This is the stamping ground of Heather Jones, a former secretary turned truckie. She's a single mum who started her business to support her two daughters and mortgaged her family home to buy vehicles.

Today Heather's female-owned multi-truck company Success Transport remains a huge, but very profitable, novelty. She spends a lot of her spare time talking to government about ways of improving life for truck drivers, like providing sleeping bays that can't be taken up by grey nomads. After all, the truckies do criss-cross the country delivering pretty much everything we need and use.

As for herself, she doesn't think she'll ever leave this stretch of the Outback. 'I love the scenery around here, the red earth and the spinifex and all the wildflowers,' she says. 'And these are uncomplicated places. There's a laidback lifestyle up here that you can't get anywhere else. You work long hours but you have freedom.'

If you're looking for a husband, the Pilbara's also the place to find one, says Heather, with 200 men for every woman. But no, she hasn't yet. Quantity doesn't always guarantee quality, apparently. 'A chap asked me to go out to dinner with him a few years ago, and we had a very nice evening,' says Heather, 45. 'Three weeks later, we were on a second dinner date, when he took my hands and told me I'd be selling my trucks when we got married. That was our second date! I looked at him and laughed, but he was deadly serious. So I told him he could enjoy my meal as well as his, and left.'

Gradually, the road is growing less red and, as the sun goes down, I catch sight of more and more animals emerging from behind the trees by the sides of the road: red kangaroos, bilbies, frogs, a few little quails hopping around, even an owl crouched by the verge, his yellow eyes glowing in the bus's headlights. By the time darkness falls, the lights are picking up what looks like a menagerie around the road. We finally arrive in Coral Bay, right outside a backpacker hostel, at half-past midnight.

I sleep fitfully at the hostel, anxious about waking up in time to catch my whale shark cruise early the next morning. In the end, I get up far too early and have breakfast at the bakery next door, waiting for the shopfront of Ningaloo Reef Dive Tours to open. When they do, I'm pretty much the first one in. I get sized up for a wetsuit and flippers.

'Yesterday, the group missed out,' says the woman who's already expertly chosen my gear. 'Unusually, there were no whale sharks around, so a couple of them are coming back with us today for another try. I'm sure our luck will change.' I feel a bit anxious. I have a flight out to Perth tomorrow, connecting with a flight to Kalgoorlie so, although a second day's trip would be free, it could be all too tricky and expensive to juggle the flights. I curse myself for never even having considered the possibility. Failure is not an option.

By the time we get out to sea on our 57-foot boat, everyone's feeling optimistic. A little spotter plane hurries off to look for whale sharks and to radio their coordinates back to us. In the meantime, we have coffee and biscuits, and we're given tips on swimming with sharks. We're told to stay together when in the water and to follow our leader, and then we're taught a set of hand signals to communicate with each other – go back, go forward, *HELP!* We also receive instructions on how to behave towards whale sharks: don't startle them, don't get too close, mind their enormous tail fins and, if they're swimming straight towards you, get the hell out of their way.

The level of excitement on the boat is steadily rising. Whale sharks date back 60 million years. Slow-moving gentle giants, it's their sheer size that's so awe-inspiring, with the heavier ones weighing in at more than 36 tonnes. Given all that, they're still (fingers crossed, Auntie Doris) no threat at all to humans, feeding only on plankton, tiny plants and animals through mouths that can reach as wide as 1.5 metres.

'Has anyone ever accidentally swum into one of their mouths?' I ask our guide. 'Er, no,' he says, with a laugh. 'Not that I know of anyway. But you could give it a try.'

One of the guides hands around a small model of a whale shark and everyone touches it for good luck. We're then divided into two groups of ten, and our group, the first one, gets changed into our wetsuits, puts on our masks, snorkels and flippers and sits on the floor. At a prearranged signal, we then shuffle on our backsides towards the end of the boat, where we all slip quietly into the water and swim out, following our guide. It's a little warm-up and practice, without the distraction of a bloody great whale shark in the water and, I guess, an exercise for those in charge to check that we weren't lying when we said we could swim.

We're all hyped up but the spotter plane radios back to say it still hasn't found one yet, and a second plane is sent up to double the chances of a sighting. We all have lunch while we wait, then sit around talking. One of the guides is from Melbourne and came to Coral Bay intending to stay only a short while. With a limited number of houses in the little settlement, and strict veto on any more being built, she spent her first four months in a tent until someone gave her an old caravan. She's perfectly happy here, though. She loves living in such an isolated place, loves the ocean life and loves introducing it to tourists. 'I feel sorry for people who live in cities and have normal jobs,' she says. 'It must be *awful*. Living out here is just so wonderful.'

Then there's a shout – there's been a sighting – and one of the guides tells us to get down on the floor. Obediently, we all dive to the floor, just as we've been taught, and the boat roars off. We stop and are told to shuffle down towards the back of the boat. No one can stop grinning. We drop one by one into the water, swim in the direction of the guide and then, lo and behold, a massive great whale shark looms up right in front of me. I'm transfixed. It's absolutely *huge*.

I put my face back up out of the water to check everyone's still with me, and then look back and just watch as it slowly powers through the water. It's a tremendous sight. I'm so close I can even see into one of its eyes.

I take a quick photo and it suddenly occurs to me that the whale shark is swimming right towards me, and that I should move away. As soon as the thought strikes, I start kicking as hard as I can to get out backwards. But he's obviously a faster thinker than I am, and slowly, very slowly, starts to dive deeper and deeper into the ocean until finally he disappears.

We all climb back into the boat, thrilled by our close encounter. We're all talking about it at the same time, and estimating his length at about 8 metres, when a cry comes – another whale shark's been spotted. We hunker down again, adrenaline pumping, speed to our next site, and then drop into the water. This one's much smaller, probably a juvenile at around 6 metres, the guide says later, but he's as cute as his uncle was overwhelming. Later that afternoon comes a third call. This time, however, only a few people see the whale shark; he's dived down before most of us have got into the water.

The boat now turns for home, as we all talk excitedly about the moment we all saw our first whale shark. I think most of us were moved by the experience far more than we imagined we'd be.

Even by the next morning, I still feel exhilarated as I catch a ride to the nearest airport, the Learmonth RAAF Base, for the flight to Perth. I sit next to an RAAF officer who asks me what I'm doing here. I tell him about Karijini, the gorges and the snake, Wittenoom and its asbestos and swimming with whale sharks. 'Isn't that shark thing pretty dangerous?' he asks.

'No,' I reply. 'I actually think it's possibly the least dangerous thing you can do in the Outback.'

He looks at me and smiles. 'I don't think so,' he insists. 'One of my friends once flew a spotter plane overseas and, on his first day, he guided a boat to a whale shark, only to realise, once everyone had got into the water, that it was actually a great white. He was back on the radio within milliseconds to yell to the guides to get everyone out. Everyone was fine except him. He nearly died of a heart attack that day, and never did it again.'

18

SEX AND NUDES AND ROCK 'N' ROLL

I've met some extraordinary women while travelling around the Outback: farmers, entrepreneurs, carers, campaigners, women from every walk of life. So I guess it was only a matter of time before I encountered someone from the oldest profession of all. Even so, in the middle of the rough-and-ready old Western Australian gold-mining town of Kalgoorlie, brothel madame Carmel still comes as something of a shock.

It's something in the way she moves, looks – a tall, elegant woman with a soft blonde bob and a silk scarf tied over a white blouse – and talks . . . in an upper-class English accent so precise, it could almost cut glass. But if I'm surprised to find a woman like that in a place like this, I'm not the only one, she says. She shocked herself too by coming here.

Carmel had been a Melbourne housewife when her second husband died. She sunk into a well of depression and asked her doctor for something that might help. He was sympathetic, but firm: it wasn't pills she needed, but something to do with all the free time she now had on her hands. He imagined the genteel woman might go off and busy herself with charity work. Instead, she saw an ad for a brothel for sale in Kalgoorlie and, to her own amazement, promptly bought it.

Nineteen years on, the refined Madame Carmel is just one of the surprises in store in the wild-west town 600 kilometres east of Perth. If there's anything you want to know about Outback men and sex, she's the one to ask. No, they're not too interested in conversation. No, they're don't like anything too fancy. And yes, they've often been away for so long from women, or their wives, that a ten-minute session is more than enough.

It may sound a strange place to go for insights, but sometimes it seems that nearly all of human life, and love, has passed through the town's brothels. From the moment prospector Paddy Hannan found a four-ounce gold nugget on the ground near Mt Charlotte in 1893, sparking off one of the biggest gold rushes the world has ever seen, and the day working women started cartwheeling down the streets to show off their knickers and drum up more business, mining and sex have both been the kinds of big business that, hand in hand, and check by jowl, have helped define Kalgoorlie.

Once, the town had a population of 143 000, the richest square mile of gold reserves in the world, and no fewer than 18 brothels ranged along either side of its own red-light district, Hay Street. Today it has just 30 000 residents and only three brothels, a result of the transformation of mining from individuals working their own small leases to the giant 'super pit' – Alan Bond's brainwave – amalgamating them all into the biggest gold open-cut pit in Australia. Other factors have been the falling quantity of gold, the shift from transient male labour to the migration of families and the deregulation of the sex industry.

'When I first came, we were so busy,' says Madame Carmel,

who's followed everywhere by her tiny chihuahua, Fifi, as she glides through her bright-pink Questa Casa brothel. The Questa was one of the first ever set up in Australia, in 1904, designed with 'stalls' at the front, in which women would sit and call out to potential customers.

'The girls used to work a 16-hour day, and the record one of them set was seeing 70 men in one shift. She could make £350 in one day and, at that point, a house only cost £4000.

'She'd see most of the men for ten minutes, but her fastest client was a man who visited for four minutes. She took off her clothes, hugged him, put a condom on him and he finished. He then rushed off, saying his mates were waiting for him in the pub.' Perhaps the slowest was the man who was discovered dead in bed.

'Men are quite simple creatures,' Carmel says. 'And in a town where there's still 20 men to one woman, we act as a safety valve for them. We've also helped many a marriage. Men will often come to us for something they don't get at home. It then helps the marriage stay together.'

Hmmm, I'm not sure what to think of that and evidently I'm not alone. One woman a few years back drove her car into the brothel, causing $70 000 damage. If her husband or boyfriend ever visited, it doesn't seem as if she was particularly grateful.

But as a result of the fall-off in the number of customers, Carmel now supplements her income by running brothel tours for tourists. It's a fascinating glimpse into the less-talked-about side of the mining industry and a startling lesson in how dramatically someone can choose to rebuild their life after encountering a tragedy.

The moment Carmel, in her posh English accent and soft sing-song voice, utters the word 'dildo', our tour is shocked into silence until one man starts coughing so hard, and turning so red, everyone fears he's having a seizure. But Carmel doesn't miss a beat.

'Other things about the business have changed too,' she says. 'The men in Kalgoorlie were all macho until ten years ago. But in the last few years, the pansies have come into town and one of the other houses has a gay man there for men looking for a man. In the old days, the men would have beaten him up.'

A few doors down is a rival brothel, Langtrees 181. The madam here couldn't be more different; she's a big, warm 23-year-old former sex worker called Dylan, the kind of 'tart with a heart' of popular culture. The speciality of her house is its range of different rooms, including the 'Holden on' room, which has a bed set in a car, complete with tail-lights and windscreen wipers; the 'Coolgardie tent' room, with its bed in folds of canvas; the 'Roman orgy' room, complete with a pool and murals featuring a number of local personalities – but with their faces disguised; the 'boxing tent', which has a bed set up like a boxing ring; and the 'underground mine' room, with mirrors and pictures of caves to give the impression of being inside a mine. 'That one isn't so popular,' says Dylan. 'Some men don't like to be reminded of work.'

With fewer men on the prowl in Hay Street, competition between the brothels is fierce. Dylan is contemptuous of Questa Casa's stalls – 'It's sad that women in the 21st century still sit in doorways,' she says. But Carmel is similarly dismissive of Langtrees' special rooms. 'There were never those kinds of rooms in brothels; you never needed them,' she says haughtily. 'I've never had a man come up and say, "If I can't have a tiger room, I'm not coming in." In an Outback town like Kalgoorlie, when a man wants sex, he wants sex.'

*

The town of Kalgoorlie is a schizophrenic mixture of the old and the new. The streets are wide and lined with fabulous old buildings from its heyday: big old hotels like the Palace, the Exchange and early government offices. Upstairs, the Palace retains all its yesteryear grandeur and elegance, with a beautiful restaurant, tables along the verandah, and a massive carved mirror – a gift from one of its most loyal customers, mining engineer Herbert Hoover, who went on to become US president. Downstairs it has a 'skimpy' bar, with scantily clad women just like Jasmine back in Port Hedland. It also has a modern reminder of what made, and continues to make, the town. High up over the town's busiest crossroads, at the top of the Palace building, a massive digital display flashes the current price of gold.

This town was built on gold, with individual miners carving out tiny shafts and tunnels all along the Golden Mile, enduring shortages of both food and fresh water for the dream of striking it rich. Life was incredibly hard for them, and many died of typhoid from dirty water. Engineer Charles O'Connor, who finally saved them by designing a pipeline to pump fresh water 530 kilometres from a weir outside Perth and thus ensure Kalgoorlie's future, also died, committing suicide after his hugely ambitious and expensive scheme sparked a bitter controversy that trashed his reputation and threatened to derail the project completely.

Yet, happily, despite all the deprivations, those old-timers probably had the last laugh, believes Matt Cook, owner of the gold-prospecting and tour business Finders Keepers. 'They took out the best of the gold,' he says. 'They dug out 37 million ounces of gold, while KCGM [the owner of the super pit] has probably only taken out 25 million ounces' worth in the last 25 years.'

But that super pit is an incredible sight. Standing on its viewing platform, I'm stunned by its size. Scoured into the red desert to the east of Kalgoorlie, it stretches 3.8 by 1.6 kilometres and goes down 520 metres – the massive house-sized dump-trucks crawling along the paths looking like tiny toy cars. Still visible, though, on all of the walls are a pattern of tiny 'mouse holes', sections of the old-timers' mines that pepper the earth. Those tunnels, if laid end to end, are estimated to stretch 3500 kilometres – about the distance from Kalgoorlie to Sydney.

Today, up to 800 000 ounces of gold are produced a year from the super pit, with around 250 000 tonnes of rock removed every day, and a tooth-sized amount of gold extracted from every tonne. Now the gold price has bounced back up, and with Australia still the world's third-biggest producer of gold behind South Africa and the US, plans are far advanced to extend the mine deeper and wider. There's also now a constant stream of newcomers to the town, either taking up the hobby of gold prospecting, or else teachers and office workers, drivers and lawyers, all wanting jobs.

On my travels around Outback Australia, I've now seen mining for silver, copper, lead, zinc, coal, iron ore and gold, as well as old uranium and asbestos mines. So what would be the best kind of mine to go for if I wanted a job in the industry myself? Matt thinks a moment about the question.

'The best would be whatever has the highest grade and is the highest yielding for the best price,' he says. 'The most profitable mines are always the best ones to work in. They just have the most money to spend.'

For a closer look at how goldmining used to be, I go along to the Mining Hall of Fame and take the 'pitch-black tour'. For this, I have to climb down a series of vertical ladders and narrow shafts into one of the old goldmines, originally dug by hand. At the base of each ladder, there are only planks to walk on before you have to bend down to shuffle onto the next one. At one point, our guide drops a stone and it feels like minutes before we can hear its splash in water at the very bottom. After a quarter of an hour, my jaw begins hurting from clenching my teeth so hard as I descend slowly down. And it's called 'pitch-black' because it is for much of the time. When the original miners' candles burnt out, they'd have to sit and wait and hope someone came by to find them. When the guide turns off his light and I stand there, in the most profound darkness I've ever experienced, I shiver with horror at how it must have been.

You'd imagine the big mining companies would be eager to support the Hall of Fame, as it's a great way to get the public onside with mining. There's a gigantic dump-truck you can sit in, gold pours to watch and displays of old miners' tents. It's very sad to learn, however, that the hall's under constant threat of closure due to a lack of funds, only being kept open, year to year, by small donations from those firms.

Years ago, I'd seen a photo of a salt lake, somewhere in the middle of Australia, with a series of steel sculptures standing lonely and stark against the blue sky and brilliant white ground. I'd vowed one day to visit and now, finally, here is my chance. Lake Ballard, I discover, is only 180 kilometres from Kalgoorlie and, since I've hired a 4WD, is easily accessible. In theory anyway. When I call the visitors bureau in the nearest town, Menzies, it seems it isn't so simple. My planned trip will coincide with the Goldfields Cyclassic, a two-stage handicap bicycle race from Kalgoorlie to Menzies and on to Leonora. The road is likely to be jammed, and all the available accommodation in Menzies is fully booked.

So near, and yet so far. But Robyn at the bureau is incredibly friendly and helpful, and enormously sympathetic. She says she'll call around for me to see if there's any solution. The next day, she emails me back. The council has a flat in Menzies that they're sometimes able to rent out – I could have that. I'm filled with gratitude.

Sometimes the Outback can be such a surprising place. When you get stuck, so often people will bend over backwards to help you in a way that, in a city, you'd never even imagine. Internet not working in the hotel? Come to the council offices and use theirs. You want a few extra hours on the hire car as your flight is later? No worries at all, no extra charge. You need a car but there are no hire cars around? Borrow mine. It's probably a lot to do with the nature of the people themselves, happy to bend the rules to get a job done, helped by a lack of bureaucracy in the Outback, where people are used to taking the initiative. And an old-fashioned generosity of spirit, of course, that's increasingly rare elsewhere.

I drive through oceans of red desert, spinifex and saltbush to the little ghost town of Menzies, pick up the keys to the flat, chat to Robyn and have a look around the visitors centre. There's been a fair bit of rain locally and she advises me to slip plastic bags over my boots when I'm on the lake, as this will stop all the mud and salt sticking. I pull a couple of bags out of my pack, ready, and then head off up 50 kilometres of vivid orange dirt track towards the lake. The best times to see it, I've been told, are at sunrise and sunset, so departing now, in the afternoon, should be pretty much perfect timing.

The road twists and snakes around until finally ending at a verge from where I can finally see the massive lake, orange close to the shore, and whiter further out with a small hillock of green to one side and the straight line of the horizon beyond.

I can't wait to get out there but, just as I set off, I notice a sign warning that no one should venture onto the lake alone, as it can be unstable underfoot after rain. Rain. There are still a few puddles on the road and the lake's foreshore, and now I examine it a bit more closely, everything does look pretty wet. I glance around but there's no one else in sight. Oh, well, I've driven all this way; I can't go back now without seeing what I came for.

There are also warnings about carrying a minimum of three litres of water. At least that's no problem. I go back to the car and put three bottles into my daypack. On my leaflet about the lake, there's yet another caution about applying sunscreen. I slap some of that on and finally set out to the lake. Too late, I remember Robyn's advice. The plastic bags stay safely in the car; my boots, with the help of the added weight of the three litres of water on my back, are soon laden down with a thick coating of orange mud and salt from the lake's sticky surface.

I trudge on, lifting each foot with effort, and imagining disappearing below the surface with every step. My progress is slow but safe, and at last I can see a couple of nude stick figures in the lake bed ahead. These are the first of the 51 sculptures set here by famed British artist Antony Gormley. He used three-dimensional scans to map the bodies of actual Menzies locals, then reduced their size by a third and cast them in an alloy containing materials found in the local rock. His display, called *Inside Australia*, was commissioned to mark the 50th anniversary of the Perth International Arts Festival, in 2003.

I finally make it to the first figure. It's only a little smaller than me and I wonder what the person it's modelled on thinks of it. But I'm sure they love the setting. I feel almost as if – and, indeed, fear – I'm walking on water here in a sea of orange and blue. I keep on going. Every time I lift a foot it makes a slurping sound with the effort of pulling it out of the mud, and I keep an anxious eye all the time on where firm land is. I can imagine, with so few landmarks and my crap sense of direction, how easy it would be to completely lose any sense of where I've come from and where I'm going, to keep walking in circles for days until every last drop of that three litres of water is drained.

On and on and on. More figures, some with pointy breasts, others with pointy penises. He's a funny bloke, Gormley. But I had no idea these sculptures would be so spread out. I find out later they cover an area of 10 square kilometres. Finally I reach the part of the lake that's all white, a shimmering, glittering, eerie world that's almost blinding in its intensity. Here there are far fewer footprints in the salt and I feel as if I could well be the last person on earth. The figures in the distance seem almost to be beckoning to me and some seem to be moving further away the more I walk towards them.

The sun's beginning to dip now too and I remember with a start that I really don't want to be out here in the dark. I'd never find my way back, and it could be weeks before anyone comes across me, curled at the feet of one of these hard-hearted sculptures. With my camera battery now almost finished, I decide I'd better retrace my footsteps and turn to go back. I'm now also dying for a pee but, of course, there's absolutely nowhere to go. Ironically, I can now see a little knot of people in the distance, who'll have a very clear view of me if I simply squat.

So while the sky puts on a splendid show for me, turning into a stunning streaked canvas of pinks and reds and mauves, all reflected in the floating white, I lumber back to shore as fast as I can. I've come all this way to see the sun set behind these strange little figures in their ghostly world of white, but all I can think of is making dry land before we're all swallowed up by darkness.

*

Menzies is a pretty dark place at night too. It wasn't always this way, though. Back in the early 1900s it was a bustling hive of gold-rush life with 10 000 people, 13 hotels and two breweries. Today, it's a town of just 100, and a mere smattering of original gracious buildings remain on the main street, which witnessed not only the first attack of gold fever in the 1890s, but also two more bouts: during the Great Depression in the late 1920s and '30s, and then in the 1980s and '90s when modern open-cut methods were used to rework some of the old mines. Yet with resource prices buoyant once more, there's now real hope of a fourth coming.

Work is going full bore at two old goldmines north of town, towards Leonora, and exploratory drilling is underway for iron ore and nickel at spots west and north-west. 'I was too young for the first boom revival, and too silly for the second, but I'm jumping on board with this third one,' says Dave McKenna, publican of the Menzies Hotel, a lovely old cream-coloured stone building in the main street. 'Those mines won't use fly-in, fly-out workers; they'll all live onsite and the trucks will pass through so it could really make this area big again. I love the quiet of the Outback here, but it'd be nice if it was a bit busier!'

The next morning, I drive back through Kalgoorlie to the place where it all began. Coolgardie, 40 kilometres south-west, was the site of Western Australia's very first gold rush in 1892, in nearby Fly Flat. Back then, it was such a significant place, Britain and Australia's eastern colonies threatened to create a new state around it if Western Australia refused to hold a referendum on federation. It conceded. Today it's another of the area's ghost towns, but one of the best preserved in the country, with wide streets lined by grand stone buildings, scattered with a few timber and tin-roofed homes.

It's such a charming place, a number of people have come through in the past and liked it so much, they never left. When Jean Anderson's marriage broke up, she sold her house and bought an old school bus and set out to drive it around Australia. She hit Coolgardie six years ago and never wanted to leave.

'I love the bush and this is a great Outback pioneer spot,' says Jean, 49, who now works in the town's museum while still living in her bus. 'There's so much to see here, and if you want some freedom, you just drive off into the bush. I think a lot of people now are buying motorhomes because when their kids grow up, they don't want a mortgage and rates any more.'

Other newcomers amass a few more possessions along with the infectious Outback eccentricity, and find it even harder to leave. Electrician Noel McKay arrived here in 1986 and adopted a wild camel. Others followed and, at one stage, he had over 170. He ended up having to buy a pastoral station to keep them all.

'I just got a bit carried away,' grins the 53-year-old. 'It's easy to do. They are beautiful animals.' Today he has 42 in the yards behind his home just outside Coolgardie, which doubles as a fascinating museum of old camel equipment, and antiques. Included among them is an example of the town's other great claim to fame, the 'Coolgardie safe', the earliest-known fridge – a box covered with a wet hessian bag. Water would trickle over it and, as it evaporated in the heat, everything inside was kept cold.

'They were smart people,' says Noel. 'The ingenuity of those in the Outback has to be seen to be believed.' Necessity being the mother of invention and all that, there must be few places in the world that forced people to be as smart.

*

The Indian Pacific train from Perth to Sydney is one of those rail journeys that every Australian should do once in their lives. Or twice. Or even three times. For me, it feels like the perfect way to return to Sydney, passing through the vast Nullarbor Desert all the way through Western Australia, South Australia and country NSW via the old silver-mining town of Broken Hill. It'll mean a break from driving long distances by car or by bus in favour of simply sitting back, watching the Outback slip by, and relaxing. Perfect.

I arrange to hop on when the train stops in Kalgoorlie for a couple of hours on the Sunday evening, and drive a last circuit of town, past the indoor beach volleyball hall – what could possibly be the point of that, I wonder – the super pit lit up at night, and four drunken blokes doing their best to trade punches in the street outside one of the skimpy bars, while a couple of the doormen look on, laughing. They wave when they notice me watching. I wave back. It's friendly like that.

By the time the train pulls out, I'm tucked up in bed in a gold-service cabin bottom bunk, with the blind open so I can see the dark shadowy landscape pass by. I want to wake up in time to watch the sun rise as we pass through the remote siding of Rawlinna, which marks the start of the vast treeless plains of the Nullarbor. But I fall asleep almost immediately, and doze right through it.

But then again, there's an awful lot more of the Nullarbor to look at. An awful lot. As we glide across the part of the line that, at 478 kilometres long, holds the record for the longest, straightest stretch of railway in the world, the desiccated flat plains spread out as far as the eye can see. It looks an endless expanse of red earth, saltbush and bluebush scrub. It makes for almost hypnotic viewing, with not the slightest sign of life to interrupt the gaze. I suppose I'd expected to see kangaroos and emus bouncing around, but beyond this train there's no indication that there's anything alive at all.

Our first stop today is Cook, just before lunch, and the half-way point across the Nullarbor. Once upon a time, this was a thriving community of 300 residents; today, after the privatisation of the railway, it became home to just four souls, surrounded by nothing in every direction, and more than 1000 kilometres from Perth and Adelaide on either side. When the train judders to a halt to refuel, take on water and change drivers, I'm one of the first to get out for a quick walk around one of the smallest, and most isolated, towns in Australia.

It's an odd feeling. There's not a lot left here: a small shop selling souvenirs for passengers, a deserted schoolhouse, a disused hospital, a tin shed that once served as the town's jail cell, a golf course with no grass, and a battered old sign, stating: ANY ARSEHOLE THAT STEALS FROM THIS CAMP WILL BE GUT SHOT AND LEFT FOR THE EAGLES TO FEED ON. What on earth would it be like to live in a place like this?

Andrea Blythman, a large, cheery 43-year-old woman, is serving at her shop when I ask her. She throws her arms open wide, as if to embrace the world around her. 'It's great!' she says unexpectedly. 'I love it. I love the country, the flatness of the land, the isolation and then the busyness when the trains come through. Life out here is what you make it. There's nothing I miss about living anywhere else.'

'Nothing?' I ask, not quite able to believe it. This would be my idea of hell. 'What about cafés and restaurants and shops?'

Andrea laughs. 'I've got coffee here, so I don't need cafés.

And while I can't cook, my husband, David, can. He used to be a cook in a restaurant. And I don't miss shopping. I phone Coles in Port Augusta and get the shopping sent over on a train or if I need to go to shops myself it's only a five and a half hour drive to Ceduna. There's nothing you need that you can't get here.'

I find it hard to believe, but maybe it comes easier to her. After all, her mum and dad lived here for years, and she spent some of her childhood here, before her parents retired and handed on the business of looking after the refuelling trains and drivers. Once Andrea left, she never imagined she'd come back but, four years ago, when they asked if she'd like to return, she decided she would. As for loneliness, even though there's only David, 49, and another couple in town, while her children Zoe, 20, and Zachary, 24, have long left home, she says she never finds the remoteness oppressive.

Each week, as well as the Indian Pacific passenger train passing through four times, twice in each direction, there are also around 70 freight trains, with drivers. 'That's lots of new people to meet all the time,' she says, grinning. 'Really, there's nowhere else I'd rather be but in my part of the Outback.'

When the horn blasts to signal the train's imminent departure, there's a mad scramble to get back on. Even though Andrea reckons it's a little slice of heaven, no one else is willing to risk being left behind to taste it too. And that's even including Margaret and Sid, whom I sit with over lunch in the dining car. They love adventure; they once went to a roadhouse's toilet in Turkey Creek, a remote township between Fitzroy Crossing and Kununurra, and ended up staying at the roadhouse for the next four weeks, helping make sandwiches so the owners could have a break.

'No, it wouldn't be for me,' says Sid, shaking his head. 'I'd find it far too lonely. And what would you do in between the trains coming in?' There's silence while we all try to imagine how it could possibly be fun, and fail completely.

The day passes in a blur of red dust, sumptuous meals, cups of tea, reading books, snoozing, announcements about where we are, information about where we're going, and chats with other passengers in the lounge. I could really get used to this. The novelty of the cabin and privacy, as well as being able to chat to others if you walk down the train or sit in the lounge or dining car, feels incredibly self-indulgent.

Every night, with the soft rocking and rolling of the train, I sleep a little better than the last, and there's the great anticipation of every stop.

We have breakfast in Adelaide and afternoon tea in Broken Hill. Afterwards, we wander around the old town, looking in shop windows and eating ice-cream. It's kind of like being on a cruise: you're a tourist but you never quite have to commit to a town. When you've had enough, you simply climb back on board into your own cabin once more.

That evening, there's a real air of sadness in the train's dining car. We eat our last supper, knowing that tomorrow will bring green hills, blue mountains and finally the great, heaving, urban suburbs of Sydney at the other end of this 1100-kilometre journey.

Even though it'll be nice to be home, for the first time I just don't feel quite ready.

When I finally hail down a cab at Sydney's main train station, the driver caught behind curses loudly through his window at having his journey held up. The cabbie tells him to calm down, but instead he jumps out of his car and bangs his fist on the cab driver's door.

The cabbie swiftly locks us both in and pulls away. He looks scared by the quite unexpected display of road rage, and I'm shaken too.

Welcome back to city life, I think ruefully. I just can't imagine, however hard I try, something like that ever happening in the Outback.

19

ARE WE THERE YET?

'It's morning! Wakey, wakey! TIME TO GET UP!'

I groan. Surely not. Surely not now.

I pull down the flap of my swag and cautiously push my nose out into the air beyond. Yes, it's about minus 4 degrees Celsius. With a superhuman effort, I open my eyes. Yes, and it's pitch-black. I pull my watch out from under the pillow, shine the torch on it and blink. It's 2.30 a.m.

All around me I hear a chorus of zips being pulled, Velcro being ripped and a stamping of feet. With the cold air now pouring into my swag, I can feel my teeth start to chatter. Please, God, this isn't really happening. Please, make this not real. This is just a nightmare and I'll wake up and it'll all go away and I'll be home in my own warm bed.

But it doesn't, and I'm not.

'Sue!' I can hear someone calling. 'SUE! Are you up?'

*

This is my last trip into the Outback and I wanted to make it special. I wanted to get up close and personal with the best that nature could offer. I wanted something challenging but fun. I wanted something you'd never find in a city, something way beyond my experience, something quite extraordinary.

Be careful what you wish for.

I've ended up on a seven-day hike along the Larapinta Trail, through some of the most astonishingly beautiful and majestic landscapes in the world. The only trouble is: I've always hated walking. And this isn't just walking. It's marching for kilometre after kilometre across the kind of razor-sharp, jagged rocks that bruise the soles of your feet and puncture the blisters on all ten toes. It's dragging yourself all the way up mountains and then careening down sheer slopes of loose stones. It's clambering over enormous boulders that rock and pitch and threaten to send you hurtling off the edge of soaring cliffs. It's trying to pick your way across fiendishly slippery stepping stones that are the only things lying between you and plunging straight into icy-cold rivers. And it's slogging up and down, up and down, up and down, until you can no longer feel anything below your waist and lose the will to live completely.

Then, just as you're on the verge of flinging yourself into the nearest gorge in despair, you finally stop, eat and go to bed in a freezing swag in a tent under siege from ten million mice in one of the worst mouse plagues in living history in one of the coldest winters Central Australia has ever experienced.

'Oh, you'll get to love it,' says Meryn, a hardened hiker who simply can't believe I'm not having the time of my life. 'You'll see. You'll get into it.'

It seems to be a view shared by everyone in our ten-person World Expeditions group. All the rest are keen walkers, happily swapping old war stories of the Overland Track in Tasmania, the Fraser Island Great Walk in Queensland, the Cape to Cape Track in Western Australia and even, in one case, the US's Appalachian Trail. Yet the Larapinta, winding 213 kilometres through the ancient West MacDonnell Ranges above the vast floodplains of the heart of Australia's red centre outside Alice Springs, is the one trek it seems they've all longed to do ever since they first managed to balance on two feet. And now they've finally made it here, for a walk doing just the best bits of the whole 21-day trek, they seem to be on a permanent high. Before I arrived, they must have each signed up to the secret Hiker's Code of Conduct: Never Complain, Never Gripe and Never, *Ever*, Admit You're Not Having the Most Marvellous Time.

Normal people would whine – just a little – about the weather: the glacial nights, the bitter mornings, the fact that the milk has frozen solid, making cereal for breakfast impossible. But no. 'Isn't it lovely and brisk!' says one, beaming, after snapping back her ice-capped tent opening. 'Aren't we lucky it's not raining?!' Regular folk might find it a touch exhausting to have to drag themselves up hills in biting blustery winds that will spare you the trouble of exfoliating for the next two years. But never. 'Wow! I can't *wait* for the view on the top,' squeals the walker in front of me. And even being told we're getting up at 2.30 a.m. one morning so we can climb to the top of a mountain to watch the sunrise provokes not the slightest murmur of mutiny. 'What a great idea!' one of the three couples on the trip exclaim. 'That will be gorgeous! Are we sure 2.30 a.m. will be early enough?'

Mind you, I was feeling anxious before we'd even begun. On our first day, we're picked up in a 4WD bus and driven to the starting point of our trek. There, we stand in a circle and our expedition leader, Marc, a mountain of a man at six foot five and 120 kilos – he could pop me in his backpack if I get tired, I hope – asks us to introduce ourselves to each other. We do, and then he gives us a little talk before we start.

'So, we'll be asking you all to give us a hand putting up tents from time to time,' he says. Fine. That doesn't sound too hard, and I'm happy we're going to have tents with all these mice scurrying around. I'd hate to share my swag with too many. But there's more. 'Make sure you carry at least three litres of water a day,' he's saying. OK, I actually read that bit on the forms and bought three big water bottles, which weigh a tonne. I can't imagine carrying them every day. 'And I hope everyone's worn in their boots before they started?' he asks. Of course. I wore my brand-new boots, bought especially for this trip, on the plane, so I'm sure they'll be excellent.

We set off and, for the first 15 minutes, I think maybe everything is going to be all right. We've meandered up a path and are now standing around at the start of our walk, at a boulder and a sign by the Overland Telegraph Station 4 kilometres from Alice announcing the start, taking photos of each other. So far, so good. I wonder just why I'd been so nervous about not being up to this, and if now would be too soon to eat the muesli bar and apple I've been given for morning tea. But the moment passes, and we head off in a straggly column, following our leader who seems to be progressing at least 3 metres with each giant, and impressively leisurely, stride. Apart from Meryn, a funny, bright woman who's ten years younger than me I later find out, everyone else is appreciably older, but they set a cracking pace, with the clatter of walking poles a few of them have brought along, the crunch of their (well-worn) hiking boots and the soft buzz of conversation.

Today's 13.5-kilometre walk is graded as medium, a gentle

introduction to the whole thing. The scenery here is already quite spectacular, with the red earth crusty beneath big clumps of spiky spinifex, mallee, acacias and bushes of wild purple fuchsia. The path is a tad rocky with loose stones, shale and quartzite that glitters whenever the sun comes out, but it's not so bad. Yet as we climb higher, along the ridge of a massive basin, my feet start hurting. My shoes are rubbing my heels and my toes feel like they're being strangled to death. Perhaps I should have gone for size 40 instead of 39 after all. My knees are also beginning to ache and the straps of my daypack, loaded down with three litres of water, are cutting into my shoulders. I'd planned to drink a lot quickly to make it lighter, but it's such a hassle taking off all the straps to get the pack off my back each time and fish inside for a bottle, I've become resigned to carrying the three litres back home again. I look up at everyone else bounding ahead. They still look as fresh as when we first set off. I'm starting to dislike them intensely.

'G'day!' The loud greeting just by my right ear nearly makes me jump out of my skin. I turn around. It's an older woman, maybe in her very late 60s, early 70s, in a T-shirt and short shorts, balancing a massive rucksack on her back. She's doing the entire 21-day trek on her own, and in a planned 12 days, carrying everything she needs – tent, water, food, the whole lot. She's what hikers call a 'true' hiker, or 'thru-hiker' as opposed to us 'slackpackers', who carry only daypacks and are doing a supported walk. I feel humbled. 'But I don't eat much,' she says cheerily. 'I have a tube of Nutella I squeeze into my mouth every so often, which keeps me going.' She asks Marc a few questions about the track ahead and then strides off. I feel a bit pathetic.

To dull the pain of my feet and legs, I try not to think about them, but to concentrate instead on my surroundings. It helps that, as we reach the top of the ridge, a fabulous view is gradually unfolding before us. Far behind and below is a settlement just outside Alice Springs; before us in the distance is the dark outline of the Northern Territory's fourth-highest mountain, Mt Sonder. 'We'll be climbing that one day,' Marc says pointing it out. 'Great!' I say, hoping it didn't sound quite as insincere as it felt. He doesn't seem to notice and tells the story of a wild bull that apparently roams these parts. I laugh, thinking he's joking, but apparently he's not. *A wild bull!* And to think I'd been worried about the mice.

We finally start descending towards our destination, Wallaby Gap. By now, my knees are screaming so loudly, I'm surprised no one else can hear them. 'Are we there yet?' I want to ask every five minutes, but I don't dare. Finally, as we walk into the picnic site, I'm hobbling but I try to smile and look like I'm enjoying myself. No one likes a whinger, and these people least of all, I'm sure. The trip's cook, Nick, picks us up in the bus and drives us to our campsite. There, all the tents and swags are stacked neatly on the ground.

I lug one of each over to a clearing and open the tent bag. There are some poles and pegs, and a great deal of material. Everyone else is busily putting tents up, but I can't make head nor tail of all the pieces. I look in vain for a little guide or plan. There's none. Eventually, I stand and look so pathetic, Nick comes over and puts it up for me. I make a secret pledge to help him with the washing-up after the meal.

I crawl inside the tent, zip it up tightly to stop the mice (and any wild bulls out there) from following me in and unroll my swag and put in my sleeping bag ready for the night to come. Then I take off my shoes and assess the damage. There's blood and pus everywhere. I take out the handy plastic snap of plasters

I've brought with me and try to open it. It resists every effort I make. I limp back out of the tent to ask Nick for a hand. He pops it open on the first attempt. I've rarely felt so foolish or helpless in my life. I wonder if I should try to impress him with tales of my boxing days, which I've discovered is an instant passport to credibility and kudos in the Outback, but then think I should save that for another occasion. This is unlikely to be the last time I ask for help. Maybe I'll just wash up twice instead.

Dinner that night is fish, baked in foil over the camp fire, and salads, with an apple crumble and custard to follow. We all hoe into it, sitting around the fire, as night slowly falls along with the temperature. True to my promise, I wash up, then sit back down next to the fire. But immediately everyone stands up as if at a secret signal. 'It's 9 p.m. and nine is hiker's midnight,' Meryn explains. 'That's the time we all go to bed.' I visit the tent enclosing the hand-dug toilet with its wooden toilet seat, wash my hands in cold water from a tin with holes ingeniously punctured in its base scooped in a bowl and hung over a branch, and walk over to my tent. I don't even have the energy to brush my teeth.

Instead, I crawl into the sleeping bag with all my clothes still on and pull the flap of the swag over my head. My feet are throbbing, every joint aches, I'm cold and I'm miserable. And, even worse, I have another six days of this. I don't know if I can stand it. If I had the energy, I'd sob myself to sleep. But I'm too exhausted even to try.

The days, just like on the cattle drive, gradually assume a rhythm of their own. We get up in the pitch-black and fumble around, having muesli and toast browned over the fire. Then, I spend a good 20 minutes wrestling with various plaster cases and wrappings (since when did they get so complicated?) and dress my blisters and scrapes, and then wonder how little water I can get away with carrying that day. Finally, we all head off.

On our second day, we walk from Wallaby Gap to Simpsons Gap, are driven somewhere else, and then walk to Standley Chasm, a steep gorge with towering rock walls, a kind of mini-version of the narrow path between cliff walls on the entrance to Jordan's Petra, but orange instead of pink, and with no donkeys towing carts to save sore feet. Instead, there's a quiet green pool at their base, a sacred site, and a lone kangaroo posing for photographs on the top of a rocky bluff. There's also a few wedge-tailed eagles swooping around and a couple of chirpy green black-faced ringnecked parrots among the ghost gums.

In our new campsite, the tents are already set up – I say a silent prayer of thanks – and we eat and chat while the hills in the distance glow crimson in the setting sun. A nearly full moon rises amid clusters of the brightest of stars. I dress my feet and we all go to sleep at 9 p.m. again. 'Are you enjoying it yet?' asks Meryn, with a grin. I smile enigmatically.

Day three, and things are looking a bit better. I'm down to carrying two litres of water a day, I've been given a fresh supply of plasters by one of the walkers, Bernie, and I'm feeling marginally more confident now about my walking abilities, although I still don't like the bits where you're forced to clamber over rocks and balance on the tops and leap onto others. I've developed my own walking style too: staring hard at the ground ahead in concentration until my new best mate, Meryn, every so often barks, 'View!' and I look up and admire whatever she's pointing out. Appalachian Trail-speak is also now creeping in, courtesy of the couple who one year did big chunks of that. I'm regularly cursing the Larapinta's PUDs – Pointless Ups and Downs, where the trail could very easily go around the hill instead of up and over all the time – and PCBs, Pointless Curves and Bends.

So as we drive to the start of our third day's trek, I'm feeling almost cheerful. Almost. That's until, of course, Marc stands by the board showing us the map of that day's endeavours, from Serpentine Gorge to Ellery Creek. There's one word on the board that jumps out at me: 'Hard'. Marc tries to put his hand over it. 'No, it's Medium,' he insists. 'And don't forget, there's no Easy.' By popular demand, he's forced to move his hand. It's there in black and white, as well as a warning about sharp rocks. I sigh. But on the plus side, there's a waterhole at our destination and I'm holding out for that. I haven't had a wash for three days now, and I stink. Dabbing at myself with a Wet One in a darkened tent just hasn't done it for me.

So, again, we walk and walk and walk. Serpentine Gorge is pretty, with red cliffs tumbling down into a cool green pool, fringed with sand. But there are constantly more hills, more PUDs, more gorges and more expansive views, although they're all beginning to merge into each other by now. The rocks are predictably sharp. It's hard going. I fall over backwards once when I tread on a sill and overbalance. Someone else falls into a big bush of spinifex, leaps out twice as quickly and spends the rest of the day picking needles out of her flesh. Some have even pierced her boots. They're pretty deadly; already they've punctured a water bladder her husband was carrying when he put his pack down too close to a bush.

Di, an older, gently spoken woman from the NSW Central Coast who's also here on her own, hangs back and walks with me for a while. She points out all the wildflowers – the buttery-coloured silver cassia, the scarlet Latrobe's desert fuchsia and the fluffy-headed pussytails – and stops to take a photo of tiny bush tomatoes. She seems to be having a genuinely good time, and is keen to share it. 'Are you enjoying it yet?' she asks.

'Are you?' I ask her, avoiding answering her question.

'Oh yes!' she exclaims, her eyes sparkling.

'Why?' I ask, genuinely curious.

'It's the beauty, the serenity and being close to nature,' she answers. 'Here, in the Outback, you can feel the land beneath your feet, you can smell nature; it's all around you. In the cities, there are so many people, and they've lost touch with nature.' We both fall silent, dwelling on her words. I think with longing of the city, of Kings Cross, of all the people and the lack of nature. But Di is evidently not thinking along quite the same lines. 'You know, I feel sorry for those city people,' she says. 'It's very sad for them.' Personally, I think she should spare her sympathy.

By the time we've reached the waterhole, across a sea of rocks, I'm full of excitement about the prospect of a swim. I stumble up to it, taking off my clothes as I go. But just on the edge, I hesitate. The pool is full of dead fish. The stink is pretty unbearable. I'm so disappointed, I think I might cry. Already everyone else who was planning to swim has turned away. But there's nothing wrong with the water, Marc's saying, it's just that sometimes it gets so cold during the winter, a lot of the algae and plants are killed off and the fish perish for lack of oxygen as a result. I only hear the first part of his sentence, that the water's fine, and I can't bear the thought of another day without a wash. So I get down to my swimsuit I've been wearing under my clothes, take a deep breath and wade in.

The water's *freezing*, but I'm committed now, and have to keep going. My legs have gone numb and it's pretty disgusting having to push layers of stinking dead fish away as I go, but I can't stop. I finally reach a part where I can't feel the sandy bottom any more and I swim, thinking it might warm me up, but bumping my arms and legs on the bodies all the time makes it not a pleasant experience. And I'm getting even colder. It's taking my breath away, but at least I feel clean, kind of, although I wonder if I'll have a faint odour of *eau de poisson* for the next four days. So I turn to shore, and see the rest of my group watching me, as well as a few Japanese tourists taking photos to show the folk back home, presumably, just how crazy Australians can be.

On day four, with even the liquid soap frozen so hard we can't wash our hands after visiting the toilet, and carrying a litre and a half of water, I realise I'm not having the worst time of any person on the Larapinta Trail. There's actually one person living a more horrible nightmare. We chance on him as we're doing our day's walk (yes, graded Hard again), from Serpentine Gorge to Serpentine Chalet Dam.

It's a tough day, with a long, long undulating climb, and lots of slithering around on rocks – which has fast become my personal bête noire – but the view is pretty good. We end up on the crest of the Heavitree Range, looking over kilometre past kilometre of plains and mountains and ridges and dips all across central Australia. My favourite part comes later, however, when we have a much flatter walk through a shady forest of gums. 'Why can't it all be like this?' I ask Meryn. She looks at me puzzled. Yes, I know, without the ups, we wouldn't have the views, and without the downs, we wouldn't appreciate them half as much . . .

We then make a side trip to Counts Point to check out another saddle view, with Mt Sonder standing menacingly in the distance, but just as we're crossing a dry river bed on the way back, we happen on a lone Irishman, sitting forlornly at the front of his tent. We greet him but there's something in the way he's sitting slumped, and barely raises his hand in response, that seems unusual. He calls us over. He's in probably his late 20s, but he looks haggard, worn out and on the verge of tears. He set out three days ago, aiming to do the whole trek on his own, but completely miscalculated how tough it would be. He has terrible, weeping blisters all over his feet and quickly ran out of bandaids days ago. He's carrying far too much stuff to allow him to walk comfortably and while he'd imagined there would be plenty of other people walking and he'd bump into them all the time, he hasn't seen another soul since he started. And the mice . . . the mice . . .

'I've never seen so many mice in my life,' he says in disgust. 'They've been eating my food and nibbling at my clothes. They're everywhere in my tent.' He indicates the tent behind him, with its front left wide open, 'I can't get to sleep at night with them running around inside and over me. And they're in my pack. I'm probably carrying half a dozen with me every step I take.' I wonder if I should pass on the tip given to me by Sonja back at MacDonald Station. Someone she knew who did the trail found taking a sleeping pill helped enormously before going to bed in an open swag. 'Then she said she didn't even notice if the mice nested in her hair at night,' Sonja told me as I stared at her incredulously. 'But I think she's a bit exceptional . . .'

I decide maybe he won't really appreciate such help and instead I just convey my sympathy. I feel desperately sorry for him. I'd probably feel exactly the same in his shoes. But some of the others aren't sympathetic at all. 'But would you ever *be* in his shoes?' someone asks. 'Why come out here when you're not properly prepared? Why not join a group, like we've done?' But from so far away, how could he have known what it's like,

I protest in his defence. 'So . . .' comes the response, 'isn't that even more reason he should have joined a group?'

It's an argument I'm obviously not going to win, so we give him some plasters, chat a while, and then head back off. I look over my shoulder back at him. He's watching us depart as if he's the last sailor on a sinking ship and we're the life raft he'd hoped might pick him up.

That evening I thank my lucky stars that I'm at least not struggling along this trek on my own, carrying my tent, food, kitchen sink and a handful of mice. Instead, I'm sitting around a cosy camp fire, having my dinner cooked for me, and just thinking how cute the mice look when they're simply running around. They're tiny things, scurrying here and there, with eyes shining in the firelight. I try to get one to come closer by offering a few crumbs of bread, but he's too nervous to trust me.

'Just stamp on him!' Marc tells me. I'm shocked, but he might be joking, I'm not sure. I don't like to ask.

'I think they're so cute,' I say. 'I'd like to catch one and teach him tricks.' Marc looks at me as if I'm mad.

Later, when I return to my tent to dress a fresh batch of blisters, I notice out of the corner of my eye a mouse run up what I think is the inside of the tent, and scream loudly. It makes him jump even more than me and he loses his grip and tumbles down. I realise then he's outside, between the tent and its outer layer.

'Are you all right?' someone shouts from the fire.

'It's OK,' I yell back, 'I just thought there was a mouse in the tent.'

'Aha!' says a voice I recognise as Marc's. 'Not so cute and cuddly now, are they?'

That night is easier. I've discovered if I put hot water into one of my water bottles – the metal one – I can hug it to get warm, and it stays warm nearly all night. It makes a huge difference. I feel almost cheerful by morning. We set off towards Serpentine Chalet Dam, with just a litre and a quarter of water in my pack, but it quickly becomes hard going, rock clambering up the dam wall. Halfway up, however, I realise we're just going up a bit further for the view, then all coming down again. I have a sudden brainwave and opt to stay where I am, ostensibly so I can take a photograph of everyone else at the top from my position. I don't think anyone really believes me.

But it still doesn't go quite according to plan. Sitting quietly on a log in the creek bed, I'm congratulating myself on my stroke of genius when I notice a loud buzzing sound. I look up and see hundreds of bees all around me. There must be a hive in the ghost gum where I'm sitting. I sit stock still, planning my escape. If worse comes to worst, I imagine fashioning myself a straw from the reeds, and dropping straight into one of the pools nearby, and staying underwater, breathing through the reed until the swarm finally goes away. Happily, after about ten minutes, they finally move off, and I'm saved my Bear Grylls moment.

When the others come back, we walk towards Waterfall Gorge and then turn off to the ochre pits. Towering walls streaked with different coloured minerals, yellow, pink, red and a dark burgundy, these are simply stunning. This is where Aboriginal people once mined the minerals for ceremonial paint, and today it has such an aura of importance about it. For the first time, I start to almost enjoy myself. Almost.

Next we go to the Finke River and, again, I have a swim and without the dead fish this time. It's pretty cold, but not as cold as the first waterhole. A couple of the group express surprise that I'm such an avid swimmer, and I don't like to tell them I'm actually not. It's just that I want to get clean and I hope the water, which is salty, might be good for my blisters, and the cold will numb some of the pain in my knees that are now nagging me constantly.

Afterwards, we go on to Glen Helen, a privately owned resort on the site of an old cattle station. It's all quite basic, with a pretty ordinary café, but its setting is gorgeous: along the riverbank, opposite ochre cliffs. Even better, it sells both ice-cream and hot showers. I buy one of each, and feel like I'm in seventh heaven.

Just two more days to go. I know that we have today to get through – although we've been warned it'll include wading through a river – and tomorrow, when we're due to get up at 2.30 a.m to tackle Mt Sonder. I'm doing my best not to think about that just yet. One day at a time.

Nick's given me some valuable advice. 'Walking is an endurance event,' he says. 'You just put one foot in front of the other and keep going and going and going. It's not about speed, it's about walking steadily, on and on.'

Another of the guys is also trying to help. 'It's like being in the army,' he says. 'At first, you don't know what to do or how things work. Then you work it out and do it automatically. You get out of the bed in the cold without thinking, you put your clothes on, you eat breakfast, you sit in a bus, then you walk. Sometimes, you can't afford to think about it too much. You just have to do it.'

So where's the fun in this? I quiz Meryn. 'It's the beauty of the surroundings,' she says. 'You're out there walking and it's a great way to clear your head. You're just out in the fresh air and you walk; it's therapeutic. It's what we were designed to do: put one foot in front of the other.' I'm still not convinced.

But today is going to be a short one anyway, because of the

early mark the next day. We're doing the Ormiston Pound Walk and while there are some jitters about the creek crossing, Marc is reassuring. He says he thinks the water will only reach our knees. It'll be cold, but we won't get too wet.

We follow the track, admire the scenery from the lookouts, and then reach sandy banks and our creek crossing. It's impossible to tell how deep the water might be. Two other trekkers appear and stride straight into the water. We watch them, mesmerised, as both slowly sink up to their armpits before reaching the other side. There's a chorus of complaints from our group. 'No, it's not that bad!' says Marc. 'There are stepping stones under the water. If you stay on those, you won't go down so far.'

He goes across to show us, then walks back to offer help. A couple of people head into the water and make it across to the other side. I walk in and beg Marc to hold my hand and show me where the stones are. I'm not proud. He guides me to them but they're so slippery, it's hard to stay on them. He almost pulls me to the other side until it's shallow enough in the sand for me to trudge the rest of the way through. A couple of the guys then ask him to hold their hands, too, as he continues to go back and forth, like a Goliath, carrying our packs for us. Another woman, admittedly quite tiny, asks if he can carry her across and he does, on his shoulders. The rest of us bitch, 'Doesn't she have any *pride*?' but mostly because none of us had thought of asking first.

Meryn then walks across, determinedly on her own, with her pack held high above her head. I admire her pluck. But not for long. One minute she's there, balancing on the rocks. The next minute, all you can see is her hat and her pack floating off. She's slipped off the rocks and become completely submerged.

*

On our last day, I'm fast asleep in the tent when the 2.30 a.m. alarm call comes. I can honestly say, it's one of the most miserable moments of my life. I don't really want to climb another mountain. I can do without yet another nice view. And I really couldn't give a stuff about watching the sunrise; you can see that any day you want in Kings Cross. But I pretend to myself I'm in the army, and I'm being called up for an important mission. Gathering all my strength, I scramble out of my swag into my clothes and into the night.

We drive, in silence, to Redbank Gorge and then form ourselves into single file. There's a full moon so there's some light, but we switch our head torches on and set off for one last time.

I go second, following behind Nick. Marc brings up the rear. What can I say? We walk and walk and walk up and down and up the winding rocky path. Every so often, we stop and regroup, to make sure no large gaps are forming between us. At one point, Nick stops and points out to me that we're on a saddle with cliffs falling away on both sides. One edge drops precariously down just half a metre from my right foot. I shudder. I would have had no idea. 'Are we nearly there yet?' I whisper plaintively, at last. 'No,' he answers. 'There's still a way to go.'

And indeed there is. This is a long, rocky track, steep in parts, and even steeper in others. I keep my eyes fixed on the ground illuminated by my torch and on Nick's feet in front of me, and just keep on going. I'm now walking so closely in his footsteps that every time he stops, I know I'm in danger of ploughing straight into him. He seems to realise this and walks a little more quickly. But every time he puts on a burst of speed, I match him. I don't want to fall behind at all and we end up stopping a number of times to allow the others to catch up.

Gradually, it grows lighter in the east and dawn approaches.

We all quicken our pace to try to get to the top before the sun rises. Here, it's rockier still but we all keep moving forward, racing, racing against the dawn. At last, we reach the lookout. It's so rocky and windy, it's hard to stand up but at least we've made it.

I flop down onto my daypack and sit quietly as the sun tiptoes above the horizon. As its rays pierce the gloom, the world below me slowly illuminates. I take a deep breath. It's like a curtain rising on the earth. At first, you can see the endless plains reaching out far into the distance, then the towering cliffs of amber and ruby and rose, and finally Mt Sonder itself is flooded with light.

At last, I feel something inside me stir.

It's true that I haven't really enjoyed much of my time on this trail through the ancient landscape, although everyone else in my group has absolutely loved it. Similarly, I started many of these journeys through the Outback with trepidation, fear and a fair bit of loathing. But I have to admit, the beauty of the Outback, the friendliness of its people, their passion about the land and the freedom of the lifestyle are gradually getting to me. I'd seen some wonderful sights over the past three months, and there must be few other places in the world with such a range of transport to get around – I'd travelled by all sizes of plane, train and automobile as well as campervan, bus, boat, foot, bicycle, horse, goat . . . I'd laughed a lot, cried a bit, whined, yarned around camp fires, fought and made some friendships I know will last the rest of my life.

And, finally, I felt just a bit closer to understanding the lure of the Outback. Gina, back in Mt Isa, had adopted me with an open heart to show me some of its secrets, Ross in the Flinders had been eager to teach me how to appreciate its beauty, and a local in Barcaldine had helped define it for me. 'The Outback isn't a place on a map,' she said, 'it's a place in your heart.' I learnt from being there that it's an attitude, how you treat people, a way of behaving. It's your belief system, and how a whole nation of Australians often long for a time when life was simpler, less complicated, more genuine.

Sitting on the top of the world up there, with the sun now on my face, and the wind finally dropping, I rise to my feet. There's a little cairn nearby, with a visitors' book on top. I walk over and open it. There, thousands of people before me have written how much they love this spot, how the battle to get there has taught them more about themselves, or how it's brought them closer to their god.

I take out a pen. 'Welcome to the Outback', I write. And for the first time in my life, I actually mean it.

ACKNOWLEDGEMENTS

When I set off travelling around the Outback, I had no idea how I would fare. But while I was on the road I met some of the most extraordinarily kind and welcoming people you'd ever find on this planet. I'd love to say a huge thank you to them all. Their friendship and help got this city girl through some of the toughest of times.

Particular thanks go to Mt Isa's Gina Scott, who's since become one of my closest friends; Patricia O'Callaghan, formerly of Mt Isa's Chamber of Commerce; Melissa Chapman; Jo Martin of Barcaldine; Jan D'Auria; Meryn Perry; Dianne Kolstad; Andrea Lingard at the Harry Redford Cattle Drive; Sonya Cullen at the Australian Stockman's Hall of Fame; Hank and Berry Cosgrove; Sonja Chalmers; Jan and Shelley Norton; George Fetting and Bruce Hutchison for their wonderful photos; Steve Jones and Clare Nash of Skytrans; Philip Alcorn; Shaun Rigby; Karin Wong; Greyhound Australia; Queensland Rail; Great Southern Rail; and Birdsville's Nell Brook.

A special mention goes to Fred Brophy of the greatest boxing tent in the world, for allowing me to take the mat – against his better judgement – and to Leo Beutel for his encouragement and advice. For their part in training me, I'm more grateful than they'll ever know to the big-hearted Carl Ehmsen, as well as to Carmen Zdroykowski, Elsie Banks, Tony O'Loughlin and Paul Isgro.

Out in the wilds, it was always wonderful to have my indefatigable agent, Selwa Anthony, cheering me on from back home. She'd ask me, 'So where are you now?' and 'Where's that?!', even though she was largely responsible for sending me off there in the first place. Selwa, I can't thank you enough.

I've always been so appreciative too of the support of Penguin publisher Andrea McNamara, who had the great idea for this book. Any shortcomings are entirely my own. A huge thank you too to editor Bridget Maidment, whose comments on the text, and suggestions for improving it, were pure Outback gold, and to designer Laura Thomas, who did a stellar job.

And a final thanks to my partner, Jimmy Thomson. He encouraged me when I lost confidence, revved me up when I got lonely, and yelled the loudest to keep me going in the boxing tent. Thanks, hon. This book is for you.